F*CK MEDIOCRITY

F*CK MEDIOCRITY

Be Powerful, Be Legendary

Caelin Kompass

Published by Game Changer Publishing

Paperback ISBN: 979-8-9877531-9-4

www.GameChangerPublishing.com

DEDICATION

DOWNLOAD YOUR FREE GIFTS

Read This First

Just to say thanks for buying and reading my book, I would like to give you a few free bonus gifts, no strings attached!

To Download Now, Visit:

www.CaelinKompass.com/Freegifts

F*CK MEDIOCRITY

Be Powerful, Be Legendary

WARNING!! READING THIS BOOK MAY INSPIRE YOU TO UNLOCK GREATNESS AND BECOME THE MAN YOU COULD BE

Caelin Kompass

www.GameChangerPublishing.com

Table of Contents

Introduction

HOW THIS BOOK WILL BENEFIT YOU

"Great people are those who make others feel that they, too, can become great."
— Mark Twain

"If you want a different life, you must be a different person."
— Benjamin Hardy

A few years ago I hit the proverbial "rock bottom".

Looking back on it now, it wasn't necessarily that big of a rock bottom but at the time it seemed like my world was ending.

I was drinking heavily.

Up to my eyeballs in debt.

No stable source of income.

Going through an incredibly difficult breakup.

Realized I had been delusional in my own life.

Got reminded how detrimental it was to be involved with my extended family on my father's side and also to my chagrin, saw a part of that dysfunction in myself.

All in all — my life was a shit show.

I knew I needed to do something different.

I knew I needed to find some way out of this hell I'd built for myself.

Therapy wasn't an option, or I should say I didn't believe in it. The people I'd seen do it got about as good of results as people who follow the food pyramid and try to lose weight. In short — not the results I was after.

After I got over my victimhood, my whining, my complaining, my anger and resentment, I realized I needed to create a new roadmap for my life.

I realized my map of the world, how I interacted with reality, how I processed things, was fundamentally, at its core, not what I needed to advance myself to the next level, so I committed to changing that.

During the course of this exploration I realized many things about myself.

I've been confused about how the world works for longer than I care to admit.

I've been waging a war within myself for as long as I can remember, trying to settle the inner-conflict I'd adopted at some point in my life.

I had no working model of the world that would allow me to actually get what I wanted or to become the man I knew I could be.

One of the biggest admissions was that I felt like I was trying to discover how to be a man.

Not what a man is, not what a good man is, just how to be the man I'm proud of, the man that I can look at in the mirror and feel proud of and that has the self-respect I want to have.

I spent years reading, researching and implementing everything I cover in this book to transform myself into who I am today.

This book will benefit you by condensing all of that knowledge into 8 pillar principles that will give you the tools and resources to transform your life as well.

On first glance, these pillars seem overly simple — and they are — that's why so many people dismiss how much weight they carry throughout life.

This book will go over in detail a set of fundamental principles that, if you apply them, carry the power to transform your life in unimaginable ways.

It doesn't matter if your life is a shit show or if your life is good and you want it to get better. I promise you that in these pages there are simple yet powerful principles that will help you become the man you know you could be.

In my heart, I'm an individualist.

I believe in the individual.

I believe in you.

I believe that all power is derived from the individual.

There are plenty of things that are out of your control, but you do have the power to control you, to take the reins in your life, to become the master of your destiny and to bring the best version of yourself into this world.

This book will show you how.

Fuck Mediocrity, Be Powerful, Be Legendary is about empowering men.

It's about empowering you to reach new levels in life.

It's the roadmap that I wish I'd had when I was younger so that I could've understood better targets in life, understood how and which standards to implement, what's driving me in the first place and how to ultimately get where I'm trying to go.

The men I've shared these structures with have all found at least portions of this to be incredibly valuable and life-changing.

Here's a single, simple example — what if you took total responsibility in your life?

Rather than running late for a meeting and saying it's not your fault, how might your life change if you were never late for anything ever again?

How would people look at you differently if you had your life in total order?

This sounds simple but it's deceptively difficult, especially in a victim-filled society.

My father taught me the best he could and I'm incredibly grateful always to him for that, just as I'm sure your father taught you the best he could.

However, as my father taught me these principles, he also taught me their opposites. Let's call them anti-principles.

For instance, perhaps when you were younger an adult in your life told you to take responsibility for something, then a short while later something happened and the adult says, "But it's not my fault. I couldn't help this. It's not my responsibility."

And just like that they exhibit incongruent behavior abandoning the responsibility they're telling you to take. They tell you to take responsibility yet then model the behavior of someone that doesn't.

Confusing, right?

Kids are far more likely to model that behavior than to listen to words only, which explains why we have so many men that are confused about how to be the best possible man they can be.

This book isn't filled with a bunch of bullshit scientific studies trying to convince you that "the science" will light your way.

On the contrary, everything presented in this book is rather axiomatic or self-evident in nature.

I'm not here to feed you information that you blindly ingest.

I want you to think about these things, to ponder them, to ask yourself if they're really true and if they are, what that means for you?

What kind of man do you want to be?

And who could you be if you really committed, you really tried, and also if you had the APPROPRIATE information to help you get there?

This book was born out of a personal frustration where I found bits and pieces of helpful information yet I struggled to piece it all together.

For example, one book would do an excellent job on discipline yet I didn't understand how to apply that to lack-luster goals.

Or that if I don't have some sort of emotional drive in the first place, this ship goes nowhere.

This book pieces together many of the seemingly disparate core fundamentals into a single cohesive volume that can be read and applied easily so you don't have to go hunt them down and then piece them all together as I did.

My goal for you is that you read and apply everything in this book and by doing so, you become the absolute BEST version of yourself.

Repeatedly throughout this book, I will come back to a fundamental principle — that you have greatness within you — that there is more to you than you know and if you'll commit to pursuing that, you'll be ASTOUNDED at who you can become in the end.

This book is written in a personally unique style that I've never attempted before.

I wanted it to read with a certain cadence and since so many people listen to audiobooks, I wrote it with that in mind.

I also believe that repetition is the mother skill for instilling empowering beliefs which is why I will continually return to reinforcing that you have greatness within you.

Whether you believe in it or not, your unconscious is always listening and if I've done my job appropriately, there is a fair amount of hypnotic language along with cadence in this book that will have you believing on a deep level that you do possess greatness within you and that it's your imperative to actually bring that into the world.

This book is about providing you with the fundamental structures to become powerful as an individual. You become powerful when you adopt rules and principles that empower you, when you have a roadmap for becoming who you wish to be.

You become powerful by building yourself into the man that you could become.

To that end, part of becoming powerful is that there is greatness within you.

And greatness is just that — greatness.

It doesn't mean good or bad, only that you have the potential to do great things, that you have the potential to become a great person. I use this semi-interchangeably with potential throughout this book purposefully to reinforce that there is this power within you.

I believe that you have greatness within you.

That the best is yet to come.

And that, as a man, you can build yourself into the person you most admire.

Enjoy the journey, my friend.

MY STORY

I have lived a not so conventional life.

When I was a kid, I climbed a filing cabinet and proceeded to fall, earning myself some staples in my head. (Ouch. I guess that explains things a bit now...)

I have 6 brothers and sisters who I'm incredibly grateful for.

As a kid, I constantly received mixed messages (mostly on my father's side of the family):

You're loved. You're not loved.

You're smart. You're stupid.

I want you around. I want nothing to do with you.

Love = yelling and fighting.

Love does not = yelling and fighting.

Anger is a great way to get attention. Anger is not a great way to get attention.

Take responsibility. It's not my fault.

I could go on and on. The point isn't to focus on any one of those, only to illustrate that I view part of the war that's gone on within myself for most of my life as simply a continuation of the war that's been going on in my parents for most of their lives.

That is until I stopped it of course.

I'm homeschooled until the 7th grade. (I've been socially awkward before and since.)

I try my hardest to be "normal" yet am distinctly interested in different things than my peers.

After graduating high school, I move to Destin, Florida with my best friend Zach and get my first glimpse at how different the world is compared to the tiny bubble I grew up in.

I narrowly avoid death in college due to riding sport bikes.

My doctor puts me on Adderall because I'm "ADHD".

I get a degree in accounting.

I stop the Adderall and realize I'm not ADHD, I'm just not suited for accounting.

Fuck.

I apply for law school.

I decide that's not right.

I spend a year back in school for a second undergrad degree in physics.

I decide I'm just punting.

I move to Round Rock, Texas with my dad and try getting into the indie acting scene.

I'm not a good actor. And I hate it.

I don't like anyone having my fate in other's hands such as casting directors.

I move to Dallas to put my hard-earned bachelor's degree to work as a male-stripper.

I spend the next 6 years becoming a legend in the industry for drinking, partying, wild sex-capades, writing erotic-romance novels and generally just being someone who loves living life to the fullest.

But, I realize it's no longer for me, so I leave and try to start a business with my dad.

It fails. Bad. It hurts my ego. My ego needed hurting.

This experience, easily the most painful of my life, turns out to be one of the biggest blessings in disguise. Through that turmoil, through that breakdown and challenging of my identity, beliefs, values and character, I emerge on the other side as a better, stronger and more capable man, resolute in my resolve to become the best version of myself possible.

I devote myself to self-improvement, to becoming the man I know I can be and to even discovering what that means and by doing that, also gain the keys to help other men solve the exact same problems I once dealt with.

Currently — I'm working to conquer the internet and help men everywhere discover how to live into their potential. Oftentimes, it's only a matter of the right information, in the right order, at the right time, and for those that are hungry.

Are you hungry?

Are you ready for change?

Good.

I believe in you.

It's time you do as well.

THIS IS A STORY OF HOPE

I want to preface this book with why I believe my message has additional value compared to the near infinite list of others on the internet.

I haven't had a natural inclination towards many of these principles I cover in the coming pages.

I've developed them, I've cultivated and used them to sculpt myself into the man I am today.

It's not been an easy journey, I haven't had all the right resources or been someone who seemingly had all the right tools from the start.

I'm not beyond brilliant like some in this space.

I don't have a genius IQ or even advanced social skills or some other ninja tactics.

While a part of me would like to tell you I'm completely and remarkably average and that the average man can transform himself just the same, that's not true.

Here's a secret, I have super powers.

I wasn't born with them, I built them, I developed them, I took my raw innate potential and harnessed it into something worth being proud of and unfortunately, there is nothing average about that.

However, you too have that same innate potential and the ability to harness that and to develop your own super powers if you so choose.

But the average don't do that.

By very definition, if you choose to go down that road you can no longer be average because the average are those that don't develop and pursue these characteristics.

I'm sure you're wondering – what are these super powers I'm referencing?

Perseverance, courage, discipline, the willingness to face myself in the darkest of times, my ability to stand in my own character even when the world is encouraging everything but that.

These are super powers, these allow you to transcend who you are today in order to become who you could be tomorrow, and when matched against your fellow man who lacks persistence, who lacks courage, the man with super powers wins by default. Every. Single. Time.

Why should you listen to me?

I've been seeking to escape the path of the mediocre man since I was young though.

I've been trying unorthodox approaches at life for a VERY long time because I saw that doing what I was "supposed" to do was not going to lead me to any place I was actually satisfied with.

Rather than go get a job and sit in a cubicle, I chose to believe in myself and to forge my own way in the world.

I wouldn't accept anything less and that's why at 34 years of age, I haven't worked for a "boss" in over a decade.

I got to have experiences most guys could only dream of and I'm still getting to have more because I simply won't tolerate anything less.

If I can do this, if I can do nearly all the "wrong" things in life that you're not "supposed" to do and sit here today, then why can't you?

Seriously.

Placing male-stripper on your resume doesn't get you any bonus points and I don't care because I'm not looking to turn my resume into anyone. I'm out to create my own path forward and even though in my twenties I'm sure I could've built more tangible skills had I chosen a different path, I also learned invaluable fundamental life skills from this experience.

Most see only the highlights of that lifestyle, the threesomes, orgies, girls begging for you to come fuck them, but there's a darker side also.

The degradation of character, the supreme unworthiness of self you develop, the costs of allowing yourself to be devalued, the addiction to adoration you develop that necessitates you stay plugged into the system so you can constantly get more and when it gets taken away, it's like your soul gets stolen.

I had a hell of a time in my twenties, seriously, did some of the most awesome, crazy, cool, wild shit you can imagine. Had sex with some of the most beautiful women on the planet, partied with celebrities, you name it.

But, it was equally marked by extreme loneliness, solitude, many nights lost in a bottle, crying as a grown ass man because I couldn't figure out how to get my life together. Having no direction or path to discover how to be the man I was proud of.

I wouldn't take it back but my life has been anything but a linear path to who I am today.

Something in me needed to go to that darker place first before I could come out the other side.

As I almost titled this book: ALL MEN GO TO HELL, ONLY HEROES RETURN.

I don't know how you feel, but when I listen to someone and it seems like their life has been one success after the next, in my mind I know that they still struggled immensely, but I also know I find it hard to relate to them.

It's like there is this pedestal and they're so high up, it's difficult to visualize myself ever getting there compared to someone who has been in the gutter, who has scrapped their way through all the bullshit, and figured out how to be good at being a man despite being their own worst enemy at times.

This is a story of hope because if I can do this, then you can also.

I'm not ashamed of saying this now – I'm a badass motherfucker and I am dedicated, hard-working, committed, resourceful and unwavering in my vision, but I wasn't always this man.

I wasn't always this version of myself.

I've built myself into this.

I've literally become more intelligent.

I've literally become more wise.

I've literally expanded the capacity of who I am through constant improvement.

Here's the thing — you're built for adaptability more than anything.

If you choose to embrace that, then you too can make the same transformation in yourself.

It's a CHOICE.

It's a DECISION.

It's a COMMITMENT.

It's time you resolve the war within yourself and get the resources to become the man you know you can be.

This book will show you how.

The Foundation

WHY ALL OF THIS MATTERS

"The fundamental question of life is, 'What is the proper orienting narrative?'" This is the same question as, 'What God do you worship?'"
– Jordan Peterson

Most men never identify what they're truly after in life.

They sort of just do this or do that and live reactively and follow along to whatever comes next.

Someone introduces them to a new game, or a new show, or a new fantasy football league, whatever bullshit comes along.

Those are largely simply distractions keeping you from identifying what you're doing, why you're doing it and where you're heading.

For men, this whole game is about power, status, respect and to borrow another concept from Jordan Peterson: "the spirit of voluntary play".

But how are you supposed to get those things if you can't figure out how to get your life in order?

Or perhaps your life is "in order" yet you don't find that you get the respect you desire. You don't feel like you're living up to the man you could be.

Sound familiar at all?

All of this matters because we're after fulfillment on an intrinsically fundamental level.

Not the kind where you stay distracted for 40 years then wake up and realize you blew your one chance at life.

We're after you achieving a sense of greatness, a sense of actualizing your potential so that when you're 85 on your deathbed, you look back on your life and think — damn, I really showed up, didn't I?

Why would you live another day in confusion? In disrespect? In not loving yourself? In a shallow or lonely existence when you don't have to?

Why would you live another day not living up to who you feel called to be in your heart?

You get greater status by becoming more powerful.

You become more powerful by mastering yourself and understanding the origins of power that come from within you.

You are the source, so if you want to change any of that, then changing you is the imperative.

And while most are reticent about that (they just want to hold onto that which holds them back), there are some who are ready to cut ties with parts of themselves in order to become a far better version that they know exists within.

SKILL SETS

To a large degree, the difference between where you are now and where you want to be is a gap of skill sets, not in personal inadequacies or inborn traits that can't be improved upon.

Plenty of people will blame all sorts of external forces, make all sorts of excuses, but at the end of the day — if they're willing to do the work, to close the gap on their skill sets, ultimately, they'll improve and develop the skills they need in order to become whoever they're trying to become.

I find presenting skill sets in this matter is often encouraging to men because they've been told this lie that they're simply born with certain characteristics and can't change them.

Nothing could be further from the truth.

With the appropriate information and the proper application nearly anyone can develop skills beyond what even they think is possible, and you're no exception.

This book covers different skill sets in depth and also has action items at the end of the chapters for you to work on.

If you simply read each chapter, do the action items and never think about them again, this won't build these in as skill sets.

Instead, you have to be intentional about implementing them in your life.

You have to constantly reinforce them until they're second nature, until they're so natural you don't even have to think about it.

Every person I've ever seen do this has become a master at the game of life.

Every person that has mastered the fundamentals of life goes wherever they desire to go and becomes exactly the person they desire to become.

It can be no other way.

"There's no key to success, it's a combination."
– Brad Lea

If you look to someone like Tony Robbins, why is it that he's done such amazing things?

He has mastered the art of not negotiating with himself so that when he says he's going to do something, he does it, no matter what.

The same is true for any other person who learns to become a master of themselves.

There is no limit to where you can go and while some learn this young and others learn it when they're older — it's a skill set and your only limitation is the degree to which you're committed.

META-GOALS

In the game of life and in the pursuit of greatness, it's important to recognize the larger game at play.

Think of this like having a weekly activity with good friends where each week there are new challenges and competitions.

While the ideal goal is to win, the real goal is to be invited back so that you can continue playing the game week after week.

In order for that to take place, if you win ALL of the time, eventually, no one will want to play with you and you'll be out of the game.

Of course, the meta-goal is the goal across all games. For Tom Brady, winning a game would be a single individual goal, but the meta-goal would be goals that span across all the games, season after season. The goal is to play the game in a way so that he gets to play more games.

In the meta-game of life, the goal is continual growth and progress which is why if you're always the smartest person in the room, you're likely failing at the meta-game.

When it comes to life, we want to identify the goals and also the meta-goals.

A goal may be to lose 30 lbs, a meta-goal may be to become the best version of yourself.

We want to identify the fundamentals and the meta-fundamentals that are really fundamentals that apply across all aspects of life.

I like to think of these things with the saying:

In life, nearly everything works some of the time and almost nothing works all of the time.

Meta-games, principles, goals, et cetera are things that work all of the time. They're integral to life.

When it comes to mindset — we don't want to adopt a mindset that only benefits us with regards to money for instance, but in all walks of life.

The same is true with how we live wholeheartedly.

We're after meta-goals that translate at every level of life, because if we really master those, we'll have a rock-solid foundation upon which to THRIVE in life.

The goal isn't just to adopt an identity that helps you get through this next struggle, yet then turns into a limiting belief at the next level. It's to adopt an identity that helps propel you through **each level of life**, each level of the game.

Most people intuitively understand this. It's like the idea around limiting beliefs.

Most people have heard of them, are aware of them, and think they just somehow got programmed in there by mistake, but that's not the case.

On some level, most, if not all, limiting beliefs started off as empowering beliefs in some form or fashion. However, as you progress in life, what started off as serving you now has come to limit you as you try to progress and grow to the next level.

On the other hand, when you focus on adopting meta-beliefs — foundational beliefs that translate across your ENTIRE life, that's where the real keys to success lie.

To illustrate, here's a quote from Nelson Mandela:
"I never lose. I either win or learn."

No matter the circumstances I run into, this belief empowers me to always be learning, adapting, changing and growing, so that I'm never stuck in loss, in failure, in a disempowered state.

This belief crosses all industries and any pursuit I'm undertaking so that I'm ALWAYS getting better.

This is a meta-belief or fundamental in the sense that as soon as you adopt it, it will empower you throughout your entire life, not only for the next year.

It will empower you in all endeavors and help you to always improve, to constantly get better, to constantly keep you oriented towards greatness.

So, the goal is to acquire some meta-principles, meta-fundamentals, meta-heuristics, that actually SERVE you rather than hinder you.

And I can't tell you how many people I see who've also adopted meta-beliefs that limit them across all categories of life as well.

"I'm stupid and can't learn or get better."

That hurts you in your job, finances, relationships and pretty much any endeavor you pursue.

"I'm not good at singing," is an example of something that is not a meta-belief and instead, does not limit you across all categories.

However, if you said — "I'm not good at singing, and never will be," that would limit you across a meta-set of categories because you're concluding that you cannot improve even if you tried.

And how much evidence do you have in your life that you can improve?

At one point, you couldn't walk — now you most likely can.

At one point, you couldn't read, now you most likely can, especially if you're reading this ;-P

At one point, you couldn't drive, and there is a high likelihood that if you can't already, you will at some point.

There is a sheer abundance of information proving the veracity of these statements, but it's up to you to actually adopt it.

The goal of this book is to leave you with a set of meta-principles, meta-fundamentals, meta-heuristics and ways of thinking that will facilitate you unlocking your potential so that you can become the powerful man you know you can be.

PILLAR I

Have Heart

INTRO

"Lack of emotion causes lack of progress and lack of motivation."
– Tony Robbins

When you ask people why they do what they do, they'll give you all sorts of reasons. Some will say you MUST know your WHY in order to do anything. Others will say they're pursuing their authentic selves. Others will say they're passionate about spreadsheets.

You'll get a bunch of bullshit logical answers and nearly all of them will lack spirit.

The entire reason we do anything we do, on a fundamental level, is to change how we FEEL.

We can come up with all sorts of stories about the whys, because of goals, or anything else, but ultimately, it's our heart that drives us all.

Our emotionality.

Desire.

It's that HUNGER you feel in your soul!

That's your driver.

This is where you get all your leverage, all your juice from.

It's why people start companies.

It's why people get out of bed in the morning.

And it's something so many men have shut off within themselves in order to fit into their tight little box of being.

That's not going to work.

So, the first principle is to HAVE HEART!

Seriously, life is an EMOTIONAL GAME and if you're denying this, you're denying yourself power. Embrace emotionality.

That's where all your power comes from after all.

It's where all your potential originates.

I get it — it's easy to miss at times.

We can get so caught up with thinking, with logical structures, with trying to make everything make sense.

But don't forget, all the greats, all the most powerful people, live with an abundant amount of heart or emotionality.

That doesn't mean they let it rule them, but it damn sure drives them.

Why would you not choose to live fiercely?

Why would you not choose to live with a fire burning in your soul?

It takes heart to get back up after you've been knocked down.

It takes heart to keep going in the face of adversity.

It takes heart to defy social norms and do something unconventional and EXTRAORDINARY!

You won't see a single top performer in the world who doesn't operate this way.

It takes immense drive, immense ambition and immense dedication to get to the top, and you sure as hell don't get there with a lackadaisical attitude.

Heart baby.

In today's world, we dismiss things when they sound too easy, too simple, too transparent.

And that's exactly the problem — it is simple, but that doesn't mean it's easy.

So instead, we busy ourselves with convoluted and complicated stories, convincing ourselves that if it were really that simple then everyone would be doing it.

Well, it is that simple, which is why so many dismiss it.

We make ourselves feel important through multi-tasking and discursive behaviors, convincing ourselves we're being so productive, when sure we're being productive and staying busy, but all on the wrong things.

Life principle — doing the wrong thing in the right way and staying busy still does not make that thing important or worth doing in the first place.

Look, all personal growth starts with the TRUTH.

It starts by getting truthful with yourself.

Truthful that you're not where you want to be, that you're not living the way you want to be, and that in your soul, you're not even really living in congruence with your heart in the manner that you should be.

There are all kinds of people out there trying to convince you to be complacent, to just be logical, to just be patient, to just take it a day at a time, to not work too hard, to take it easy.

FUCK THAT!

Fuck what everyone else says.

FUCK PATIENCE!

You need URGENCY MOTHERFUCKER!

You need to be IMPATIENT about your life.

You need to stop letting others tell you to cool it and instead embrace that emotionality and step on the gas.

This is your juice, why are you depriving yourself of it?

Bro, get pissed.

Get serious about your life.

Get excited for your life.

Get whichever way you need to be to harness that fire in your soul.

Don't back down from this, let it burn and fuel the man you could be.

When I say HAVE HEART, I mean have emotionality about your life.

Embrace the fact that life is an emotional game and when you understand this and can LEVERAGE those emotions you feel into positive, productive forces, they can help you transform yourself and your life.

You can have all the best logical information in the world and it not mean a damn thing. It's that emotional leverage that moves mountains.

For me, it started with giving myself permission, having courage, acknowledging who I wanted to become, becoming present and having gratitude, and then doing the things I needed to do no matter what.

Now, when I coach other men, this is where I start. I make them convince me that they truly want to change their lives, that they can NO LONGER stand being the same person they are and that they MUST evolve into a better version of themselves.

I have a friend, I'm not going to name names, but he's IMMENSELY talented. He could do anything that he wants in life, yet he mopes around talking about how he'd like to make more money, have a more enlivened life. Yet in the same sentence will also say how he just can't get himself to care enough.

FUCK THAT!

You can't muster enough FUCKING HEART for your own life?

What kind of man are you, bro?

The goal is NOT to be like that.

The goal in this pillar is for you to understand and internalize that adding emotionality to your life is like adding fuel to a fire.

If you don't have any gas in the car, you're not going anywhere.

I've been there before, been in this broken spot where I just couldn't seem to muster the emotionality necessary to affect the proper change in my life.

But once I realized how to get leverage on my life, how to tap into that power, I've never been the same, and neither will you.

This isn't a maxim to be an emotional train wreck, it's a call to start playing at a higher level.

You know you're a level 10 person who's just gotten stuck at level 4 somehow.

Just go watch any sports player who's in a tight situation and either pulls through or drops the ball.

Their reactions are EMOTIONAL.

That's because they're INVESTED.

Why would you not be invested like that in your OWN life?

Why would you not give yourself permission to have the courage to actually put that much emotion into your life?

I know plenty of men who put more emotion into watching their favorite sports team compared to designing the life they dream of.

Fuck that!

You're not going to be that guy and this guy will help show you how.

LET'S GO MOTHERFUCKER!!

CHAPTER ONE

The Permission Factor

PERMISSION

Noun

— Approval to do something

— The act of giving formal authorization

Dreams plagued my sleep as I tossed and turned.

Something had snapped within me, I just didn't realize it yet.

There are times in everyone's life where tectonic shifts happen and most of us have no idea why or how they occur. I know I didn't on this most propitious of mornings. I only knew that some sort of irreversible reaction had happened, that some sort of chain of events had clicked into place and I would never be the same.

There are always two yous in the room — your conscious and your unconscious.

What most people don't realize is that your unconscious is still there working all the time and there is nothing "SUB-conscious" about it.

As Carl Jung said —

"Until you make the unconscious conscious, it will direct your life and you will call it fate."

On this fateful morning — Wednesday, April 13th, 2011 — I gave myself permission to go a different way, to choose a different route in life, to avoid being just another statistic, just another individual that does what they're told to do, and instead gave myself permission to pursue who I could be.

I was in college at the time, pursuing a second undergraduate degree in physics. The first had been accounting — big mistake.

As I opened my eyes — I realized I was pursuing the same strategy all over again.

I wasn't evolving, I was revolving.

I was pursuing a second degree to stay in college because I had no clue who I was, what I wanted, what I valued and what I was actually seeking in life.

That started me on a journey that's less linear than most, a journey that eventually led me to who I am today — a man that helps other men unlock their potential and become the best, most powerful version of themselves.

But, it wasn't easy, it wasn't simple, and it damn sure was anything but traditional.

However, it all started with PERMISSION.

Giving myself permission that day to hope for something different.

To believe I could be something more.

To trust in myself enough to weather the uncertainty life would throw at me.

Permission to explore who I could be,

To forgive myself when I made mistakes.

And I made A LOT of mistakes.

Ultimately, it's been this sense of giving myself permission that has led me through constant iterations in my life.

As Naval Ravikant says —

"It isn't 10,000 hours that creates outliers, it's 10,000 iterations."

Giving myself permission that day led to a cascade of events I never could have predicted, most of all, being right here right now, doing what I'm doing:

Taking all the experience, knowledge, resources and aptitude I have and using it to help other men become a better version of themselves.

The first step to living with HEART is actually giving yourself permission to do this.

When I tell people this, they often think it sounds silly and maybe it does, but so often we fail to give ourselves permission to actually go somewhere, or do something, or BE something or someone.

We have all these judgments, these hang-ups that keep us stuck.

Most of the time, when inspected, we find that the disempowering stories we're telling ourselves aren't true at all.

You have to give yourself permission to feel those emotions, to get that drive back in your life.

That it's okay to be happy or sad, or satisfied or dissatisfied.

To admit that you're not where you want to be and also know you could be somewhere else, somewhere better.

In order to get there, you have to free yourself up, to give yourself permission to admit these things.

So many of us are beyond locked up emotionally, locked up internally to the point that we can't seem to break through that metaphorical wall.

I've done tons of work on myself yet I still find that I'm a work in progress, always in giving myself permission:

Permission to cry

Permission to care about someone or something

Permission to live

Permission to pursue greatness

Permission to not beat myself up over mistakes for the next 30 years like so many do

Permission to forgive

Permission to have a relationship with myself that I enjoy

Permission to actually be worthy in my own life

Permission to be human

Permission to pursue a LEGENDARY life

It sounds trivial, however, it's anything but that.

I should go ahead and clarify for those men who're thinking, if I just listen to how I feel all the time I won't get anywhere.

We're going to cover this more in depth, but I'm not saying to only listen to how you feel. Only to allow your emotions to fuel you towards big goals in life rather than tamping them down so you're just a programmed robot.

We've become so enamored in our society with logic, with trying to take all the emotion out of everything, yet in the end— LIFE IS AN EMOTIONAL GAME.

The entire reason we do anything is to change how we FEEL.

There are plenty out there who would say "real men don't cry" or "real men are stoic" or whatever else but those are also oftentimes the most passionate of men.

What they're really trying to say is to learn how to control those emotions, not to not have them. I can tell you, I would far rather face an emotionless opponent than a passionate one who has learned to direct and focus that passion with absolute precision.

That's what you're after.

However, if you have followed what society has imparted on so many, then perhaps you've revoked your own permission to feel.

This is the first step to getting back on the path of being a man of power.

You were born with power.

You have always had it there, inside of you.

Have always had this huge amount of potential.

Yet so many of us simply haven't given ourselves PERMISSION to actually pursue that potential.

To even ADMIT that GREATNESS is something we feel inside of us.

Say it outloud — I BELIEVE I HAVE GREATNESS WITHIN ME!!

And you do — I BELIEVE THAT YOU DO.

And I'm not afraid to tell you.

YOU HAVE GREATNESS WITHIN YOU MOTHERFUCKER!

It's time you give yourself permission to actually believe that also.

To give yourself permission to pursue what you've always known to be true — that there is greatness within you and it's up to you to make that greatness known in the world.

This is the permission factor.

As Zig Ziglar said —

"One person with commitment is worth 100 with only interest."

Are you going to give yourself permission to have the commitment that your life deserves?

So many people toy around with the idea that they could be great, or would like to pursue their dreams, or wish to elevate themselves, to be something more in life.

But — that's exactly it — they TOY around with it.

They don't give themselves PERMISSION to actually live the MISSION.

They don't give themselves permission to 100% COMMIT to pursuing the life they really want and so they settle for a life of MEDIOCRITY.

As Mark Twain said —

"Don't dream your life, but live your dream."

At what point did you REVOKE the innate permission you were born with to chase your dreams? To chase being that person you envisioned you could become?

We all had those dreams as kids.

But at some point we stopped focusing on who we could become.

We stopped focusing on who we could BE.

And instead started focusing on what we could have.

And then bought into the rat race where you're now stuck.

Why is it that we let others be the ones who decide what we have permission to do or not do in life?

We need the teacher's permission to use the restroom.

Our boss's permission to take off.

Our partner's permission to go to the gym.

Our family's permission to support us in our pursuits.

Society's permission to deem what is acceptable or not.

We're stuck wondering who will judge us if we publically decide to announce that we want to pursue our potential.

We're stuck wondering how those around us will react, will judge us, will support or not support us, will either give love or take love away from us.

That's because so many of us have abdicated our very own BIRTHRIGHT to give ourselves permission.

Hear me now — you were not born to be average. You were not born to be a slave to anyone. You were not born to abdicate your permission factor to others — that is yours and yours alone.

And make no mistake — it can be a lonely and tough road in the trough of pursuing a legendary life and greatness.

People don't talk about it so much in the personal development world but when you start getting better, it starts becoming a reflection on everyone else around you, and people don't like having their inadequacies revealed.

But, the life you get on the other side of it is not even remotely comparable.

It's the life you know you should be living and up until this point, simply haven't given yourself permission to truly pursue it.

Or maybe you have and you've failed once or twice or even multiple times.

Well as Zig Ziglar said —

"Failure is an event, not a person."

Sometimes you just have to give yourself permission to keep going because almost invariably, if you don't stop, you'll get to exactly where you want to be.

In order to have heart — you must give yourself permission to do so.

And this can't be a wishy-washy sort of decision.

This can't be a sort of, well maybe today I feel like this sort of thing.

This needs to be a REAL FUCKING DECISION.

The kind that burns the boats so you are forced to take the island.

The kind that you feel all the way into your soul.

In order for things to really change, you need to believe that things MUST change.

You need to feel it so deeply that it's like a bolt of lightning hitting you, where you realize that you've been cheating yourself out of permission and that you've had the power within you all along.

To unlock your potential, you have to actually get some LEVERAGE on yourself.

This is what so many are lacking these days because they've given their permission to everyone else and they're so locked up emotionally that they can't seem to get any leverage — because guess what?

All leverage comes from your emotions.

You can logically know you should change.

Logically know that things would be better if you did.

Logically know that there is greatness within you.

But if you can't get behind that emotionally, with a big enough emotional punch, with lots of emotional leverage, it means nothing.

You'll see absolutely no change because the entire reason we do anything is to change how we FEEL.

So, give yourself permission to start feeling.

Give yourself permission to admit that there is greatness within you and permission to actually pursue that.

Give yourself permission to be who you could be.

To chase that version of yourself you know is within you.

To BE LEGENDARY!

Give yourself permission to start building that muscle.

It took you years to shut it off, it may take a few weeks or months to fully turn it back on.

If you go to the gym, you don't get muscles the next day.

It takes time.

It takes commitment.

It takes giving yourself permission to commit and persevere for as long as it takes to get there.

The same is true with giving yourself permission to have heart.

This isn't something that automatically happens over night. Give yourself some grace and permission to not beat yourself up over it, if and when it doesn't happen immediately.

Give yourself permission to treat yourself as a friend that you care about, that you would encourage along the path to greatness, to simply show up each and every day to pursue the man you know you could be.

And when you don't, give yourself permission to just start back over again the next day because that's what heroes do.

They may fall off, but they never give up.

ACTION ITEMS

- Where have you revoked your permission in your life?
- How can you give yourself permission today to have heart?
- How would your life change if you gave yourself permission today to pursue GREATNESS?
- Who could you be in 5 years if you gave yourself permission TODAY to actually become that person and then allowed yourself to commit fully to that vision?
- Look in the mirror, actually stare into your own eyes, and verbally give yourself permission in whichever ways you need it. Do this each morning for the next 30 days.

  I give you permission to have heart

  I give you permission to be kind

  I give you permission to love deeply

  I give you permission to BE GREAT and pursue greatness

  I give you permission to live deeply

  I give you permission to be the man I know you can be

CHAPTER TWO

Courage

"You will never do anything in this world without courage. It is the greatest quality of the mind next to honor."
– James Allen

I wipe tears from my eyes.

I'm going through a break-up with my girlfriend and we'd just had it out.

I keep engaging in self-sabotaging behaviors and I have no idea why.

It's compulsive. I'm unable to get a handle on it.

I struggle to be honest with her about what I want and especially about what I'm not going to tolerate such as how I feel she disrespects me.

I tell her I'm going to figure out what's going on with me and why I do the things that I do.

I look in the mirror while she's in the other room.

I don't understand why I'm here, how I've gotten here in life.

I'm 30 years old and supposed to be successful by now.

I'm supposed to have life figured out to some degree and on the contrary, it seems like I had it figured out more when I was younger than now.

Now I'm just an emotional train wreck that can't figure out how to solve the war raging within myself.

I'd had a hell of a time in my twenties living a life most guys can only dream of, but I've brought that to a conclusion and can't seem to figure out how to turn it into something else. Something constructive.

For me, there's only a single path.

As Ryan Holiday wrote, The Obstacle Is The Way.

And **I am the obstacle.**

Despite all my flaws, having the courage to face myself may be one of my biggest redeeming qualities.

Having the courage to emotionally sit with that pain, that discomfort, that realization that I'm the common denominator in all my problems.

Looking in the mirror, I commit to becoming the man I know I can be.

I affirm to her that I'm going to figure out how to be a man that I'm proud of.

We're still breaking up, I can't do this with her, too much has transpired between us.

But, it still takes immense courage to push through that emotional pain, to stay on the path and push forward to who you can be.

Emotionality. Heart.

It takes courage to fully feel your emotions, but that's exactly what's necessary.

"Life shrinks or expands in proportion to one's courage."
— Anais Nin

Courage is really the backbone of what it means to have heart.

It takes courage to swim upstream, to go against the flow of social norms, to follow your heart when it calls you to GREATNESS, when it calls you to LEGENDARINESS, when everyone around you encourages *complacency, compliance* and *conformity*.

But, that's part of your job as a man.

Even if we lived in a society where greatness were something that everyone pursued, it would still take immense courage to do so.

To pursue your potential, to even admit it in your heart, takes courage because it means creating a standard.

It means risking failure.

It may seem far easier to not care, to pretend like you don't want to be great, to pick the nihilistic path, but are those people ever truly proud of their lives on their deathbed?

Too many people assuage their sense of pride by focusing on being good, so that they don't have to feel the pain of not being great, so that they don't have to grieve their lost potential.

But we all know that GOOD is the ENEMY of GREAT and it takes courage to put yourself on the line, to step up to the plate and swing that bat because there is the possibility of striking out.

Yet what so many miss is that you're still great even when you strike out.

Because you still had the COURAGE to step up in the first place.

It's sad but people all around you will discourage you from following your heart.

They'll try to convince you of your mediocrity.

They'll encourage you that you can do anything, yet when you express the desire to do it, they'll then tell you that you can't do that much.

They'll tell you to just be complacent.

Or to keep doing the same thing that you've always done.

Be compliant.

But we all know that isn't the path to being legendary, to being great.

That's where courage comes in.

"Courage is not the lack of fear. It is acting in spite of it."
— Mark Twain

People will tell you how you're just hyped up from this message whether you read it, hear it on audio, or experience it in person.

They'll tell you it's all RAH-RAH stuff and you'll return to normal soon.

Maybe you will.

Or maybe you won't.

My question is — what are you committed to?

Is this really just RAH-RAH stuff, or is it that this message resonates and resonates for a reason?

Perhaps it's that the entire world is telling you to supplicate, to just be a good little boy and shut the fuck up, and like any hot-blooded male you take umbrage to that message.

Perhaps it's really just that this message gives you PERMISSION to believe in yourself, to believe that there is power within you, to acknowledge that power and maybe, just maybe, give you enough courage to pursue your potential.

Courage doesn't mean not having fear.

Courage is progressing forward in spite of the fear.

Maybe you are scared, but you choose to do it anyway.

There is a saying — Have fear fuel you instead of rule you.

As Derek Sivers says:

"Don't be on your deathbed someday, having squandered your one chance at life, full of regret because you pursued little distractions instead of big dreams."

Most people major in minor things because they haven't given themselves permission to have the courage to pursue their potential.

So they live a life filled with little things, then get to the end and finally realize — LIFE WAS ALWAYS GOING TO END ANYWAY.

So why didn't they go ahead and do the things they wanted to in the first place?

As Teddy Roosevelt said —

"The only man who never makes mistakes is the man who never does anything."

And here's the thing that nobody tells you about personal development —

It can be really fucking difficult.

Here's a quote from Steve Jobs —

"I've always been attracted to the more revolutionary changes. I don't know why. Because they're harder. They're much more stressful emotionally. And you usually go through a period where everybody tells you that you've completely failed."

That's what pursuing your potential is, by the way. It's REVOLUTIONARY changes and it's not all daisies and roses.

These days, so many people get rewarded and praised for signaling that they're working on themselves, or focusing on their "mental health" or trying to be better.

Yet oftentimes with no accountability towards the RESULT.

So you'll hear them saying that they're working on themselves for a decade and at some point you start to wonder what the hell they're doing other than just talking about it.

They're getting SATISFACTION with NO ACTION.

Or maybe they're taking action yet still not getting the result, in which case, CHANGE YOUR APPROACH.

Don't just keep doing the same thing over and over again, expecting a different result.

We all know that's INSANITY!

But it really does take serious courage to make revolutionary changes in yourself.

That's because it's difficult, and working to make changes actually requires you to — ding ding — MAKE CHANGES.

When you MAKE THE DECISION to go down this road, you'll need courage, because for a lot of people, it gets lonely in the middle —

You're making changes.

Your existing friends don't know how to treat you because the social dynamics are being challenged.

It's reflecting their own inadequacies back to them.

You're cutting the people off who you've known you should for some time yet haven't had the courage to.

Maybe you're firing that employee that has been ruining life for 20 other people yet you've held onto them under the guise of caring about them.

What about the other 20 they're sucking life from?

Did you not care about them?

And on the other side of that, you're building new relationships, sculpting a new life and ultimately — developing a NEW IDENTITY.

Make no mistake, becoming the man you could be will be an arduous journey, and it requires a lot of heart and courage.

However, if it wasn't hard, it wouldn't be worth anything in the first place.

If it was easy, everyone would do it and it would have no value.

That's the great thing about being a man — you get to build your value in this world and if you're committed to it, there is no limit to who you can become.

As Tony Robbins says —

"If you can't, you must. If you must, you can."

So, let me ask you, what will it cost you if you don't step up to that plate?

Life is about progress.

It's about growth.

It's about creating a meaningful life.

You don't do that in the pursuit of complacency or mediocrity.

You do that in the pursuit of GREATNESS!

So FUCK your MEDIOCRITY and BE LEGENDARY MOTHERFUCKER!

ACTION ITEMS

- What is your heart calling you to do that you've not had the courage to do?
    - How could your life change if you had the courage to do this thing?
- Courage is a muscle — list out 3 ways you could practice exercising that muscle.
    - i.e. Asking for a discount on coffee.
    - i.e. Call a friend and tell them you care about them.
    - i.e. Post something vulnerable on social media.
    - Go do all 3 of these things in a given week period consistently for the next 8 weeks.

- Who is someone you admire that seems to have courage? How can you surround yourself with people who encourage you to be more courageous?

Fear Busting Exercise

- Identify – Is this imagined or real?
- Worst Case Scenarios or Repercussions.
- Minimization — How could you minimize potential outcomes?
- Focus on Solutions — How can you focus on courage rather than fear?
- Clean up the aftermath — repair worst case scenarios?
- Still in fear? Stop it. That which you resist persists. Focus on courage.

CHAPTER THREE

Acknowledge The Call to Greatness

It's difficult to hit a target that you haven't appropriately identified.

I needed to say it outloud. I needed to verbalize it to another, to declare it to the universe.

I was taking a walk with a friend and I knew this was the time.

"This may sound crazy, but I need to say this aloud. I want to be great. I know there is a better version inside of me and I seriously want to meet that dude."

"That doesn't sound crazy," they reassured me.

"This just isn't something I'm used to saying aloud. I want to be rich, like filthy rich, like 100 million dollars in the bank rich. It's not even about the money, it's just that I feel like I have that sort of potential."

"If that's what you want, then why be reticent about saying it?" my friend prodded.

"I didn't grow up in a family where people vocalize things like that. Most people dream of things yet never actually put them out there and commit to them fully — And I don't want to be most people, so I'm putting it out there. I'm no longer going to be shy about vocalizing what I want and who I want to be.

"I want to be the baddest MFer I can be and I don't see anything wrong with that. I feel called in my soul to do something great in this world and I don't want to keep hiding that.

"I don't want to be like so many out there, afraid to share their dreams, afraid to take a chance on themselves, afraid to bet on themselves, won't even have the courage to acknowledge that they too feel this same way."

My friend looks at me and smiles. "Do it then."

There is something powerful in declaring things to the universe, to the world, to other people.

Do you think all the best people in the world got where they are by just hoping on it?

No!

At some point, Tom Brady said to himself and others that he wanted to be the GOAT. And guess what? We all know he is.

It was this very process that helped me along the path I'm on right now.

I eventually had to declare what I was about.

I couldn't play the humility game any longer.

I had to admit I was out to do something great and that meant having the confidence to say that I am great and there's nothing wrong with wanting great things.

This goes against lots of people's programming where they're told to be humble, to try not to stand out, to give up on their dreams, to never actualize their potential.

But you already know that's not what we're about in this book.

Jim Rohn said —

"You cannot change your destination overnight, but you can change your direction overnight."

Ever since you were a child, you've had heart. It takes heart to fall over and get back up, over and over, and over again.

It takes heart to fail then get back up just one more time.

To face all the uncertainties of the world and persist anyway.

To struggle to take your first breath.

To struggle to adapt to a world where so many things are trying to crush you.

The sheer force of gravity is trying to cave you in, yet you've resisted this from the moment of your conception.

You've been called to greatness since the moment you were born and maybe even before that.

I believe there is GREATNESS within you.

I believe it takes ACKNOWLEDGING that you have a CALLING within your very soul to pursue that greatness, to pursue a LEGENDARY LIFE!

To pursue the man you've always known you could be.

As we age, the world begins to take its toll.

We begin to give in, to start selling ourselves a bit short.

To look around and see others giving up on their dreams.

Others giving up on believing in pursuing their greatness.

And slowly, we begin to abdicate our own right to greatness.

We begin to believe it's too difficult, or just an ideal, or maybe for others but we could never do those sorts of things.

We feel this gnawing in our hearts, this calling, yet we stuff it down in lieu of false promises.

Promises that a life of mediocrity is better.

That a life of complacency is easier.

That we'll be far happier and fulfilled if we're not the driven type.

If we're not the type that pursues what we all have felt called to in our hearts.

Maybe, if we can just keep our heads down, then we can have a good and pain free life.

But you and I both know that's a lie.

According to Bronnie Ware who wrote The Top 5 Regrets of the Dying — the number one regret of the dying is:

"I wish I'd had the courage to live a life true to myself, not the life others expected of me."

Think about that.

The reason that this is a step in the HAVE HEART pillar is that you need to consciously acknowledge this calling you have.

If you don't, then who will?

If you don't, then you'll just keep lackadaisically wandering through life without ever getting to the point of truly igniting that spark within you.

If you feel like I feel,

And you believe as I believe,

Then you too, feel as though you have this calling within you.

And then perhaps, you also, can believe in yourself the way that I believe in you.

This is a crucial step.

It's a pivotal moment.

It's in our DECISIONS that we DICTATE our DESTINY.

At some point — you need to choose to WIN at life.

At some point — you have to make the DECISION to step up and become that man you know you can be.

To pursue that potential within yourself.

As Robin Sharma said —

"Don't live the same year 75 times and call it a life."

It's time to answer that calling you have in your heart.

It's time to step up to the plate and start pursuing your purpose in life.

This one will be a lot of fun.

I hear a lot of people talking about how they're searching for their purpose, or trying to figure out what they're passionate about, or if they could just find their purpose then they could get on with their life.

I'm about to drop the hammer on you:

Your purpose is to pursue your potential.

Your purpose is to become everything that you could be in life.

To pursue your potential relentlessly, so that when you get to the end,

The version of yourself, of who you could've been,

Is the same exact version of yourself, as who you became.

That is YOUR PURPOSE.

Your purpose is to acknowledge the calling you have in your heart to pursue greatness, then chase that version of yourself down.

To become the man you could be.

To become a hero to yourself.

To become a hero to those around you.

To become a beacon of what the human spirit stands for.

To become LEGENDARY.

That's your purpose.

It's incredibly CLARIFYING once you get to that point.

Because then you realize you've first of all altered course and cleared up misdirection in your life and now can get on to searching for what you're really searching for.

What you're really searching for is the most appropriate VEHICLE for you to actually pursue that purpose through.

Tom Brady currently pursues his purpose through the vehicle of football.

Michael Jordan pursued his purpose through basketball for a time and now in different ways.

Your vocation is merely the vehicle with which you choose to actually pursue your purpose which is pursuing greatness.

And I agree, selecting the most appropriate vehicle is important to actually pursuing your potential.

But, it's awfully confusing when you've been taught that the vehicle and your purpose are one in the same, and awfully freeing when you realize they're not.

The first step is to acknowledge that calling you have in your heart to pursue your purpose, to pursue your potential.

With this first step, you've made a DECISION and we'll go into this more later, but in that decision, you then open yourself to everything else you need.

As Ralph Waldo Emerson said —

"Once you make a decision, the universe conspires to make it happen."

Target selection is wickedly important — by that I mean selecting the most appropriate way to develop yourself, your talents, to develop into the man you could be, to pursue that version of yourself you know exists within you.

We're going to get there.

But right now, this is about answering the call to actually make that COMMITMENT with yourself and to the WORLD.

That you're acknowledging this call within you and your commitment to pursue it.

I think Les Brown sums it up well in this quote —

"You don't have to be great to get started, but you have to get started to be great."

I know it's scary.

I know it's intimidating.

I know it takes courage to actually acknowledge this.

That it gives you hope when sometimes you feel scared to even hope for hope.

That it can feel daunting.

That it's easy to placate yourself with thoughts of having an easier life by ignoring your call to greatness.

But we both know that's a lie.

That there has never been a harder life than one lived in COWARDICE.

Than one lived in AMBIVALENCE towards one's TRUE PURPOSE.

Another quote by Les Brown —

"Most people fail in life not because they aim too high and miss, but because they aim too low and hit."

You feel the calling.

You have it in you.

Acknowledge it.

Then aim towards it.

Pursue that greatness relentlessly.

BE LEGENDARY.

ACTION ITEMS

- Right here, right now, make a commitment with yourself that you're acknowledging your call to greatness and that you're 100% committed to pursuing that and becoming the man you could be.
  - This is a proclamation to the universe that you want to be the man you know you can be.
- Declare it to the world — tell someone that you want to be the baddest version of yourself you can be. Tell them that you want to live up to your potential and what you know is inside of you.
- What regrets will you have on your deathbed one day if you don't acknowledge this call and live congruently with it?
- How are you committed to seeing your life change over the next 5 years by acknowledging this call?
- Link MASSIVE pain to not taking the actions to follow through on your call to greatness.
  - In 5 years, how will you feel knowing that you're only a fraction of the man you could have been if you took this material seriously, right here, right now?
  - What bad habits or practices will you still be doing that are sabotaging you in 5 years if you don't make the decision to answer this call and change TODAY?
- Now, link MASSIVE pleasure to changing.
  - How will your life transform into the one you desire, into abundance, by acknowledging and answering this call?
  - Who will you be in 5 years because of it? What are the bad habits you will have stopped and the more desirable habits you'll have in place?

- What characteristics will you have compared to who you are now?

  Will you live more presently?

  Have more gratitude?

  Be more honest?

  Be more compassionate?

  Be a better father?

  Be a better leader?

  Have more abundance?

CHAPTER FOUR

Be Present & Have Gratitude

My buddy was talking, trying to penetrate my morose mentality on the world and give me some words of encouragement, but I was nowhere to be found.

"Bro, are you listening?" he asked.

It's not his question that jars me from my ruminations but the change in tonality.

"Yeah, absolutely man," I lie.

"You're going to get through this. I know it's tough right now but this is just character building."

I thanked him as he left and sat down to wallow some more in my victimhood.

This is exactly where you don't want to be.

There are superpowers in this world and when you learn to master them, you become an insanely powerful individual.

Being present and having gratitude for your struggles is one of them.

Gratitude is a super power for your heart, your mind, your entire life, and gratitude occurs in the present.

It would be years later until I mastered the art of actually applying this to my life, but when I did, I stopped the noise. I stopped constantly losing power to all the little things in my life, to all the leaks, and was then able to direct myself wholly and singularly towards my goals.

"I have realized that the past and future are real illusions, that they exist in the present, which is what there is and all there is."
— Alan Watts

"The ability to be in the present moment is a major component of mental wellness."
— Abraham Maslow

Becoming a man of power doesn't happen in the past, nor does it happen in the future — it happens by living presently.

So many of us will dream about the future, dream about how things ***could*** be in order to avoid facing how things ***are*** in the present.

Or, we'll escape to the past, to a better time to likewise, escape our current, crushing reality.

But, if you're going to truly have heart and tap into your potential, that requires you to be present.

To be fully engaged.

Right here.

Right now.

To be locked into the present so that you can experience reality and then bend it to your will.

If you're off daydreaming whether in the future or past, it prevents you from maximizing yourself in this moment.

Life is meant to be lived yet when I look around, I see so many who are simply trying to escape, trying to avoid being present, trying to shy away from and avoid actually tapping into their potential.

I get it.

It can be difficult to be present.

It takes courage.

It takes a certain amount of faith and strength to face reality.

It isn't always easy to shoulder that responsibility.

It isn't always easy to look adversity in the eye and smile.

I've succumbed to cowardice in my life more times than I can count, and each time, I've never felt better about myself afterwards.

The only person I fooled each time was myself, trying to convince myself that I was something other than what I was.

But we all know in our hearts who we are and who we could be.

The antidote to the crushing weight of reality of course is gratitude.

I've now found I can have gratitude no matter what life throws at me.

I've gotten past the idea that I know what the right decision or wrong decision is.

That there is a right way and a wrong way.

That there is a surefire way that life *should* happen.

That's not reality.

Just because you think the world *should* be some way, doesn't make it so.

And just because you think you know the formula for the right decision and wrong decision, that doesn't make it so either.

Let me ask you — have you ever made a terrible decision that led to a wonderful outcome?

How about a decision that you are absolutely certain is a great decision that turns out to lead to some of the worst experiences?

I know I sure have.

That doesn't stop me from trying to make the best decision I can, but it does mean that I have gratitude for the experiences either way.

Both being present and having gratitude are fundamental to having heart and you need both.

Without the ability to be present, you miss all the great things that make up this experience we call life.

You miss the laughs, the tears, the meaningful moments, the pain, the hardship and the sweetness of the moment when you overcome a seemingly insurmountable obstacle.

If you can't have gratitude for these things, then they'll be meaningless, which is really, in my opinion, just about the worst outcome one could have in life.

You're sure to have pain, you're sure to have struggle, you're sure to have obstacles.

But with gratitude, you give all that pain, struggle and obstacles meaning, which is what we're really after anyway.

A meaningful life — what more could there be?

You live a meaningful life by unlocking that potential you have within yourself and becoming the man you could truly be — that in and of itself is extremely meaningful and purposeful.

But, in order to truly live a great life, you have to have heart, which also means being present and having gratitude, even in the depths when life feels insurmountable.

"He who has a why to live for can bear almost any how."
— Friedrich Nietzsche

In the following sections I'll go into more detail about the past and future and how we can tap into those to actually create the future we want, to create future memories and to alter the past, but for now, the main goal is to actually be present and have gratitude in those moments.

To stop and smell the roses.

To actually find something great about a seemingly horrible situation.

To be present in the pain so that you can create a different outcome.

To realize that while pain may be inevitable, suffering doesn't have to be.

You can't have gratitude without being present and while you may be able to be present without gratitude, that leads to a miserable existence and unfortunately a great many people choose this option.

That leads people to shut down emotionally.

To find the world too painful a place.

A place not worth being present in.

A place where they're simply trying to escape because they haven't realized that they have a choice in how they experience reality.

There is a better way and all the greats have known this.

You may not get to choose all of your experiences in life, but you do get to choose how you will perceive and contextualize those experiences and what you will take out of them.

This may sound simple or like common sense,

But if you master this alone — this is a SUPER POWER.

We don't get to choose which time in history we're born.

We don't get to choose which zip code we're born into.

We don't get to choose our height, or sex, or skin color, or hair type or a variety of other things.

But we do get to choose how our experience on this big rock floating around the sun will be.

We may not get to choose how we're raised, or what we have to deal with, but we do get to choose how we'll view those things.

We do get to choose if we'll be present or not.

We do get to choose if we'll have gratitude even in the most painful of moments or not.

We do get to choose whether we'll choose to believe that life is always working for us or against us.

We do get to choose whether we believe life is a gift or a curse.

And we do get to choose what we're going to do with this thing called life.

That's powerful.

That's unbelievably powerful.

You have that power within you,

So choose greatness, choose life, and become legendary!

ACTION ITEMS

- What are 3 of your top go-to strategies for not being present?

  i.e. Social media? Cleaning? TV?

- How can you create a habit-loop-trigger to change those so that instead, they empower you to be present?

  - Habit-loop-trigger – When you pick up your phone to look at social media, you create a trigger warning in your brain to ask if you're doing this to avoid being present in another situation.

- Create a mental trigger warning so that when you engage in these activities, you ask yourself what you're trying to not be present for?

  i.e. I'm on social media and someone tries to talk to me. I have a mental trigger warning that says to lock the phone and put it down to be fully present for that conversation. I can pick the phone back up later.

- How could your life be so much sweeter, deeper and better by being present even when you don't want to be?

- What sort of routine can you put in place so that you consistently are looking for opportunities for gratitude?

  i.e. habit-loop-trigger so that when you experience pain, you automatically reframe it as a learning experience that you're grateful for, and also then focus on learning so you can find the origin of the pain so that you don't make the same mistake on repeat like most of us do.

- Implement a morning gratitude journal where you list 3 things you're grateful for. Do the same for an End of Day journal.

BONUS SECTION — FRACTIONAL LIVING

One of the biggest ways people avoid reality and being present these days isn't through constant daydreaming, but instead through constant distraction.

So many people are convinced they're more productive than ever, busier than ever, have so little time, yet when asked for an accounting of productivity or busyness, they fail to produce anything of substance.

The problem here is fractional living — multi-tasking, constant entertainment, a constant information flow coming in towards them at warp speed that they can't actually be present and focus on one thing because they always have so many channels blasting them.

But, it's also in vogue to practice gratitude and be more aware. So you have this entire group of the population that has convinced themselves of their ability to be present, to have gratitude, to be *enlightened*, yet in the same sentences will complain about their crushing anxiety, depression, binge watching shows, their disenchantment with their life they just can't seem to articulate.

They're practicing having gratitude while watching TV, browsing social media on their phone, listening to the news on their computer, and drinking a gluten free, soy mocha latte with extra pumps of sugary bullshit.

Look, I get it.

You're BORED.

You have no compelling future.

No compelling story for your life.

No compelling desire to do anything.

No compelling possibilities and you're BORED.

Or perhaps you're scared.

Perhaps you're scared to actually start your own business.

Or to ask for a promotion.

Or to show up in your relationship fully.

Or to believe that you could make a million dollars.

Or to believe that you're even worth that.

So you've convinced yourself how busy you are.

You've created a rigged game for your life where you only engage in FRACTIONAL LIVING so that you never have to face being present.

So that you never have to face actually looking in the mirror and having some accountability with yourself.

So that you never stop long enough to sit with the uncomfortability that is the present, that is whole living.

It's not the busyness that's keeping you from greatness.

It's not the resources.

It's not the money.

It's not the relationships or other EXCUSES.

It's YOU.

It's you and you even know it.

So you've devised an elaborate illusion of busyness to ensure that you only engage in fractional living with the warped idea that it will somehow get you where you want.

It won't.

Look at any of the greats through history — they don't engage in fractional living — and neither should you.

Even someone who's extremely busy with 5 minute time block schedules throughout the day isn't living fractionally.

Hell, if you only have 5 minute time blocks then you had better show up at a damn high level in order to execute. You're not going to be checking twitter, texting and eating while also in the middle of attempting to have a meeting. You're going to be fully present, fully dialed in and fully engaged in whatever the topic is here.

Single-tasking trumps multi-tasking just as whole-living trumps fractional-living.

Fractional living leads to just that, a fractional version of yourself.

You're split and therefore lack wholeness.

You lack integrity.

Integrity comes from the latin word integritas, meaning "one" or "whole".

Instead, you're living in plurality and that's massively painful and confusing.

You're not present and therefore don't get the benefits of being present.

I know it's difficult to make the transition from constantly entertained, constantly distracted to actually allowing yourself to sit with boredom, to sit with nothingness so that you can also focus with the entirety of your being and live wholly.

It's uncomfortable to make changes but the rewards you get for learning to be present and have gratitude cannot be overstated.

To close, and my last thoughts on fractional living,

Cut that shit out.

ACTION ITEMS

- List your top 3 bad habits for fractional living.
- List how you will set up habit-loop-triggers so that you stop these habits and implement 3 new, better habits.
- Make a commitment, right here, right now to stop fractional living and instead to be present and to live with gratitude.

CHAPTER FIVE

Do It Anyway

"When mental energy is allowed to follow the line of least resistance and to fall into easy channels, it is called weakness."
– James Allen

I wake up. It's still dark outside. My body hurts. I haven't slept enough, and everything inside me is screaming to get back into that warm cozy bed.

I go to the bathroom, flip the light on and stare into my crusty eyes.

Fuck that.

Fuck getting back in bed.

Fuck not hitting my goals, not keeping my word to myself, to keeping my commitments to myself and others.

I splash some cold water on my face and let that fire inside me roar.

Having heart is about listening to those emotions that help encourage us towards our long-term goals and future vision, not those short-term, temporary emotions that lead to regret and lack of fulfillment.

This is something I see men misconstrue when they're first introduced to this concept of leveraging their emotions more.

Having heart isn't about listening to how your each and every little emotion feels and giving into that.

It's about putting those in their place in the overall scheme of things so that they drive you.

You'll look back on a hard day that you didn't think you could make it through with pride knowing that you did.

You'll look back on a hard workout that you were certain wasn't going to happen with pride for pushing through the pain and adversity.

That's how life works.

Adversity is not the adversary.

This isn't a pillar about being a little bitch.

It's a pillar about leveraging all that emotionality towards purpose and goals so that you can become that man you know is inside of you.

Part of learning to be a man is learning to do all the things you don't want to do in the short-term so that you can be the man you most desire to become in the long run.

Men aren't built without struggle.

As Wes Watson says:

"Adversity introduces a man to himself."

Having appropriate expectations in life is extremely helpful to never being disappointed.

I used to wish for a problem and pain-free life.

Now, I realize that without those, there would be no growth.

That without the struggle there would be no value on the other side.

No one looks at an athlete that's showing exceptional heart during a game and thinks he's had a struggle-free experience.

We respect him precisely to the degree of STRUGGLE he is in fact overcoming.

Maybe he is making it look easy because we all know he put in the work but each and every person can also see that he's not leaving anything on the table — and that's why it's respected so much.

Do you think every ounce of his body isn't screaming to tell him to stop?

Do you think his muscles want to keep pushing through exhaustion?

No!

But guess what?

He does it anyway.

That's because he has heart and that's what it's going to take for you as well in life.

It doesn't matter what you do or don't feel like doing, you just have to do it anyway.

That's part of being the man you know you can be.

If it were easy, you'd already have done it.

If it were meant to have no value, it wouldn't be worth doing.

This is the struggle and why I've spent this much time on this pillar.

Emotionality sets winners apart from losers.

How bad do you want it?

How hungry are you?

How committed are you to your vision?

People who listen to their each and every emotion over-value short-term pleasures while those who have learned to leverage their emotions appropriately value long-term vision and harness their emotions to give them the leverage to actually achieve these.

All the leverage comes from emotionality though.

If you watch people who've risen quickly over the last 15 years, people such as Tim Ferriss, Grant Cardone, Wes Watson, Ben Greenfield, Joe Rogan, Jordan Peterson or any other person you wish to name — they are all driven and motivated as hell and why is that?

They're passionate.

They're excited about life.

They're on a damn mission.

They're committed to being unstoppable.

Do you think it's their superior thinking or logic that got them there?

Hell no!

It's their unrelenting drive in their mission which stems from having so much heart that they bend reality to their will.

You can do this also.

Don't shy away from those emotions, but also don't give in to them. Don't give power to the emotions that tempt you to compromise on your vision.

To quote Wes Watson again: **"Life is about being and becoming."**

You don't become the baddest motherfucker alive by being soft or by listening to your each and every emotion.

You do it by harnessing them and directing them towards who you're trying to become.

When you hold that vision in your mind, all those little temptations are just that, only temptations.

When people ask me what to do when they don't feel like it, I ask them if they know what they need to do. Oftentimes they know, so then I tell them it doesn't matter how they feel — do it anyway.

Don't compromise.

Do it anyway, motherfucker!

ACTION ITEMS

- What have you been avoiding doing (that you know you need to) because you haven't "felt" like it?
- How can you utilize your long-term vision to give you the emotional leverage to do the things you need to now so that you can become who you want to be tomorrow?
- When you do things today that you don't "feel" like doing, begin the process of anchoring how good you feel afterwards at overcoming yourself in that moment and doing it anyway.
    - Anchor reward and pleasure to that. Literally stop, look in the mirror, give yourself a fist pump or "Hell yeah, motherfucker!" in the car to actually recognize this accomplishment.

Imagine if you were playing in the Super Bowl and played your heart out then at the end there was no reward, no reinforcement, no anything to make you want to do that again. This is what it's like if you don't anchor Ws (wins) in your life.

You have to stop, to recognize and stack those Ws so that you build up confidence and anchor pleasure and progress to overcoming adversity.

- When you give in and don't do the things you need to because you don't feel like it, anchor how shitty you feel because of that and how you never want to feel that way again.
    - Anchor pain to this. Same process except don't let it eat you up. You can both simultaneously feel that emotional pain and forgive yourself so that you're not stuck in a downward spiral.

      Forgive yourself, leave it in the past and get back to focusing on stacking Ws.

CONCLUSION

Life is an emotional game.

Having heart is the foundation upon which everything else in this book is built upon.

The more deeply you're able to tap into that emotional well, the more leverage you will carry with you in your life.

The more emotion you bring to life, the more power you tap into.

One of my favorite quotes is from the movie Speed Racer.

"You don't climb into a T-180 to be a driver. You do it because you're driven."

— Racer X

The same is true with all race car drivers today. They're not climbing into the cars to be a driver, they do it because they're driven, they're passionate, they're obsessed, they're driven by something so deep, so primal, so powerful that nothing can deter them from their mission.

In short, they have heart and **heart has them.**

Needless to say, if you haven't learned how to manage your emotions, this can make for a very difficult life.

Just as a toddler can't control their emotions, they suffer outburst and fits and a time of uncontrolled turmoil, so too will your life be if you don't learn to manage yours.

However, in the journey of learning to manage your emotions, it's important to remember to not over-correct so that you're devoid of them, which is what I see so much of today.

Having heart is about empowerment.

It's about giving yourself the tools and resources necessary to become the person you truly can be in this life.

We're here to unlock your potential and it starts by getting some serious fuel and thrust behind you.

All the legends that we associate greatness to throughout history have understood these principles. They've all battled against their own demons yet in the end, conquered them through multiple levels to become the people they became.

Remember, to put a spin on the famous quote by Rumi —

"What you seek is seeking you"

Or

When seeking greatness, greatness seeks you also.

Give yourself permission.

Have courage.

Acknowledge your call to greatness.

Be present and have gratitude to fuel you.

And when you don't feel like it – do it anyway!

Choose to be GREAT my friends.

PILLAR II

Implement Non-Negotiable Standards

INTRO

"What you put up with, you end up with."
— Brad Lea

Non-negotiable — not open to negotiation or discussion.

Five years ago, if you had asked me about my standards, I would have rattled off what I thought they were.

However, upon even a modicum of inspection, I would've seen that I wasn't actually clear on my standards.

More importantly, that they were very open to interpretation or negotiation.

That made them guidelines, not standards.

Guidelines that I followed and broke occasionally when it was convenient for myself.

That was a recipe for disaster.

Invariably, that led to hitting rock-bottom and having a hard reckoning with myself in the mirror.

And that was the best thing to ever happen to me.

Because it made me get absolutely clear about my actual standards.

What they were,

And to strategically implement them in my life.

That is the day my entire life changed.

When I took my "standards" from CASUAL guidelines, to NON-NEGOTIABLE, that set me on the path to becoming who I am today.

If you also do this, your life will change the same.

CHAPTER SIX

Take Responsibility and Extreme Ownership

"The moment you take responsibility for everything in your life is the moment you can change anything in your life."
— Hal Elrod

"You must take personal responsibility. You cannot change the circumstances, the seasons, or the wind, but you can change yourself. That is something you have charge of."
— Jim Rohn

In 2008, my father and I are rescued by helicopter from an island located in an alpine lake in the Lake Tahoe region. The next evening amid raspy breaths from my aching lungs, I received my first real lesson on personal responsibility.

I sat across from Ed Seykota, legendary trend trader and all around savant, and expressed how it really wasn't my responsibility that I'd been rescued.

"Someone should have put a sign up," I argue.

"The park rangers should have brought life vests rather than a helicopter."

"It wasn't really my fault. I was enticed into it by some overweight girl on a nearby rock who had done it and I wasn't about to let her show me up."

This was the one. I wasn't to blame. It was my ego. I couldn't be helped for that.

Ed was having none of my bullshit excuses though.

He instructed me that blame and fault are more political terms to obfuscate responsibility.

It didn't matter who was to blame, who was at "fault, only that it was my responsibility for somehow landing myself on a rock in the middle of a lake where I found I didn't feel confident swimming back.

How embarrassing.

Here I could go swim a mile nonstop in a pool at the local recreation center yet couldn't muster a simple 100 yard return swim.

My ego was shattered yet I was blustering, trying to assuage myself and avoiding having to look in the mirror and actually take responsibility.

Ed taunted me back, "Why should someone put a sign up? You're responsible for what you do, aren't you?"

"Well, if I'd known better then I wouldn't have done it," I try to counter.

"Even if you had known better, you're still responsible for what you do. If you'd cared to know better, couldn't you have researched altitude acclimatization and known better beforehand?"

"Well, yes. But I didn't think to."

"And that's your responsibility. If you'd taken responsibility beforehand how I'm telling you to, perhaps you would've acted differently in the first place."

"Well, I can't take responsibility for everything," I counter.

"Why not?" he said rhetorically. "I do. I take responsibility for me and everyone else also."

"I don't understand," I confess.

"Look, I'm here on this planet just like everyone else, so when something happens to someone else, or the planet, or otherwise, I have to take responsibility for my role in it. That doesn't mean I can change all of it, or am to 'blame' only that I have to take responsibility in my personal capacity."

"That doesn't seem right," I argue.

"It doesn't matter if it is or isn't. The most powerful and capable people on the planet all believe and behave this way. When you accept this on a deep level, you then start changing the world because you take responsibility for your role in it."

"Well, what if I'm driving down the road and a semi-truck suddenly and even purposefully decides to swerve and run me over?" I counter, thinking I've got him on this one.

"You managed to find yourself in that spot, in that time, in that location, beside that madman didn't you?"

"I guess," I mumble.

"And no one made you do that did they? And even if they did, then you would've put yourself in the spot to have someone make you be there at that time. No matter how you look at it — it's your responsibility.

"You have the ability to respond and how you choose to do that dictates the results you get in life. That's where your freedom lies and also your responsibility."

I mull over this conversation for the coming weeks and even put it into action for a time and get terrific results from living this way. Then, I promptly decide to forget all about it on a deep, emotional level and revert to my old ways of blame and fault and get my old results.

On the surface, I profess to abide by this principle, yet in my core and as reflected by my behaviors, thought processes, and results, I'm not truly living this way.

And my life reflects that.

So it devolves until I finally take absolute responsibility.

That was the moment I began to change everything in my life, again.

Extreme ownership is one of the most overlooked fundamentals that's simply mis-applied today, especially in the area of personal growth and development.

Taking responsibility is foundational to everything you do in life.

The results you get in life are DIRECTLY PROPORTIONAL to your capacity and ability to take an EXTREME level of OWNERSHIP over your life.

On a logical level, most of us know and even acknowledge that we need to take responsibility, yet we're also invariably caught up in the social games of blame and fault, resulting in the profession of taking responsibility yet ending with the absolution of extreme ownership.

We profess to believe in taking responsibility.

We virtue signal it to others, and end up getting "satisfaction with no action" according to Derek Sivers.

While we anchor ourselves in our "professions" in our "intentions" the RESULTS fail to testify that we've truly actually taken an extreme level of ownership over our lives.

If you had, then you wouldn't be where you are currently.

It's that simple.

I know it stings.

It's tough to look in the mirror, to see and acknowledge a truth that you've been strategically hiding from yourself.

But you and I both know it's true.

As Richard Feynman said:

"The first principle is that you must not fool yourself and you are the easiest person to fool."

Words of wisdom to live by.

This is one of the critical missing structures in so many lives I see today despite their professions of believing in taking responsibility.

But here's the thing — people that are truly great don't do that at all.

They don't profess one thing and do another thing.

They take a RIDICULOUS level of responsibility and relentlessly own it.

They understand it and it's not something that's **casual** or even logical.

It's something that they truly live by, it's a mode of operating for them.

You can logically take responsibility or ownership of something but it's only when you truly take responsibility in your heart that you start getting results.

Logically, I took responsibility for years, while on an emotional level eschewed it.

I masked my own inadequacies and results from myself, convincing myself that I was taking responsibility, all the while, knowing that I was not truly in accordance with myself.

And of course, this deteriorated my relationship with myself.

Deteriorated my congruence with myself so that I diluted my power, my focus, my results, all because I was in conflict with myself.

My life glaringly reflected those results.

That's what this is about by the way — this is results based responsibility.

If you want RESULTS in your life, then RESPONSIBILITY is the way.

When you take an EXTREME OWNERSHIP level of responsibility that's burned into your very soul.

When you admit that you're the common denominator in your life.

That you're the centerpiece of all your problems,

And take responsibility for that.

EVERYTHING will change.

"I know you would like to blame the world, but the fact is that life is an 'up to you' thing."
— Richelle E. Goodrich

People who get rapid and massive change in their life take responsibility for the fact that it's up to them to bring that about, and when they do that and feel that in their heart — that's exactly what they get.

It's strange but we're plagued by victimhood, by mediocrity, by nihilism.

By so many around us preaching complacency, telling us to lay off the gas.

But if you want results in your life, then you internalize that it's your responsibility to be in the driver's seat of your life.

"The victim mindset dilutes the human potential. By not accepting personal responsibility for our circumstances, we greatly reduce our power to change them."
— Steve Maraboli

This is really at the core of being great.

Call it responsibility.

Call it extreme ownership.

Call it radical responsibility.

Call it personal responsibility.

Call it what you will but taking control of your life, becoming who you could be, all starts with having the courage to take that level of extreme responsibility and that doesn't happen on a purely logical level — it happens when you feel it in your bones.

Let me ask you — how would your life change if you took an extreme level of responsibility for all aspects of it?

Could your relationships be deeper?

Could you make more money?

Could you have more time spent in empowered states and less in anxiety and overwhelm?

Could you finally solve the problems that have been plaguing you that you haven't wanted to fully own?

Could you finally get on the path to the person you're truly capable of becoming?

Would greatness no longer be an aspirational call, and instead a way of life?

"The price of greatness is responsibility."
— Winston Churchill

Listen to me closely — your entire life will change when you begin to take an extreme level of responsibility.

When you take responsibility for every single aspect of it and OWN it!

Here's where I get plenty of push back from people.

But… I have this or that problem or excuse…

Constantly trying to avoid responsibility and to displace blame or fault.

To avoid looking at their inadequacies or taking responsibility for their life.

Here's the thing — your excuses may be valid.

You really may have been dealt some bad cards or whatever else.

The problem is, nobody really gives a fuck.

That's harsh but it's true.

I get it. Life is not fair.

Life can be BRUTAL.

But you still have to take responsibility for it.

It gets better when you start owning the truth and taking responsibility because then you're at least in the driver's seat.

At least then you have an empowering perspective that will allow you to go and get the results you've been desiring for so long.

If you're not responsible for those results then who is?

If you can't change your life then who can? Who will?

If you don't have any say over your situation then why do you try at all?

Because in your heart, you know you have far more say than you've been allowing yourself to take responsibility for, and it's painful when you get there.

It's painful because then you realize that you're the architect that got you to this very point, right here, right now, and that you're responsible for everything you don't like in your life.

"One day I realized that everything that I get out of life, is exclusively a result of my actions. That is the day I became a man."
—Nav-Vii

All personal growth starts with truth.

If you want results in your life, that starts with you taking responsibility for the fact that you're the driver behind those results and you have to own them, good or bad, no matter what. When you do, suddenly you realize that you have a lot more power than you thought.

To segue, there is a difference though between taking universal responsibility compared to universal fault.

It may not be your fault if your house or business is struck by a meteor but you still have to take responsibility for it.

It may not be your fault if someone drops a baby giraffe on your doorstep at night, but you have to take responsibility for it.

It may not be your fault if a tractor trailer hits a patch of ice and plows into you, but it is your responsibility to recover.

When you start looking at life this way, then you start acting differently on a micro-level.

When you take extreme ownership of your life, if there is bad weather, you check reports so you can avoid any crashes due to ice.

If there is a baby giraffe left on your doorstep, don't waffle around trying to blame others or create fault — you take responsibility and figure it out.

This is one of the biggest linchpins behind all the GREATS in history.

Because they didn't just logically know it, but knew it in their hearts.

They operate differently because of this deep INTERNALIZATION and acknowledgement.

That's why they turned out to be the greats.

They weren't greats and then took responsibility.

It was the process of taking responsibility that turned them into greats.

George Washington wouldn't blame anyone else for a battle he lost.

Abraham Lincoln didn't blame his generals when they failed him. He took responsibility.

How about another one:

During a solo descent of Bluejohn Canyon in southeastern Utah, Aron Ralston dislodged a boulder which caused his right arm to be pinned. Unable to free himself and after 5 days, Aron had to break his own arm, then cut through the remaining tissue with a multi-tool.

Aron knew no one was coming to save him or at least save him in time so he did the only thing available — he took extreme ownership of his situation and himself and did what was necessary to survive.

Responsibility is the crux behind all progress.

If you're not responsible for you, then who is?

Look, it may not be your fault that you're having health issues, or that you grew up in a family that was less than ideal, but no one else can take responsibility for you.

"There is an expiry date on blaming your parents for steering you in the wrong direction; the moment you are old enough to take the wheel, responsibility lies with you."
— J.K. Rowling

You are the ONLY one that gets to choose your response.

Your ability to respond.

As Viktor Frankl said —

"Forces beyond your control can take away everything you possess except one thing, your freedom to choose how you will respond to the situation."

That is your responsibility.

"There are two primary choices in life: To accept conditions as they exist, or accept the responsibility for changing them."
— Dr. Denis Waitley

It's not enough to logically "know" you need to take responsibility.

This is something that must be internalized, must be completely etched into your being.

It's so easy to understand this, to comprehend it, yet then to get around friends or family and fall into the same lazy, unhelpful or disempowering thinking patterns.

Jim Rohn said:

"You are the average of the five people you spend the most time with."

Something most people miss is that this includes you also.

You can constantly profess to taking responsibility, but a more accurate way to see if you actually are or not is to look at the results you're getting in life.

Your results will ultimately be a lagged reflection of the degree of responsibility that you're taking.

If you're around others that do nothing but avoid responsibility, do you really think you'll end up taking the degree of it that you need to in order to create the change in life you're after?

I think not.

"Accountability breeds responsibility."
— Stephen R. Covey

It's critical for you to design your life in a manner that supports you taking this level of extreme ownership.

That supports you having this level of vulnerability, this level of truthful self-reflection, this level of commitment.

This is a NON-NEGOTIABLE STANDARD to be implemented into your life.

It's important for you to feel congruent with this in a deep manner, as I said, in your bones.

We can logically know that eating stuff we shouldn't isn't good for us, but if we don't really care, it doesn't matter.

"We all think of ourselves as independent thinkers who reason based on facts and evidence. But the truth is that our brain spends most of its time justifying and explaining what the heart has already declared and decided. And there's no way to fix that until you've learned to recognize what the heart is saying. "
— Mark Manson, author of The Subtle Art of Not Giving a F*ck, — Impact Theory Podcast

It's only when we have internalized our responsibility into our core that we get that level of congruence necessary to make massive, rapid change, to truly start actualizing your potential.

You have to decide and declare this to yourself repeatedly.

You must evangelize this concept to yourself until it's so deeply ingrained that you don't have this concept — instead, this concept has you.

This is about becoming the most powerful man you could be.

This is about developing the tools within yourself to be that person.

Only you can take responsibility for that.

Only you can take ownership of your life.

The day you truly decide to and do,

That's the day everything changes for you.

That's the day you decide to walk the path of legend.

ACTION ITEMS

- What are 3 areas where you have been abdicating responsibility that you need to OWN right now?
- How can you COMMIT to taking EXTREME OWNERSHIP of your life from this point forward?
- If you took complete ownership of your life in your heart at this point, how could your life change over the next 6 months?

  I could lose X pounds of fat.

  I could get out of a relationship I have been avoiding taking responsibility for.

  I could deepen my relationship by taking responsibility for showing up in a partial manner.

  I could make X amount more money by taking responsibility for my ability to generate wealth and abundance in my life.

- Oftentimes, the best way to fully learn to implement extreme responsibility into your life is by having accountability. Who can you get to help hold you accountable to your new definition of responsibility?
- You have GREATNESS within you. It's your RESPONSIBILITY to unlock that. Here and now, do you give your absolute COMMITMENT to unlocking that greatness and taking extreme ownership and responsibility for your life from this point forward?

  I take complete OWNERSHIP and RESPONSIBILITY for EVERY aspect of my life from this day DATE:____________ forward. Signed: ___________________________.

RESPONSIBILITY DEEPENING PROCESS

To understand taking responsibility more, take a few minutes and answer the questions I've listed out.

- How are you complicit in creating the circumstances in your life that you profess to not want? (Hat tip to Jerry Colonna.)
- How have you assuaged your ego and placed blame or guilt on other parties rather than taking responsibility in these circumstances?
- What does taking responsibility mean?
- What are 5 things you can think of off the top of your head that had you taken radical responsibility in your life instead of blaming, would have you in an entirely different position in life?
- If you had taken radical ownership of those things, what might have been the result instead?
- What are 5 areas where you can implement radical ownership in your life right now?
- In the future, when you find yourself blaming or assessing guilt on another party, how could you stop and remind yourself to take responsibility?
- How deep is your level of commitment to operating from this extremely powerful technology?
- Who are three people you can tell about this, so that you solidify it in your mind and actually reinforce it as a teacher, and also so they can help hold you accountable to this? Hint: if you can't teach it, you don't know it.

CHAPTER SEVEN

Be Unreasonable, Intolerant & Unambiguous

"The world needs many more dreamers. Unreasonable souls who fight the urge to be ordinary."
– Robin S. Sharma

On March 7th, 2022, Joe Rogan released an episode on his podcast — The Joe Rogan Experience — featuring Jimmy Donaldson, otherwise known on the internet as "Mr. Beast".

At the time, and also as of this writing, he is the largest YouTuber in the world. He's merely 23 years old and raking in BILLIONS of views and also millions of dollars.

Perhaps you're thinking — YouTube — who cares, how much could he really be making in the first place, according to Forbes, it was around the tune of $54 million in 2021.

So yeah — YouTube.

But that's not actually the point of this story.

In the interview with Joe Rogan, Mr. Beast reveals how he arrived where he is today, all starting with the discovery of YouTube at age 11.

Jimmy became OBSESSED with the platform.

He immediately got it. He immediately loved it. At 11, he probably wasn't thinking about money nearly as much as simply making content, and doing the things he loved.

However, this led him to building his entire life around this platform.

He became unreasonable, intolerant and unambiguous about this mission.

When Rogan asked Jimmy if he'd seen SouthPark, Mr. Beast said it wasn't on YouTube so he hadn't seen it.

As the interview continues, you begin to see just how committed Jimmy is to doing what he loves.

He does that to the EXCLUSION of all else.

Jimmy has implemented NON-NEGOTIABLE STANDARDS in his life and those act as the filters of what he says yes to, and also what he says no to.

This is part of the secret to becoming the man you could be — you make your world bigger when you make it smaller.

You can only say yes to an extremely limited number of things, so it's imperative to only say yes and commit 100% to the things that have massive upside and that are meaningful to you.

Jimmy does this impeccably.

If it's not on YouTube, he doesn't really care.

He's not focusing on what he's missing out on, he's focusing on what he's able to do.

He's not focusing on trying to put himself into a box like so many other people, he's focusing on being unreasonable about his life and it's that unreasonableness that has led to him having what so many would consider is an unreasonable life.

As George Bernard Shaw said:

"The reasonable man adapts himself to the world; the unreasonable man persists in trying to adapt the world to himself. Therefore, all progress depends on the unreasonable man."

It's this commitment to a cause that defines so much in life. And just so we're clear, commitment is defined by the sacrifice you're willing to make in lieu of it.

During the interview, Jimmy said that at one point, he formed a mastermind with several other YouTubers where they got on Skype for around 1000 days in a row.

Imagine all the things other kids were doing, all the things that Jimmy was missing out on, all the things he was sacrificing to make this level of commitment.

But, that's not how he saw it at all.

Mr. Beast was intolerant of anything less.

Jimmy wasn't missing out.

Jimmy was perfectly comfortable saying NO to an infinite number of other things because he had optimized his life around what he most wanted to say YES to.

So many people end up saying yes to so many things that are wishy-washy, that are only partially enjoyable, where they never get to do the things they truly want to do.

I heard Ed Mylet say that Malcom X had coined a favorite quote of his:

“That which you do not hate, you will eventually tolerate.”

It’s only when you become INTOLERANT that you actually begin the process of not tolerating all the things that are watering your life down.

It’s when you’re intolerant of saying yes to things that aren’t actually optimized for the life you truly wish to design.

When you’re intolerant, you’re not missing out on all the things you could be doing — you’re strategically saying yes only to the HIGH-VALUE activities that truly move the needle for you.

And we’re not taught this in school.

We’re taught to “be tolerant” to “share” to “say yes to things even when you don’t want to because otherwise you’re selfish”.

BE FUCKING SELFISH!

We’re talking about becoming the most powerful man you can be here.

You can’t do that if you’re out serving everyone else’s desires for you.

You can’t do that if you’re unable to say NO and truly mean it — for it to be a no where there is absolutely nothing the other party can offer you in order to change your mind.

Don’t you think that’s exactly what Jimmy had to do as well?

The level of dedication he had meant he had to say no to the Friday night games, to all the random conversations about nothing and instead have conversations only around YouTube.

He had to be intolerant of anything that deviated him from that path.

If you want a formula for failure then:

Be tolerant.

Accept anything from anyone.

Have NO standards.

Be unable to tell anyone no, including yourself.

Share your time freely with those who also have no direction in life.

Allow others to pressure you into what they want you to do, otherwise you're selfish.

See how that works?

The formula you've been taught is wrong if you want to actually become the man you know you could be.

You don't need to be reasonable, you must be unreasonable!

You don't need to be tolerant, you must be intolerant!

You will never succeed if you're operating from ambiguity — you must have CLARITY.

Ambiguity is the dream killer.

What if Mr. Beast instead had said he simply wanted to be an internet personality so jumped from platform to platform trying to become this ambiguous definition instead of focusing intently on what he truly loved?

It's likely we'd have zero idea who he is, because as Ray Dalio says:

"While you can have virtually anything you want, you can't have everything you want."

It's only when you're UNAMBIGUOUS about what you're after in life that you can be unreasonable and intolerant of pursuing that.

If you're unsure, then you have to be unreasonable and intolerant about gaining clarity over that ambiguity.

Jimmy "Mr. Beast" Donaldson is a remarkable human being with a riveting tale and while you're going to hear more about him in the next section, suffice it to say that nothing I write can do him justice in the magnanimity that he constantly displays.

On the show, he also revealed how he is a philanthropist, helps deliver meals to locals in need and is a force for good in the world.

That is greatness. Never take your eyes off the prize.

This is about becoming who you could really be and who you could really be is also someone that can impact and change the world and positively affect all those around you.

To segue from Jimmy's story, I want to dive deeper into how implementing NON-NEGOTIABLE STANDARDS around being unreasonable, intolerant and unambiguous can massively transform your life.

These are really just standards after all.

We hear standards talked about all the time.

People say things like — want to change your life, raise your standards.

It's 100 percent true.

When you raise your standards, your life absolutely will change.

Unfortunately, oftentimes that's simply too ambiguous.

It doesn't really give people the nitty-gritty that they need to fully understand it.

It doesn't prepare them for processing the things they'll supposedly miss out on, or how to really stick with those commitments, or truly anchoring why they're doing that in the first place.

There is such a negative connotation associated with being unreasonable, but isn't it really the unreasonable person that moves the world?

As Steve Jobs said:

"The people who are crazy enough to think they can change the world are the ones who do."

We're all taught to be reasonable, to be fair, to be COMPLIANT, in short, to be watered-down.

That works if you want a life of MEDIOCRITY where you don't actually become the man you know you could be.

Naturally, we need a certain degree of reasonableness because we are social creatures after all and we do need to get along with others.

However, the degree to which we need that is FAR different than how reasonable we think we need to be.

Perhaps 100 years ago this might have been different, but now, if you're unreasonable and want to have your life revolve around YouTube, you can, and you can find your tribe along the way also because the internet makes connecting possible where it never was before.

You're not stuck in a small village where you can only connect with others there and that has to remain your existence.

You have access to go out and find and create your own community and you have to be unreasonable about that.

If you're not, that's fine, but you won't actually find that or live the life you could.

The world is set up to further the existing hierarchies, to benefit and further the existing power structures, the meta-institutions of society if you will.

I get it, we need a certain amount of that.

But greatness stems from the individual, and that only happens when you become unreasonable about accepting anything less than greatness.

It was unreasonable for Arnold Schwarzenegger to think he could be 7-time Mr. Olympia when NO ONE had done it before, but that didn't stop him.

It was unreasonable for Joe Rogan to do what he's done with his podcast when there was zero evidence of it becoming what it is now. He lost money for years, yet stayed unreasonable about his vision and there's a reason that he's now the largest podcaster in the world.

No one gets to greatness by being reasonable.

You don't do something worthwhile CASUALLY.

You don't do something worthwhile and meaningful trivially.

You're competing against every single other person and most importantly — yourself.

It's only when you're unreasonable that you break through those barriers and go to that next level in your potential.

People think I'm unreasonable when they invite me out on a weekend night and I tell them I'm dedicated to what I'm working on.

That's okay — people don't have to understand my reasoning.

I only have to answer to myself.

I have a calling in my heart to become the man I know I can become.

I'm dedicated to being unreasonable about that pursuit.

I find people oftentimes hear these phrases and they simply don't register the degree to which these things need to be applied.

When you start becoming unreasonable you also begin realizing that you can't keep up with all the Netflix series that your friends are, or that you can't say yes to all the events you used to, or that you can't live your life as casually as you had before.

That's tough for a lot of people.

It's tough when you realize that if you have a vision for your life, unless your friends and family or whoever else gets on board, that train is rolling out the door and they're going to be left behind.

Some would view this as sacrifice, others would view it as an opportunity to gain new friends that have shared values and are also on a similar mission.

This brings up obvious questions — your commitments are defined by that which you're willing to sacrifice in order to keep them, so what are you really committed to?

What you're really committed to is your identity after all, so if you're committed to greatness and to becoming that person, then it's important to recognize that sacrifice is involved.

But, when you're clear on your vision, you also understand it's not really sacrifice. It's only the process of growth.

You realize that you're not actually missing out on things in life — you're strategically saying yes to the most high-value activities and behaviors.

You're optimizing for who you truly want to be.

And you're being unreasonable about that.

Once you realize that you really only care about making YouTube videos, it doesn't bother you to miss out on Thursday night bowling. It just doesn't matter because you've gotten rid of the ambiguity about what's meaningful to you, and optimized for what is actually meaningful instead.

Depending on where you're at in life, I also think it's helpful to not optimize prematurely.

Kevin Kelly talks about this and how it's important to actually explore life if you're uncertain what to optimize for.

For Jimmy, it was an easy choice because he found what he really cared for early on, but for most, it's not so clear.

Yet, they simply accept this rather than being unreasonable about dispelling that ambiguity in their life.

Where would Jimmy be if he'd never been introduced to YouTube in the first place because he hadn't been inquisitive or seeking things out in life?

You too must be inquisitive, to try different things on in order to see what fits.

It really is important to be unreasonable about this because so many people want to push others to optimize pre-maturely, to pick "something" and try to force them to stick with it for the next 40 fucking years.

On the other hand, I think the world is changing vastly, and in the future we're going to see people pick things for 5 to 10 year increments with large cataclysmic shifts in their pursuits in life as their character and values develop.

Think about it.

Most people have different values today than they did 10 years ago. Do you?

That's okay.

Isn't it a little absurd to try to have people pick something and then put them in that box and never let them leave?

I don't know about you, but people change, people grow and some people prefer to stay stagnant.

Regardless, I find it entirely absurd to try to pressure people into prematurely optimizing.

Maybe it's okay to not be a millionaire by 30 and have everything figured out.

Maybe it's okay to be perfectly okay right here, right now, exactly where you are, and to realize that it's exactly where you need to be in order to truly become the man that you are meant to be.

In order to truly find that uniqueness, to truly find what you find most meaningful and your direction in life, it takes an unreasonable soul to plod through all the noise in order to uncover the real gems in life.

That's where you have to be intolerant of anything less than that.

It's so easy to capitulate, to acquiesce to social pressures, to simply conform to who you think the world wants you to be.

However, we both know it's not really that easy.

It seems easy on the surface, but in reality, you'll get to your deathbed one day, you'll be 80 years old and realize that the hardest thing in life was actually

SACRIFICING who you WERE for what you thought people wanted you to be.

You'll realize that you sacrificed your potential, your uniqueness, all that made you YOU, because it seemed easy at the time.

And you'll realize that you paid for it with your SOUL.

You'll realize that you paid for it by never developing yourself into who you were capable of becoming.

That would be a tragedy.

Because you really do have greatness within you!

And I believe you can be LEGENDARY!

It's only when you become intolerant of anything less, that you'll start getting everything more.

I know it's divisive when I tell people that they have to become intolerant in their lives.

Everyone has so many sensitivities where they're trying to be abundantly tolerant with everything but is that really the way?

Didn't Abraham Lincoln become intolerant of slavery?

Didn't we as a country become intolerant of being ruled by a king across the Atlantic?

JK Rowling was turned down by 12 publishers before finding success with Harry Potter. But she was intolerant of anything less than having her books published.

What if instead she had stopped at the first one? What if she had been tolerant of rejection and failure and just moved on with her life?

It's our intolerance that defines us.

"You get what you TOLERATE."
— multiple citations and unclear who first said this.
I've heard it most prominently from Tony Robbins.

It's only when you become intolerant of having a semi-passionate relationship that you change it.

It's only when you become intolerant of being overweight that you truly change it.

It's only when you become intolerant of not having the success you want that you truly change your direction in a moment.

This is why these things go together.

"Only those who will risk going too far can
possibly find out how far one can go."
— T. S. Eliot

It's only when you're willing to risk going too far, when you're unreasonable about what can be done, when you're intolerant of anything less than you believe possible, that you shatter barriers and have the breakthroughs you desire.

That's where being unambiguous is critical.

You may have zero clue what you wish to optimize your life for, but you can have absolute clarity over the desire to be great and be the man you know you could be.

It takes being unreasonable and intolerant of anything less where you're willing to truly explore and not allow yourself to become complacent.

So many people never figure out what they're trying to do in life because they're reasonable and tolerant of the ambiguity that they face in life.

They treat it as if it's just a part of life and that there is nothing they can do about it.

But that's not the case at all.

The people who are truly dedicated to unmasking the ambiguity in their life, to discovering exactly who they want to be and could be, are the ones who actually do just that.

But how could you do that if you never commit to it, if you never believe it's possible, if you never develop any standards around this thing?

You couldn't.

It's only when you're dedicated to your life, to actualizing your potential, to becoming the version of yourself that you know exists within you, that you start actually becoming that person.

"We only see what we aim at. The rest of the world (and that's most of it) is hidden."
– Jordan Peterson

I know this is counter-intuitive.

I know this goes against what society would have you believe is the way to become the person you want to be.

But it's still the way.

When you implement these non-negotiable standards into your life, I can guarantee you that is the moment your life begins to transform.

Stop tolerating an ambiguous existence and instead pursue greatness with a clear vision of who you're committed to being and then be entirely unreasonable about that mission.

Right now, we're just laying the groundwork for your success so if you're thinking I don't know what to be intolerant or unreasonable about, that's okay, we're going to get there soon enough.

Stick with the journey, my friend.

ACTION ITEMS

UNREASONABLE

What are 3 areas of your life you'd like to change right now?

How could being unreasonable about those areas having to change now, actually create the change you've been wanting?

List action steps for how you could implement being unreasonable around these 3 areas to get change started NOW.

What gets rewarded gets reinforced. How will you reward yourself for adopting this unreasonableness around your goals and who you're committed to being?

How can you work to design your environment so that it encourages you to continue this unreasonableness? Speak to friends or family and have them also encourage you in this? Join a support group online?

INTOLERANT

How could becoming utterly intolerant of any change that's LESS THAN the desired change you have for those 3 areas?

How could you become utterly intolerant of accepting any change from yourself that's LESS THAN what you're capable of?

How could this intolerance drive this change home to completion compared to a wishy-washy commitment?

How can you reinforce this intolerance repeatedly until it becomes second nature? Get a coach to help hold you accountable? Write it on your mirror? Listen to a recording 3 times a day?

How can you design your environment to help reinforce this intolerance? Remove the chips? Create major friction between you and doing something you're trying to stop?

Take a piece of paper, draw a line down the middle and write all the things on the left that you will tolerate and all the things on the right that you will no longer tolerate.

LEFT i.e. I will only tolerate real commitments from myself.

RIGHT i.e. I will no longer tolerate not showing up each day at 100%.

UNAMBIGUOUS

How can you get infinitely clear on exactly what you're trying to do? Not just "lose some weight" but instead, "lose 2lbs per week for 8 weeks, then slow to 1.5lbs per week until I lose 30 pounds and also drop below 12% body fat, with a certain amount of desired lean muscle mass."

Get HYPER-SPECIFIC.

How can you reinforce that PRIORITIZATION of these 3 things you're trying to change?

You don't prioritize your schedule, you schedule your priorities.

If you have more than 3 priorities, you have no priorities.

List out all the other things you could do instead of focusing on these 3 things, pick out the most tempting ones and reorder them first, then hang them up somewhere with a DO NOT ENGAGE AT ALL COST sign above them until you meet your other 3 priorities.

You have to be entirely unambiguous about what you're trying to do and recognize that distractions are the enemy. Define them beforehand and then feel the satisfaction you have in knowing that you're not really missing out, you're just reprioritizing in order to accomplish what's truly meaningful in your life.

CHAPTER EIGHT

Embrace The Obsession

"When I started studying other obsessive types who were super successful and stopped seeking advice from those who were settling for average lives, average results, average money, average everything and who were never obsessed with anything except defending average, that's when I began to really live."
— Grant Cardone

"Make it your daily obsession to make the most of your potential."
— Tom Bilyeu

"Until you become completely obsessed with your mission, no one will take you seriously. Until the world understands that you're not going away — that you're 100 percent committed and have complete and utter conviction and will persist in pursuing your project — you will not get the attention you need and the support you want."
— Grant Cardone

"Be great because nothing else pays."
— Grant Cardone

Whether you love him or hate him, you've probably heard of Grant Cardone.

If you've ever been fortunate enough to sign up on his email list, you know he's truly an obsessed person and not in the least bit shy about sending so many emails it seems like you can't get away from him.

But, if you turn the clock back 15 years, practically no one knew who Grant Cardone was compared to now.

He grew up in a small town in Louisiana and lost his father at 10 years of age. From there he slipped into drugs as a teenager and finally landed in rehab leading to his sobriety at 25 years old.

From there, he committed himself to auto sales at first, then started a training program and seminar business where he taught auto-dealerships how to improve their sales process.

During the crash of 2008, Grant nearly lost all he had worked for and finally had an epiphany.

He was settling.

He had become soft and was merely doing the things everyone else was and that nearly led to his financial destruction.

And that wasn't okay.

Grant realized that so many around him were giving him advice to lay off the gas, to ease up a bit in life, yet all those people were precisely average.

It was only the OBSESSED individuals that truly moved the world, that truly got what they were after in life.

And so that's what he did — he embraced his obsession and used it to launch one of the most unique and fast-scaling campaigns to take him from an unknown, from near total obscurity, to a household name that evokes strong opinions both ways.

But, that's just part of it — you're always going to have haters when you're doing big things, when you're obsessed.

Grant became obsessed with never being in the position where he faced financial destruction again.

Grant became obsessed with not being a watered down version of himself.

Grant became obsessed with maximizing his potential.

That's how Grant went from an unknown to a known.

From someone with huge potential to actually turning that potential into reality.

From mediocre and average to extraordinary and great.

"The dictionary defines the term 'obsessed' as 'the domination of one's thoughts or feelings by a persistent idea, image, or desire.' Although the rest of the world tends to treat this mindset like a disease, I believe that it's the perfect adjective for how you must approach success."
— Grant Cardone

Obsession has become such a pejorative in our culture, yet hasn't it been the obsessed who've given us the great things we enjoy now?

Think about Edison and the lightbulb — he had to be obsessed in order to reach the final iteration where it actually worked.

Think about Benjamin Franklin and electricity and how you no longer hear about building fires caused by lightning strikes from his discoveries.

Or more recently, Steve Jobs' obsession with creating amazing products.

The people we all look up to and add to the greatness and legendary categories have all been obsessed.

Yet, those closest around you all tell you to "lay off the gas, bro" to "take it easy" and to not want so much.

It's confusing.

People profess to want you to express your greatness and your potential yet then discourage you from it when you actually do start embracing it.

We could go deep on why they do that but the critical factor is to recognize that an ordinary amount of dedication in today's day and age just isn't going to cut it if you're attempting to become the man you could be.

We're all trying to keep up with a million different things, to be able to talk about all the Netflix shows we binged, while also keeping up with the news, and also being an expert on the next hot topic.

I have news for you — that's a recipe for ordinary and average.

To tap into who you actually could be, it's critical that you embrace the obsession.

Yes, there are some people who seem to magically do it all and to make it look easy, and to treat their pursuits with a sort of triviality, but they're the exceptions.

I don't pursue life chasing unicorn strategies.

Everyone who has been truly great, that's lived up to their potential, at some point became obsessed with their life.

They became obsessed with chasing that potential down and became who they knew they could be.

I want that for you also.

Obsession is a blessing, it's a gift that must be unapologetically embraced in order to actually become the person you know you can.

As we discussed in the previous section, it's really only when you're obsessed that you can truly buckle down and stay focused on the things you need to in order to maximize your life.

For some reason, we all want to believe this lie that we can go through life in a *casual* manner and then somehow have life give us back all these great things.

It's not true.

That doesn't mean that you only have to study a single thing for the rest of your life.

Charlie Munger follows the expert-generalist methodology and reads INCREDIBLY broadly so that he's truly an expert in multiple fields.

But, he had to be obsessed in order to do that and get there.

I suppose that's why Warren Buffet cites him as the best business partner one could ask for.

I've read incredibly broadly with an average of 50 plus books per year for well over a decade. I've done that because I've been obsessed with learning, with getting better, with sharpening myself into the man I know I could be.

That's something no one tells you.

Somehow we've been convinced that convenience and comfort are to be sought out and desired after — yet that's exactly the opposite of what it takes in order to be the man you could be.

"Comfort is a disease. And it's what the media wants you to do. It's definitely what the big pharmaceutical companies want you to do. They

want you to get comfortable. All the big money on this planet actually wants you to get comfortable so you just sit back and become a passive spectator in the game of life."

— Grant Cardone

Let me ask you this — at what point did you start giving up on yourself?

At what point did you start embracing the comfort and sacrificing your dreams and who you could be?

At what point did you start selling yourself out for this thing called comfort rather than embracing the internal obsession you felt?

Most kids are obsessed with learning, obsessed with getting better, obsessed with all the things that they can do and will do in the future.

And then, at some point, whether it's social pressures, academic establishments telling them to calm it down, or perhaps they simply model their parents and see how they've given up on themselves, so they start doing the same.

This is bullshit and you and I both know it.

You make your world bigger by making it smaller.

You make it bigger by saying yes to the things that MATTER and have meaning to you and then obsessing over that.

You make it bigger by forsaking all the things you think you should be engaging in that you don't actually care about that much.

You make it bigger by getting comfortable saying NO to all the things that don't interest you.

You make it bigger by actually becoming MORE.

And you become more as you clarify your vision for who you could be, who your future self could be and then chasing that dude down.

"I'm as proud of many of the things we haven't done as the things we have done. Innovation is saying no to a thousand things."
— Steve Jobs

Again — you make your world bigger by saying no to extraneous things and being proud of yourself for making those decisions.

A few years ago I hit a total rock-bottom low point in my life, and that was the point that I decided everything had to change.

That was the point where I decided I was no longer going to tolerate who I was being and start becoming the man I knew could become.

I decided to stop wasting my potential and wrote down on a piece of paper:

It's time to sculpt this MOTHERFUCKER

And that's exactly what I did.

I took that saying, I took my drive and embraced an obsession level of commitment to sculpting myself into who I could be.

It was then I realized that I had been buying into the lie.

That I had been led astray, had been duped in how to live my life, in how to be the person I knew I wanted to become.

So, right now, it's also time for you to commit.

For you to make the decision to sculpt this motherfucker.

To stop playing around with your potential.

To stop believing the lies.

To stop treating obsession as something to be feared and instead something to be lusted after.

To no longer apologize for your desires or drive or your commitment to being obsessed with your life.

You only have one of them.

This one life, that's it.

So why not be obsessed with it?

Why wouldn't you give it everything you've got?

Why wouldn't you try to live the best life that's ever been lived?

And be obsessed with sculpting yourself into the man you know is just waiting to come out of you?

There is more to you than you know.

Just like the stone is slowly stripped away on a sculpture, so too must you strip away the parts that aren't serving who you could be, so the obsessed part of you can arrive and then step up to the plate in life.

In an episode of Impact Theory hosted by Tom Bilyeu, Tom's guest, **Brendon Burchard**, a high performance coach, broke down the difference between passion and obsession.

"There is a difference between passion and obsession.

And high performers have obsession about the topic.

They are obsessed about the topic in which they're trying to learn, master, grow into, and so that obsession is real.

And I tell people — here's how you know the difference between the two.

When you're passionate, everybody cheers you on.

They're stoked for you. Oh you found your passion — awesome. Follow your passion. Live with passion. Be passionate. Chase your passions.

Passion, passion, passion, passion.

Passion is good.

The world is going to be like — YAY, passion.

When you're obsessed, they're going to be like — why you gotta be so crazy?

Why can't you be satisfied?

Why do you always gotta get things so perfect?

Why do you spend so much time here?

When you're obsessed, people think you're nuts.

So it's different.

And it's like — I always tell people — if no one thinks you're crazy, you're not yet operating to the outer limits of your potential.

You're not there yet.

Because somebody in your life should say — 'man, you really care about this in like a crazy way.'

And when you get there, you know you found your thing."

Brendon goes on to say how most people obsess over their shows on Netflix or thread count of their sheets more than about their life or the impact that they're making in the world.

I tell people — you don't have to know what you're passionate about, you don't have to know some huge purpose in the world, you just have to make the commitment to become obsessed with your life.

When you do this, all the other stuff will show up when it's time.

But first, you have to commit to yourself.

First you have to give yourself permission to actually be obsessed with your life.

To actually be obsessed with who you could become and not be dissuaded when those around you attempt to convince you to water yourself down.

You don't water greatness down.

Instead, you actually water greatness like a plant you'd like to see grow.

You reward obsession.

You reinforce that it's this commitment that will have you proud of all the things you said no to, because you also knew the things you most wanted to say yes to.

Say yes to obsession.

Say no to mediocrity.

Say FUCK NO to complacency.

Become UNAPOLOGETICALLY YOU and proud of the person, the man that you're sculpting.

Become relentless in your pursuits.

I'll close with this last quote from my man Grant Cardone,

"There is no way God put us here to be ordinary."

I agree.

You weren't put here to be ordinary.

You weren't put here to be average.

You were put here to be fucking great!

You were put here to be a LEGEND MOTHERFUCKER!

There is greatness within you and it's just waiting for you to embrace it.

ACTION ITEMS

VISUALIZATION

Go to YouTube and search for Caelin Kompass Obsession Visualization to play this in the background. If not, read then perform it here.

Imagine yourself standing in front of a mirror 5 years from now.

Look into your eyes.

Look into who you've become.

Look into the man you're now proud to be.

Feel the smile on your lips turn up.

Feel the swell of pride in your chest as you inspect this person you've sculpted yourself into.

Imagine reading this book 5 years ago and putting these strategies into action.

You became obsessed with your life.

You became obsessed with THE MAN you knew you could be.

And you made that commitment and followed through relentlessly.

Imagine all the hardships you faced.

The friends or family trying to step in, trying to dissuade you from being who you knew you could be.

The friends or family members who are no longer around.

The joy and peace you have knowing that where you're at now is so different than where you were.

That looking in the mirror right here, right now, you understand that those friends and family members are still the same people they were 5 years ago.

But you no longer are.

You've grown.

You've developed yourself.

You've sculpted yourself into someone you're proud of.

And also that the people you have in your life are proud of.

That your community is proud of.

You've become a hero, not only to yourself, but to those around you.

A beacon of hope.

An inspiration.

Think of all the tired nights.

All the missed dinners with friends who are still having the same dinners and still in the same places.

Think of all the Netflix shows you missed out on.

But also, all the beautiful experiences you've gotten in return.

The vacations you traded in, in lieu of those shows.

The destinations and life you've gotten to live instead of living vicariously through a TV.

Imagine standing there in front of that mirror again, and feeling perfectly content and peaceful, knowing you haven't missed out on a single thing.

That you had the courage to say yes to the MOST important things.

And to say NO to the things that weren't truly meaningful.

Feel how proud you are that you pursued meaning and impact.

That you pursued living life to the fullest extent.

That you transformed yourself and in the process, all those around you as well.

Take a last moment and really look at yourself in the eyes.

See the pride there.

See the dedication and how much it means to you.

Tell yourself — "I'm so proud of you. I'm so proud of who you've become. You did it. You chose you and here we are together and isn't this beautiful."

Take one last look and go ahead and open your eyes.

- How would your life change if you embraced obsession?
- Who could you become if you became obsessed with discovering just that?
- Now is the time, right here, right now, to commit to becoming obsessed with your life. Write down your name and date and your commitment to becoming obsessed with your life. To becoming obsessed with sculpting yourself into who you really could be.

CHAPTER NINE

Tell The Truth

"The object of the superior man is truth."
— Confucius

"The real question is: How much truth can I stand?"
— Friedrich Nietzsche

So many of us have bought into the lie that it's appropriate and even to be rewarded to lie, to not be honest, to not tell the truth.

Now you're thinking — no way — I grew up learning it was bad to lie.

Yes, you probably did.

Then you watched your parents or others around you lie.

Not directly, not always, but subtly.

When they did lie directly, overtly, there was always a good enough reason that made it okay, that JUSTIFIED that lies bullshit.

So you watched, and you learned, and you — modeled.

You slowly began to adopt this nuanced form of deception, this nuanced art of telling the truth or mostly the truth while artfully leaving out the things that just weren't "appropriate" or that would cause issues, or just may not be polite.

Slowly but just as surely as the sun rises, you began to weaken your sense of reality, of what's real or not real.

Why?

Because you can't ascertain the truth.

You ask someone, does this make me look fat?

That person then responds with a *softener* — no, it accentuates your features.

You hear from another — money doesn't matter, it won't make you any more happy.

And then accept their justifications for why they're broke.

You have a "friend" in your social circle that makes everyone uncomfortable, but no one will actually tell him or her because you're all too cowardly to not be "nice".

Here's the thing — that's not nice.

It's not nice to deprive that person of the feedback necessary for them to make changes, to grow, to become a better person so that they don't make everyone uncomfortable.

You think — I really care for my partner but they're not meeting all my needs and I can't be honest about it, so I'm going to lie to them, to convince them that they are meeting all my needs while simultaneously going out and having other sexual or emotional relationships to actually fulfill my needs.

Then justify it as CARING.

Because you care…

You lied and didn't tell him or her and didn't tell the other guy or girl because of course, you're "nice".

Look, I'm not the morality police here. I'm not here to tell you what your relationships should be or if you should have multiple partners or a single one or anything like that.

There are plenty of people in a relationship where it's a don't ask, don't tell situation and each partner knows the rules and that's fair.

But if you're with someone who thinks they're in a totally committed, monogamous relationship and you do this, maybe you should consider having a hard look in the mirror.

I know it's oftentimes easier to ask for forgiveness rather than permission but you deprive yourself and your partner of the opportunity to actually face the situation when you're not truthful about it.

This is coming from someone who disagrees with a lot of the traditional American models of relationships. Trust me, if you're a high-value man in the world, and actually become who you could be, there are plenty of women that will be just fine being in a relationship with you while also allowing you to have your freedom.

I just wouldn't marry them in the West because it's geared against men having rights.

Don't believe me? Nearly 50% of first marriages end in divorce, 60% of second marriages and 73% of third marriages with 69% of divorces being filed by women.

If I were to tell you these are the odds of losing 50% of the things you work for over the next 20 years by working for one company or you can go with another company where there isn't a 50% chance of loss, which would you go for?

That's right.

Believe it or not, I am actually pro-nuclear family, pro-marriage if that's what you want, and pro-fathers and children. I just think it needs to be looked at within the context of where you're at and the available options.

At the very least, consider a prenup. Don't be naive.

If that's what you want, more power to you, but at least get truthful with yourself about it and don't try to force yourself into a traditional American relationship while then trying to get it to also fit the norms of different cultures.

Back to our scheduled programming.

You think it's caring when you make up stories to justify your lying to yourself or your partner or anyone.

But, we both know that's all a lie.

We both know it's not nice to lie.

It's not nice to not tell the truth.

It's not nice to fuck with people because we're too COWARDLY to actually live truthfully.

And that's what it is in the end, right?

COWARDICE.

"If you don't say what you think then you kill your unborn self. When you have something to say, silence is a lie."
— Jordan Peterson

I know this is heavy.

I know this has taken a turn.

But it's necessary.

As a society, we have stopped having the HARD conversations because we're all caught up in trying to be too "nice" at the EXPENSE of the TRUTH.

It's not good, man.

It's not good at all.

Rather than being able to have difficult conversations around certain topics, now many people automatically apply a derogatory label to anyone who disagrees with them and end the discussion with an ad hominem attack.

It has taken the turn to stifle any that dissent with your perspective of reality.

And it has left no room to attempt to ascertain the most important thing — the truth.

As Friedrich Nietzsche said —

"There are no facts, only interpretations."

Telling the truth MUST BE a NON-NEGOTIABLE standard.

That doesn't mean that what you're saying is always the truth.

But it is your current iteration of it, and if you have any hope of getting to the next, you have to start with the present.

The truth is only the beginning, a starting point to expand upon, so that you can make progress, grow and become the man you could be.

The truth isn't stagnant, it's not set in stone, it's not absolute — it's something to be sought after, to be revered, to be cherished.

Even while it's painful at times, it's the building block upon which all else is built.

Another quote by Friedrich Nietzsche —

"The snake which cannot cast its skin has to die. As well the minds which are prevented from changing their opinions; they cease to be mind."

The truth as we're talking about here, isn't about embracing dogmatism — never that.

It's about implementing the standards necessary for you to be the man you know you really could be.

It's about providing a starting point to be built upon with which we can all interact.

To do that, we have to be skeptical of ourselves, of our believed truths, while also remaining committed to ascertaining the actual truth no matter how many layers deep we must go in search for it.

If we stop telling the truth, then how do any of us get the necessary feedback in life to get better?

To grow?

To improve?

Imagine if you had a coach who wouldn't tell you the truth?

Consider this parable:

There was once a young boy who wished to be the greatest fighter the world had ever seen. In a nearby kingdom, it was rumored that a master of the arts had taken up residence in the mountains to pursue a life of solitude away from the fighting he was so masterful at.

Upon hearing this, the boy took off to seek out this master.

When the boy finally located the master, the master explained that if he wanted to train under him, it would be a long and arduous journey of 10 years.

The boy agreed and began his apprenticeship.

The apprenticeship didn't begin in the way the boy expected but instead by simply serving the master, then as time wore on, slowly the master began to reveal more and more secrets.

The boy practiced diligently and the master assured him that he was progressing well, that his training was just as he knew it would be — that the boy was a natural talent, and under the master's tutelage would be the best fighter the world had ever seen.

Mid-way through his training, the boy began to have doubts as he heard whispers from the local villagers yet when he confronted them, they all expressed their jealousy at being so fortunate to train under such a revered master.

As the time grew near for the boy's training to be complete, the boy expressed doubts to his master, only to have his master scold him and remind him that he was the most formidable warrior alive until the boy would take the helm.

The boy, now a young man, was full of doubts as his training was coming to an end.

Yet all the villagers and his master assured him that he was in fact to be the most feared, most revered warrior to ever walk the earth.

The master, sensing that his apprentice was becoming impatient, declared a final challenge for the young man.

He would have to travel to a distant land, and defeat their local champion in combat.

The young man did as his master directed and traveled to the distant land and challenged the local champion.

The young man found himself in combat with a sword for the very first time yet felt confident.

The master had told him that due to his exceptional training and knowledge of his body, the sword would be as a natural extension of him, and he would know exactly how to wield it effortlessly.

Upon the first blow by the local champion, the sword flew from the young man's hands. He stared at his shaking hands, stunned, unable to reconcile this betrayal.

And the last thing he thought was that he hadn't been trained to be the world's best fighter, but instead had been the world's biggest fool.

And the last thing he felt was how saddened he was that not ONE person had had the COURAGE to tell him the TRUTH.

All progress starts with the TRUTH.

Oftentimes, the most difficult thing is not only telling others the truth, but telling YOURSELF the truth.

To quote Richard Feynman again on the same quote—

"The first principle is that you must not fool yourself and you are the easiest person to fool."

It's not nice to lie to yourself.

It's not nice to lie to others.

If you're going to become the man you know you could be, you have to tell the truth.

If you don't, then how can you be pursuing greatness?

The truth is foundational to getting where you want to go, and how can you get there if you can't be honest about where you are at?

Greatness is telling the truth, and telling the truth leads to greatness.

Telling the truth means getting honest with yourself about where you are, where you want to go, who you want to be, what is no longer acceptable, what you've been accepting that you shouldn't be and where you've been lying to yourself to assuage your ego, or pride or because you've been too cowardly to actually confront it.

Great cultures and people are built upon the truth.

And great cultures and people crumble when they no longer have a foundation of truth.

I know this will be unpopular.

It shouldn't be, but I know it will.

Everyone knows they should tell the truth, like really tell the fucking truth and also let themselves feel the truth in their heart, yet we're also resistant to it.

It can be painful.

It can be hard to see our imperfections, our flaws, how we've subjugated ourselves to being less than we could be, how we've fractured ourselves when we know we have greatness in our hearts.

That's where courage comes in.

I know it's painful.

I know the truth can cut deep, yet the lack of truth is far more pernicious, far more deadly.

As Friedrich Nietzsche said —

"Sometimes people don't want to hear the truth because they don't want their illusions destroyed."

I understand.

I really do.

I lied to myself for years.

I was the BIGGEST liar in my life, and I paid for it at great cost.

I lied to myself, telling myself that I was on my way to doing something with my life even as I'd chug an entire bottle of vodka.

I'd lie to myself that I'm somehow smarter, somehow more intelligent, all while demonstrating remarkably average intelligence.

I'd lie to myself that someone would notice me drowning in my own unworthiness and save me until I finally realized I was the ONLY one that was going to save me.

I'd lie to myself that I didn't have any problems, convince myself of the veracity of this, all while trying to hide my problems in the closet.

I'd try to lie to myself that I wasn't fucked up inside, yet all my actions and results I was getting in life told exactly the opposite story.

It was only when I finally came to that *threshold* with myself, that point when I couldn't take it any longer, that my illusions were shattered and everything changed.

It was only when I broke down and was forced to sit with the truth of my life, with the truth of where I was, of who I was being, of my utter brokenness, that everything changed.

This may sound motivational as you're reading it, but it didn't feel like it at the time.

When that wall came down, it was darkness. It was painful. It was sweet relief mixed with a tsunami of emotional turmoil — and man, I ugly cried — hard.

I bawled my eyes out like a baby, sitting on the floor, all alone, full of shame, full of disappointment, full of anger, full of sadness, full of fucking victimhood.

Yet, through all of that, one thing rang out profoundly from that darkness — HOPE.

I felt like I finally had hope because I'd also gotten to a cold, hard truth, and I knew I could build upon that.

All progress begins with truth.

Oftentimes, we're not told the consequences of not telling the truth or we don't fully understand them.

In my world, each one of us has a ledger in our unconscious mind and that ledger is always being tabulated and is especially influenced and weighted upon our thoughts, actions and the emphasis or meaning we place upon those.

So when we don't tell the truth, our unconscious knows this, and it keeps a record in that ledger.

If that something we don't tell the truth about is a big deal, has a large emotional meaning, it's weighted heavier in the ledger.

This ledger is constantly running, constantly being tabulated, so when you lie to yourself and others, you begin to erode the confidence you have with yourself.

You tell yourself you're going to go to the gym — your unconscious says — who are you kidding, you lie to yourself and others all the time, we know you're lying here also.

That's part of keeping your commitments also.

You make commitments then don't keep them, then you wonder why you can't get yourself to follow through on other commitments — it's because you've eroded that trust you have with yourself.

It starts with telling the truth — owning that —and recognizing that there are serious downstream consequences when you don't actually do what you say you're going to do, or you don't tell the truth when you know you should.

Look, this isn't rocket science.

This isn't some sort of new idea.

But somehow it is something that's lost on a lot of us or perhaps we've forgotten, or perhaps no one has ever explained the true magnitude of downstream effects that not telling the truth has on us.

Either way, this isn't something most of us hear once and just snap our fingers and are like — poof, that's it, all problems solved.

It's a constant learning, a constant process of improvement.

Telling the truth is actually a **skill set**. It's something that the more you practice it, the better you'll get at it, so long as you're actually rewarding yourself accordingly.

Remember, **what gets rewarded gets reinforced.**

If you only focus on the pain of telling the truth and give that a disempowering meaning, you won't want to do it for very long.

But if instead you focus on the reward that's gained in that hardship, you'll be hooked and won't be able to do anything but tell the truth.

More thoughts on telling the truth by Nietzsche —

"I'm not upset that you lied to me, I'm upset that from now on I can't believe you."

This sums up what I'm describing perfectly.

Your brain is saying that it can't believe you when you say you're going to do something.

And why the hell should it?

You say you're going to go for a 5 mile run and stop at 3.

You say you're going to earn more money next year, yet sit on the couch eating potato chips rather than actually making that a reality.

You tell everyone how passionate you are about doing something, yet don't follow it up with any action.

Your brain is saying — you're not passionate about that thing at all — you're passionate about telling people what you're passionate about and getting their reward for your "passion".

Your brain is saying — you're only passionate about cheap satisfaction motherfucker, about having your ego assuaged by others because you lack the internal sense of validation of actually doing something of merit that you truly believe is of merit.

You can fool other people, but you can't fool yourself.

Your unconscious is there with you all the time, and it's much, much smarter than you are.

It's only when people realize that **they** are the biggest obstacle in their life that they get serious about trying to get truly congruent — and when that happens, they discover they're far more powerful than they ever dreamed.

"If you do not tell the truth about yourself you cannot tell it about other people."
— Virginia Woolf

Truth starts first by telling yourself the truth.

And it's an emotional game a lot of the time.

It's not always this logical thing we think it is.

So much of life is in our emotions, not in this raw logic, or 1 or 0, or on or off, or binary code.

Being the man you know you can be starts with telling the truth.

This is non-negotiable.

That doesn't mean telling everyone, everything all the time. By all means, if you think someone's baby is ugly, please do not say that and then say I told you to.

But do listen to your conscience to a degree and decide where that line lies for you so you can start choosing your values rather than simply the ones you adopted and modeled from life.

ACTION ITEMS

- What 5 truths have you been hiding from yourself that you need to confront?
- What truths have you been harboring that you haven't shared with others who need to hear them?
- How would telling the truth allow you to gain congruence and accelerate your path in life?
- How would telling the truth allow you to gain greater congruence so that you would do the things you tell yourself you're going to do?
- How can you empower yourself emotionally to actually confront the truths you've been hiding from?
- How can you use all the steps we've covered up until this point to confront the truth? To give yourself permission, to take responsibility...
- How would telling a truth that is painful today lead you to be where you truly want to be in 5 years?
- How will you fail to become the person you want to be if you continue lying to yourself and others?
- What will your life look like if you don't stop this behavior?

- How will your life transform if you give yourself permission to change this behavior and follow it up with ruthless action?
- Your ability to tell the truth is what separates you from the greatness inside of you. How committed to this principle are you? How willing to confront your fears are you to become the person you could be?

CHAPTER TEN

Demand Orderliness, Discipline & Professionalism

"There is one thing that gets you out of bed in the morning, and that is discipline. Because your dreams and your goals are not there waking up for you in the morning."
— Jocko Willink

"No one can give you heart. No one can give you discipline. No one can make you unstoppable. Those are things you must decide for yourself. But make no mistake, it's a decision. It's not a genetic gift. It's a mindset."
— Tom Bilyeu

Whether you love him or hate him, Andrew Tate has polarized people all around the world. For some men, he's a beacon of hope who says all the things they wish they could say and for others, he's a misogynist, a bully and deserves to be banned.

As someone who values free speech, I fundamentally disagree with those who call to ban someone, especially when it's unlikely that they've fully inspected what that individual is saying in full context.

Regardless, during an interview with Patrick Bet-David, Tate sat down and at one point elaborated on some of the standards in his life. Here's what he had to say:

"And general professionalism. I've developed a habit where I punish myself for the smallest of improfessional actions.

If I misplace my keys or misplace my phone and it takes me more than 10 minutes to find it, I'll punish myself for that.

Regardless, whether I don't spend money this week, or I don't go here, or I'm canceling that, or I'm going to defer buying something I want — I punish myself religiously so that next time I put my phone down, I know where I put my phone.

Next time I put it down, I know where I put it, all the time.

When I put it down, I know where my phone is.

So when I'm around people who are like, "Hey, I lost my keys or Hey bro, I forgot."

When I'm around sloppy people, I don't like it.

I like people who have their lives in order.

When I detect sloppiness, I don't really want them too close, cause gaps are where things sneak in."

When was the last time you set standards like this for yourself?

When was the last time you were intolerant of sloppiness in your life?

In my world, I demand orderliness, discipline and professionalism.

Why?

Because I'm trying to become the man I know I can be and the only way to get there is through daily incremental improvement.

Here's a secret — I was not naturally born this way, nor have I yet become naturally this way.

I impose my WILL on myself to become the man I know I can be.

I'm not some story of always having positive habits since I was young, of always doing what I needed to, and then having a track record of 30 plus years of being that way.

On the contrary, my story is one of doing the work necessary to transform myself and instill these traits within myself because that's what's been necessary in order to become the man that I'm proud to look at in the mirror.

To reiterate - this book is about becoming powerful as a man. You do that by bringing order to your world, imposing discipline upon yourself and developing a sense of professionalism that you're proud of.

What if you were never late again?

What if you stopped making all those sloppy mistakes?

What if you stopped allowing the comfort of your bed to seduce you and instead became the master of how you show up each and every day?

As David Goggins, the hardest man alive, says:

"We are all great. No matter if you think you're dumb, fat, been bullied, we all have greatness. You gotta find the courage. It's going to be hard work, discipline, and the non-cognitive skills - hard work, dedication, sacrifice - that will set you apart."

This pillar is all about implementing NON-NEGOTIABLE STANDARDS into your life.

You don't develop these things overnight, it takes time, it takes repetition for you to build that competence and confidence in yourself.

The more you demand this of yourself, the better you get at delivering it to yourself.

One of my biggest struggles over the previous years was keeping commitments.

Why?

Because I was weak. I kept saying yes to things I didn't really want to do, then would make up a bullshit excuse at the last minute to ditch and not keep my commitments.

I mastered the art of this during my time as a male dancer where this was actually encouraged and the norm. After years of that, I realized it had come to wreak havoc on my life.

Once I left, I found this behavior and character trait persisted.

I wasn't proud of it yet lacked the proper knowledge, understanding and discipline to actually change it until going down a road of personal discovery and development.

Now, this is something I coach other men on, the importance of keeping commitments and agreements and also how to do that.

"It's pretty self explanatory. The more discipline you have in your life, the more freedom you have in your life. People are always looking for a remedy or a shortcut to make hard things easier. Things are hard for a reason. If they were easy, everyone would do them. If something is hard, I don't care – I'm just gonna do it anyways."

— Jocko Willink

We cover this more extensively later, but I demand orderliness, discipline and professionalism from my life — that means I ONLY say yes to things that I fully intend on following up on.

That also means that my automatic answer to most things is NO.

Your commitments are your word — you don't break that casually.

How would your life transform if you had this as your standard?

People may not like that you say no to most things, but they'd respect you for at least having your priorities straight.

They'd respect that when you say you're going to do something — you're damn sure going to follow through with it.

They'd respect that you only commit to high-value activities and also only surround yourself with high-value people because you don't want to be surrounded by sloppy individuals.

I'd like to aspirationally think we all understand the impact that our direct social circle has on us, but truthfully, I don't think most people do.

I'm not convinced most people understand the true magnitude of just how important it is to be surrounded by other people who are at least heading in a similar direction.

It's unlikely that if you're sloppy, a group of people who are orderly are going to just welcome you into their circle.

They're going to demand you get better and shape up as a man.

But, you can find a group of other men who may also be committed to implementing a better set of standards and all accelerate each other's growth.

"Most of this generation quits the second they get talked to. It's so easy to be great nowadays because most people are just weak, if you have any mental toughness, any fraction of self-discipline – the ability to not want to do it, but still do it – you'll be successful."
— David Goggins

I'm not here to necessarily tell you where to apply discipline in your life, where to apply orderliness, or even professionalism. I'm here to convey how important they are to have in your life.

For some, my house would be considered sloppy, for others it's insanely clean. You have to find where that line is for you and also within your social circle.

They'll give you feedback about what's acceptable or not and whether it's up to their standards or not.

Here's the thing about these principles though — there's no magic bullet shortcut. You can read 100 books on discipline or orderliness or professionalism, but at the end of the day — you must IMPOSE them on yourself.

You must DECIDE that this is how you're going to be, then be that way.

Here's a little preview of mindset:

You act out your beliefs.

The results you get in life are a reflection of the actions you take based upon your beliefs.

And your beliefs are reinforced by the ACTIONS you take.

When your behavior consistently reflects that you're the TYPE OF PERSON that is disciplined, that is orderly, that is generally professional, then guess what?

You actually BELIEVE that's who you are and it's part of your IDENTITY.

That's what we're after in the end here anyway.

We're after you becoming the most powerful and capable man you can be which involves you UPGRADING your identity.

When you consistently impose these standards on yourself, you begin the process of actually affecting identity level change and before you know it, it's just who you are.

"If you don't think you are disciplined: It is because you haven't decided to be disciplined. Yet."
— Jocko Willink

What does this look like for me in my life?

Show up on time.

Don't leave dishes in the sink.

Don't allow things that need to be done today to be put off until tomorrow.

Do what I say I'm going to do.

Never misplace anything.

If I make a mistake, analyze it in real-time so that I can avoid it next time.

Show up like I view future Caelin in 5 years would show up.

Be respectful yet maintain ruthlessly high standards.

Demand more from myself than I would ask of others.

Stack WINS daily so that I reinforce my identity of a disciplined, orderly and professional man.

These are just a few of the standards I have for myself and while I may not be perfect at all of them, I'm certainly far better at imposing them onto myself through daily practice than I would be if they weren't part of my standards.

"You cannot aim yourself at anything if you are completely undisciplined and untutored."
— Jordan Peterson

In your journey to become the man you know you can be, selecting proper targets and aim is critical, then possessing the discipline to see yourself through on those goals is integral to actually becoming that version of yourself.

It doesn't matter where you're at today.

It doesn't matter if you're totally undisciplined or you have a solid amount of discipline already instilled in your life — we can always get better, always become more, always create a better version of ourselves. The key is to stack those daily wins for incremental improvement.

If you want to be a man of power, a man who taps into his potential, it's time you begin IMPOSING your will onto yourself and implement non-negotiable standards around discipline, orderliness and professionalism.

Think of how you feel when you go somewhere and everyone is utterly professional from head to toe.

Think about when you're around a person who's like this.

You don't have to worry about them being late, you don't have to worry about them dropping the ball, you don't have to worry about them acting unprofessionally or disorderly.

It just works.

Now imagine if you were that person for everyone in your life.

You were just the man that bends reality to his will, imposes his standards on life and life reflects those standards back to him.

How would people look at you?

How would you respect yourself?

How would you contribute by being a beacon of the qualities that make a man most desirable?

In order to be fully transparent, I want to add the caveat that if you've been implementing these at 40% and then implement them at 80%, your life will get MASSIVELY better.

There are those on social media who create the illusion that they're 100% strict or committed or that they have zero deviations in their life – and perhaps they do, I'm not there watching their every movement – but from the one's I've met and interacted with, they hit their targets more like 85% of the time.

Totally fine either way. I have zero judgments. I just don't want to present these things in a false or misleading manner. Perfection is not necessarily the goal, progress is.

Look, I drink occasionally. I fuck off occasionally. I drop the ball just like every human does and forget to call someone back or make a scheduling error.

You're human, treat yourself as such.

That being said, because of years of implementing these as standards, I find that even while drinking or making a mistake in some situation, I still maintain a greater degree of orderliness, discipline and professionalism than most of my peers from this practice.

That's the difference.

This is not to say that you have to live a perfectly ascetic, never-make-mistakes life.

Only when you make this your lifestyle, your life will simply work increasingly better and better over time.

Do these for 3 months and you'll see an improvement.

Do these for 3 years and you'll look back on yourself and won't even recognize the man standing in front of the mirror.

To close, you have nearly unlimited potential, unlimited capacity for who you could become.

Make the decision today to impose your will on yourself and your world.

Become the man you know you could be.

Become an example of how a man can transform from sloppy, undisciplined and unprofessional to orderly, disciplined and professional beyond all reproach.

I believe in you.

It's time you believe in you too.

ACTION ITEMS

- What are 3 areas where you could impose orderliness on your life?
- What are 3 areas where you could impose discipline on your life?
- What are 3 areas you could bring a greater degree of professionalism to in your life?

LEVERAGE: PAIN

If you ignore these 3 things, how much will it cost you?

Will you be in the same place in 5 years, still unable to impose these principles on yourself?

Will you never have the respect you desire?

Will you never gain the social status you desire because of a lack of these things?

How will you look back on your life from your deathbed one day and regret, so painfully, regret not doing the difficult things today in order to become that version of yourself you know you could be?

LEVERAGE: PLEASURE

If you implement these 3 principles today, where could you be in 5 years?

How could your life MASSIVELY transform for the better?

Imagine looking into your eyes in the mirror 5 years from now having lived by these standards each and every day. Imagine the pride, the respect, the gratitude you have for yourself today for taking care of your future self, for loving yourself enough to live by a higher standard.

Feel that gratitude, feel how much it means to you, how hard it was at times but how the struggle gave the journey so much value. How you lived up to who you knew you could be and are that version of yourself you're most proud of today.

CHAPTER ELEVEN

Act Like Your Own Hero

"If you are not the hero of your own story, then you're missing the whole point of your humanity."
— Steve Maraboli

At the Academy Awards in 2014, Matthew McConaughey took the stage to accept the Best Actor award for his role in Dallas Buyers Club.

During that acceptance speech, McConaughey defined who his hero was and how he landed on that as delivered below:

"And to my hero, that's who I chase.

Now, when I was 15 years old, I had a very important person in my life come to me and say, 'Who's your hero?'

And I said, 'I don't know, I've got to think about that. Give me a couple of weeks.'

I come back two weeks later, this person comes up and says, 'Who's your hero?'

I said, 'I thought about it. It's me in 10 years.'

So I turned 25. Ten years later, that same person comes to me and says, 'So, are you a hero?'

And I was like, 'Not even close! No, no no!'

She said, 'Why?'

I said, 'Because my hero's me at 35.'

So you see every day, every week, every month, and every year of my life, my hero's always ten years away.

I'm never going to be my hero.

I'm not going to attain that.

I know I'm not.

And that's just fine with me, because that keeps me with somebody to keep on chasing.

So, to any of us, whatever those things are, whatever it is we look up to, whatever it is we look forward to, and whoever it is we're chasing.

To that I say: Amen.

To that I say, All right, all right, all right.

To that I say, just keep living, eh?

Thank you."

There is a reason that Matthew McConaughey won that award and part of that reason is that he adopted an empowering philosophy early on and truly lived it.

As we talk about implementing non-negotiable standards, I find this is one so many people don't think to embrace.

It's only when you start behaving differently that your life actually changes.

And how do you know how to act like?

You envision who your hero would be — you in 10 years — and then you act like that person would.

How would that person make decisions?

What standards would that person hold themselves to?

What would that person be committed to?

"It is not the past, but the future, that drives a person's actions and behaviors. All goals can be placed in two categories: approach or avoidance. Connected to your Future Self, you can appreciate, embrace, and love the present. Connection to your Future Self creates purpose and meaning in the present. The more connected you are to your longer-term Future Self, the better and wiser your decisions today."
— Benjamin P. Hardy, Be Your Future Self Now: The Science of Intentional Transformation

It's your vision for who you could be that matters vastly more than who you are currently.

It's the goals you have for yourself that matter more than your innate personality.

It's what you're oriented towards and intent upon that drives who you're being today.

As Jordan Peterson says:

"Specify your damn goals because how are you going to hit something if you don't know what it is?"

How are you going to become your own hero if you don't admit that's what you're after?

When McConaughey identified that he wanted to act like his own hero, he was identifying the best parts of himself and orienting towards those.

When you make the conscious decision to act like your own hero, like someone you're responsible for, you actually start acting like that person.

You ACTUALLY start becoming your own hero.

That's how you 10X your life in lightning like speed.

This is a NON-NEGOTIABLE standard.

When you start reflecting on your behavior, start running it through this filter and start creating that expectation for yourself!

Wake up in the morning with the conscious awareness to act like your own hero that day.

Own that you're after doing just that.

This is uncomfortable for a lot of people.

Most of us struggle to accept praise, to accept flattery.

Why?

Why should you be embarrassed about being the hero that you really could be?

Why should you diminish yourself?

To follow-up with another quote by Jordan Peterson:

"Often people won't specify what their goals are because they don't like to specify conditions for failure. So if you keep yourself all vague and foggy

which is real easy because that's just a matter of not doing as well - then you don't know when you fail."

If you identify as your own hero, then don't behave accordingly, then we associate failure to that, and of course — that's painful.

But, it's far more painful to go through life in ambiguity.

It's far more painful to get to the end of your life and meet the HERO that you could've been, yet realize you never actually became that person.

When you start acting like your hero in 10 years, you start becoming that person TODAY.

You actually start the process of changing your entire physiology, your brain structure, your very chemical make-up to act in congruence with that version of yourself.

That's why it's so powerful.

Because there is greatness within you and to unlock that greatness, it's incumbent upon you actually embracing that you're the hero of your own story.

That's a thought most don't ever think about — you are the hero of your own story.

Why not start acting like it?

Why not start acting like the hero you know exists within you?

As surely as the sun sets, you will arrive 10 years later and you'll still be stuck with yourself.

The question is will you be stuck?

Will you be the same?

Will you be closer to becoming your own hero or further from it?

Will you be more of a hero to those around you, a villain or an anti-hero?

Who will you be?

You're sure to arrive either way, and that arrival will either have taken place with conscious planning and intention or with careless abandon and you'll be left questioning how you arrived where you are.

I get it — it's tough to admit you want to be better.

That you actually want to be your own hero and acknowledge that.

But that's part of the call to GREATNESS.

That's part of your call to answer that question in your heart as to who you could be.

"People will do anything, no matter how absurd,
to avoid facing their own souls."
— Carl Jung

Facing yourself, your inadequacies, isn't easy.

It's a challenge to hold that vision of who you could be in your mind and stay true to it.

This is why it has to be a standard.

It has to be non-negotiable.

It has to be something you integrate into your soul.

You have to commit to chasing that person down, just like Matthew McConaughey is chasing himself down as his own hero.

You have to actually start acting like your own hero in 10 years and you will act your way into a new way of being.

"It's easier to act your way into a new way of thinking than to think your way into a new way of acting." — multiple authors through the years

One thing I do find when I coach people is that the 10 year horizon is often too far in the distance for them to really internalize it, for it to have any real immediacy in their lives.

Most of us operate off a shortened time horizon and place much greater emphasis on that, so rather than picking something that's unimaginable, it can occasionally be helpful to pick you as your hero in 6 months or in 1 year.

When you look at people who've truly committed to transforming themselves, a single year can absolutely take you from zero to hero.

I have a friend, we'll call him Tyler only because that's his name, who stopped drinking one year ago.

In that relatively short time span, he has totally transformed himself from being someone who was spending thousands of dollars per year on alcohol, getting into bar fights, driving drunk and acting completely irresponsible, to now being nearly an entirely different person.

One year later, he's sober, on a path to becoming his own hero and becoming the man he knows he truly can be.

As he continues this each and every year, in 10 years, he won't even recognize that former version of himself, that version who he used to be.

What I will say though, is I'm excited to see who that man is. I'm excited to see who Tyler becomes in 10 years because I know if he keeps chasing down his potential, there's virtually no limit to who he'll become.

It takes commitment.

It takes persistence.

It takes owning your life.

It takes admitting to yourself that you are going to orient towards this goal.

It's this way of pursuing your future self that drives everything in life.

Once you lock onto this, you have hope, you have direction, you have orientation.

You have a methodology that will lead you to becoming the person you know you really could be.

And that's BADASS!

Because you are a badass!

As McConaughey said, this isn't about ever actually getting to be your own hero.

This isn't about getting to a single destination then stopping.

That's not how life works.

You can always get better.

You can always grow, and that's mostly what life is about anyway.

It's orienting to the proper things in life so you can actually be that person you know you could be.

This is a modus operandi that you live day-in and day-out.

I once heard Charlie Munger in a clip on the internet somewhere comment on an aging Warren Buffet who was somewhere around the 80 year old mark at the time.

To summarize, Charlie said that Warren is only getting better, not declining at all.

And now, with Warren at 92, we can see Charlie was correct.

Most would call it a day, throw in the towel, stop acting like their own hero in 10 years, but not either of these guys.

Perhaps that's also why they're both over 90 and have been partners in one of the most successful businesses in history.

This is a simple principle, one that few ever truly implement in their lives.

But if you'll implement it today — you'll be amazed at who you become tomorrow.

It worked for Matthew McConaughey.

It's worked for Benjamin Hardy who is a best-selling author and Ph.D. who overcame immense inertia to build a highly successful business and amass a huge presence online with a dedicated audience.

If you're still dubious, in an interview with 60 minutes, Tom Brady, the legitimate GOAT, was asked which superbowl ring he liked the best.

His answer — **The next one.**

Always the next one.

He is always oriented towards a bigger and better future.

He is always making his future brighter than his already sparkling past.

Because he is his own hero in 10 years.

You can be your own hero in 10 years, too.

It's time you COMMIT.

ACTION ITEMS

- Who could you, as your own hero, be in a year from now?
- What would that man be like?
- What are the characteristics that person would have?
- Who would that person associate with?
- How would you be proud of acting like your own hero over the previous year?
- Who could you be in 10 years, acting like your own hero each and every day?
- Who could you impact and influence by acting this way?
- Who's hero could you actually become by becoming your own hero?
- If you had adopted this 5 years ago, how could you be totally different today if you'd put it into action?
- If you don't put this into action, how will you be the same person in 5 years that you are today?
- What beliefs would future you hold?

CONCLUSION

Non-negotiable standards are imperative for you to become the man you could be.

It's easy to talk about raising your standards, but I think you see that's not enough.

You have to get specific.

You have to remove the ambiguity.

You have to get laser focused on exactly which standards you're going to implement, then be relentless about doing just that.

You have to find the line of what you'll tolerate or not, because if it's negotiable, then it's really not a standard at all — it's just a casual guideline or something you profess that holds no water.

NON-NEGOTIABLE means just that.

These aren't to be trifled with or set and then implemented casually.

If these are weak, when you come up against what Wes Watson calls "The Convenience Factor" you'll capitulate and fall back to whatever is comfortable.

It's during times of INCONVENIENCE, of struggle, of adversity that your standards are most tested and that's why it's important to train them even on the best of days so that you're prepared for the worst of days.

Take responsibility.

Be unreasonable, intolerant and unambiguous.

Get obsessed with your life.

Tell the truth.

Demand orderliness, discipline and professionalism in your life.

And lastly, act like your own hero man, because you surely are or can be for others if you do.

You're here to change your life.

You're here because you have greatness within you and it's putting these in place which will bring that potential out.

Become the most powerful version of yourself today.

Become LEGENDARY!

PILLAR III

Upgrade Your Mindset

INTRO

"Circumstances do not make the man, they reveal him."
– James Allen

Mindset is a BEAST of a subject.

I want to set the expectation right here that this book introduces you to the subject of mindset, that this is more of a guidebook rather than a full blown exploration into all its possible nuances. However, I have never met someone who truly mastered this subject that was anything but wildly successful in all aspects of their life.

Dismiss this at great peril.

That being said, you don't necessarily have to go down the rabbit hole on mindset or its subsets, you can actually ascertain much of it on your own if you truly want to sit down and think. But, why would you try to reinvent the wheel if you don't have to?

People write entire books on different categories that are merely parts in the whole of mindset. Habits for instance — there are tons of books on this category which make up only a small portion of what mindset really is, and that's precisely why it's so hard to nail down as a concept.

Life is complicated. More than that, it's often hilariously paradoxical which throws even more people for a loop.

Mindset isn't always complicated, in fact, I think more people dismiss it due to its simplicity. Yet trying to fit the puzzle pieces together cohesively needs to be done in somewhat of a strategic manner.

As it turns out, doing the right thing at the wrong time usually doesn't lead to the desired result.

If you read a book on discipline, and read a book on habits, and read a book on self-management, they're all really helpful. The key is your ability to tie them all together so that you get RESULTS.

That's what you're really chasing after, right?

You have greatness within you and the goal is to tap into that potential.

We're going to focus more on getting results, on empowering you to radically alter your life and achieve major transformation.

I've written this section over 3 times now and this is the 4th attempt — not because each of the others weren't good, but because trying to distill a large concept down into an easy to digest, clear picture takes work.

After all, wasn't it Leonardo da Vinci who said:

"Simplicity is the ultimate sophistication."

I definitely don't want to even attempt to pass this off as the ultimate sophistication because I'm sure I'll look back on this in 10 years, having continued to learn more, to refine my thinking more and opine on how elementary it is, but that's just how life goes.

We grow, we get better and we keep progressing — those of us who choose to, that is.

If you're new to this subject, enjoy!

If you're a veteran to this subject, I still think you're going to find some real gems that no one has talked about in this manner before and you'll walk away with a clarity that you didn't realize you'd been missing in the first place.

CHAPTER TWELVE

Mindset Breakdown

I had blown up my life.

I was in debt up to my neck.

I felt extreme hostility toward my Dad and Grandmother and blamed them for my situation all while claiming to take responsibility.

I had quit my previous job over a year prior and hadn't had cashflow for that entire time.

I was drinking 1.5 GALLONS of VODKA per week. Depending on who's standards for shots or drinks you're looking at, that's roughly 20 per night.

I could barely stand to look at myself in the mirror.

My body had devolved. I was soft and inflamed with chubby, puffy cheeks and the classic dark swells under the eyes from someone who sleeps yet never gets rest because their body is constantly in a state of survival from being poisoned on a constant basis.

My life was in utter shambles and I was the ENTIRE reason for this predicament.

I was also going through a break-up with my girlfriend at the time where I couldn't even muster the courage to be honest about what we were really breaking up over.

I felt UNWORTHY in every way possible.

I felt unworthy to simply take up space for breathing.

I felt like a complete and total failure where I couldn't even picture how to drag myself out of this dark space.

I was in the middle of hitting rock bottom.

As Stephen Covey said:

"Admission of ignorance is often the first step in our education."

I called my mother one day crying, professing how I didn't know how I'd gotten here.

Of course, she had no idea where here was. I wasn't about to tell anyone the depths of my actual despair or problems. I had to keep an air of having my life together for ego sake.

I confessed that I had just had the realization that I was delusional.

And I was.

I had been delusional about who I was, about what I was pursuing, about how it would happen, about how that might transpire.

I kept telling myself I would magically pull out of this hole, that I was destined for more, that I was going to be somebody, to do something — all while not doing the necessary things to actually make those things happen.

Naturally an argument could be made that I was doing exactly what I needed to do considering that I did end up pulling myself out, but only after I came to this realization.

I had to pull the blinders off my eyes and realize what it would truly take, the level of sheer FORCE OF WILL, of CONSISTENT DEDICATION, of the work and fortitude it would take to drag myself out of that hell and propel myself to where I knew I should be.

But here I am, a grown-ass man, crying to his mother.

It felt good. So good.

I had become so locked up, I was struggling to let anything out yet here the flood gates had opened up.

I saw myself for what I was.

I was delusional — thinking that someone was magically going to come save me, that I was magically going to turn things around without the serious effort and consistent work it takes in order to do that. Without the dedication necessary to effect that change.

I think I largely modeled this from my dad.

He always had large, grandiose plans and would build them up in his mind and start down that road a little ways but never follow through.

That was me. I was dreaming of all the grandiose places I was going to go, keeping myself in a delusional fog to only mask the fact that I wasn't going anywhere.

Of course I could keep deluding myself until the end of time but then I'd eventually wake up one day and realize I'd wasted my entire life believing my delusions, all while never living my actual dreams.

That was ground zero for me.

It was a few weeks after that when I finally sat down and made THE GREATNESS CONTRACT with myself.

That's another book to come, but for now, suffice it to say, I drew a line in the sand, raised my standards and made the commitment to sculpt this motherfucker into the person who stands before you today.

I had spent years reading and applying all the tactical hacks for speed reading, for multi-tasking, for improved efficiency, for agile development, yet somehow missed the most fundamental of lessons.

I had ignored all the principles of mindset that were also included in those lessons.

I wasn't here for lack of ambition or drive or motivation.

No, I was here because I had ignored the most fundamental of principles — primarily that I was the biggest obstacle in my life and until I confronted myself and my mindset, I wasn't going to move past this point right here.

I was going to continue REVOLVING rather than evolving. I was going to stay stagnant, repeating the same mistakes over and over and over again until I buckled down and learned the things I needed to.

I had always assumed that I knew how to develop my mindset, that I had adopted a paradigm that would bring my success, that I had a way of thinking that would allow me to be successful, that my view of the world would yield the results I desired.

But nothing could be further from the truth.

The fact is — the world was merely reflecting back to me my actual mindset.

As Stephen Covey said:

"We see the world, not as *it is*, but as *we are*—or, as we are conditioned to see it."

I didn't realize at the time, not only do we see it as we are, but it reflects that view back to us, so the very results we're getting in life are merely a reflection of the mindset we have about the world.

What a mind-fuck, right?

This became the pivotal moment in my life, where I decided to no longer use discursive pursuits as a way to practice creative avoidance in dealing with my mindset.

I made the decision to no longer engage in my problems the way the world was telling me to.

I didn't need to talk about them more, to process them more, to ruminate over them any longer, to wallow in my victimhood over what happened to me as a child.

I know that works for many and I never want to discount therapies that are helpful for some, but for me, as the man I am, these things simply aren't helpful.

I don't need to focus on problems, I need to focus on solutions.

I don't need to talk and process, I need to act and build.

I don't need to focus on fault or blame but instead take responsibility and learn the art of recontextualization so I'm empowered.

In short, I know traditional therapy helps many people today and if you need it, I encourage you to seek it out, but for me, I found it just kept me stuck and revolving rather than evolving.

I'm a fucking man and as such, mostly we need to go out and conquer things, to change our environment, to better ourselves, to build our value rather than wallow in all our victimhood.

I didn't need a therapist, I needed a coach.

Someone to tell me to get off my ass and get it together.

I needed a role model.

I needed someone to help me learn what it means to be good at being a man.

I was struggling. I still do. I'm still learning and very open about the fact that I'm in a pursuit to really learn how to be the best man I know I can be and what being good at being a man means for me.

I tell that to some men and they laugh, but others get it.

I'm choosing to build me, my legacy, my life, and so I need to confront these things, not simply accept that which I was taught because it damn sure wasn't nearly as good of a model as I can come up with by learning and modeling from the best of others.

I decided to conquer my mindset, to focus on the only thing that really mattered to me — to go down this path of personal growth so deep that it would be impossible for me to fail.

If I was the biggest obstacle in my life, I'd just have to chase that sucker down as deep and as long as was necessary to repeatedly break through those barriers.

Over the coming months and years, I learned, absorbed and put into practice all the tools and strategies I could and completely transformed myself.

In retrospect, I realize there were multiple factors playing out in my life and each one had their unique story and emotional intricacies to deal with, yet I also realize that it was partly due to just not having the appropriate information.

"The way we see the problem *is* the problem."
— Stephen Covey

I didn't want a bunch of WOO information.

I didn't want someone telling me from a theoretical pedestal how to live my life. Someone with a PhD who thought they were smarter than everyone else and cited a ton of research.

I didn't and still don't give a shit about that. I've read enough books to know that can be spun any which way and all the people who think they're so brilliant probably aren't nearly as brilliant as they think they are. I was one of them, after all.

I needed a coach, I needed another man to help give me some direction, and not to coddle me but to show me how to step it up and get it the fuck together.

Well, I didn't necessarily find that sort of 1-1 mentorship, but I did find A LOT of mentors in books, courses, seminars, YouTube and all the other avenues available to anyone with a smartphone today.

So I gave myself a masterclass in this very topic and transformed my life.

First, I had to be open to these things, to have heart, to give myself permission to actually admit and state the transformation I was after. Once I was committed, the rest took care of itself. The information I needed started trickling into my life because once you make a decision, the universe conspires to make it happen.

I realized that while I could've tried multiple things over and over again, until I got the right information, until I got the appropriate TOOLS, I was never going anywhere.

Incidentally, I arrived at quite a few principles on my own from sheer persistence and necessity, but I also learned an enormous amount from others along the way.

"It's important to realize that on the journey to achieving big, you become bigger."
– Gary Keller, The One Thing

I've read anywhere from 50 to upwards of 150 books a year for the last decade.

When you do that and you actually put those things into practice, your life is just about guaranteed to change.

So, albeit a bit late, I discovered the MASSIVE importance of MINDSET and how it is generally the make-or-break factor for most people in their lives, assuming they have some level of desire, ambition, courage, et cetera.

And there isn't anything wrong if you don't. Like I said before, I'm not the morality police over here or someone telling you how you "should" live your life.

I am someone saying that if you do have these drives, and do have a desire for greatness, that I have some excellent tools I've discovered along the way that can greatly expedite your journey.

So, let's dig into this more and actually learn about how to upgrade your mindset.

Greatness is a mindset, and mindset leads to GREATNESS.
— Me

One of the biggest things I struggled with as I entered the personal development world was wrapping my head around what mindset actually was.

On the surface, the concept of a mindset seems obvious. As I dug into it more and more, however, I realized it was the amalgamation of many different things we think about. While each is important, having so many facets makes it difficult to distinguish the different areas to focus most heavily on.

"The mind is just like a muscle - the more you exercise it, the stronger it gets and the more it can expand."
— Idowu Koyenikan

Here are several definitions, and while helpful, I don't think they actually encompass the totality that is mindset.

Originally, it was used in the 1930s to mean —> habits of mind formed by previous experience.

According to vocabulary.com, mindset is —> A person's usual attitude or mental state is his or her *mindset.*

or

a habitual or characteristic mental attitude that determines how you will interpret and respond to situations.

or

According to Wikipedia — mindset is an established set of attitudes, esp. regarded as typical of a particular group's social or cultural values; the outlook, philosophy, or values of a person; (now also more generally) frame of mind, attitude, disposition. A mindset may also arise from a person's worldview or philosophy of life.

For our purposes here, we're going to say that mindset sits at the intersections of all these different things.

It's your philosophy about life, your outlook, your habitual or characteristic mental attitude, your world view, your mindset muscle or discipline of mind, your habits of the mind, frame of mind, et cetera.

Generally, I think these are better understood in metaphor.

We hear about people such as David Goggins who has built a rock-solid mindset where he can push through seemingly insurmountable odds, pain and adversity. That's one way to think of mindset, such as the more you impose discipline on yourself, the greater your ability is to do that in greater amounts, or the more you lift weights, the stronger your muscles will get.

You expand your capacity by training just like anything else.

Mindset is every bit as much a skill set as is lifting weights or developing the discipline to sit down and study for 5 hours.

We also hear about mindset such as your philosophy about life or mental attitude. Carol Dweck popularized the idea of a growth mindset or a fixed mindset which is really your outlook on life about how the world works, what you're capable of and what you can ultimately achieve.

Here's a metaphor:

A shoe company sent a representative to a foreign country to assess whether it would be a good market to move into or not.

When the representative arrived, he looked around and immediately wrote home saying — "Coming home. No potential market here as nobody wears shoes."

The CEO could hardly believe it as a close confidant had advised him that the country was ripe for his shoes.

Rather than capitulating, the CEO decided to send another representative to get a second opinion.

Upon arrival, the second representative sent a letter back home immediately — "Send all the shoes you can make as quickly as possible! No one here has any shoes, the market is nearly unlimited!"

Two different people, two different mindsets.

While they both saw the same thing, they arrived at polar opposite conclusions.

This is why you can have a good attitude about going to a job you dislike while simultaneously believing that you don't deserve anything better than that job.

You can tell yourself — I may as well have a good attitude because I'm stuck at this position no matter what I do.

Or you could tell yourself — I'm going to have a good attitude while here and learn the necessary skills because this job is really just preparing me for my next and better one.

The very same person, two different mindsets, and they'll end up in entirely different places in life.

My goal here is to give you the tools and resources to start changing your mindset TODAY, so that you can start getting results sooner rather than later.

Part of mindset for me was simply learning how to think better or to develop more helpful heuristics with which to view the world and make decisions.

It was learning a better way to BE.

Once I did that, really internalized that, everything shifted.

Rather than trying to change my outer world, I made the shift to changing my internal world.

Life is contextual and when you master the art of RECONTEXTUALIZATION — everything changes.

"To try to change outward attitudes and behaviors do very little good in the long run if we fail to examine the basic paradigms from which those attitudes and behaviors flow."

— Stephen Covey

Mindset took me from UNRESOURCEFUL to RESOURCEFUL.

From blaming my lack of resources as the problem to understanding that it had been my lack of resourcefulness.

The problem was how I was showing up to the problem, it was how I was approaching the problem, it wasn't the problem itself.

It was me. It always had been me.

That shift happened because I learned at a fundamental level what the real drivers behind mindset were and then how to manipulate those levers.

As Stephen Covey said:

"If we want to make relatively minor changes in our lives, we can perhaps appropriately focus on our attitudes and behaviors. But if we want to make significant, quantum change, we need to work on our basic paradigms."

The bolts and nuts of mindset are that beliefs and values are foundational, ground-level on what everything else is built upon.

Your paradigm or worldview or philosophy of life is an amalgamation of these two things.

You've made DECISIONS throughout your entire life about how the world works, how you work, how the universe operates and how you're going to handle those things.

It's all these decisions that turn into BELIEFS that then form the different mental maps which you use to view the world.

It's your values that work in a sort of psycho-cybernetic loop along with your beliefs to create all these belief systems.

For instance, maybe you value relationships and people so you have a greater propensity to give people the "benefit of the doubt" when red flags are raised. It's these values that influence what you believe or the conclusions you draw from a certain situation.

All of this is happening all the time and it's largely your UNCONSCIOUS that's in the driver's seat more than you know.

FRACTIONAL REALITY

On a fundamental level, you always have a fractional view of reality and are only perceiving small bites of the whole. Our brain tells us stories that we're getting the entire picture, all the while we know we're only truly getting snippets at best.

You can really only consciously pay attention to 7, plus or minus 2 things at a single time, so it's your unconscious mind that's running all the rest in the background.

There are some people who choose to refer to it as your "subconscious", but there is nothing "sub" about your unconscious mind.

As Carl Jung said:

"Until you make the unconscious conscious, it will direct your life and you will call it fate."

Your unconscious is with you, in the room, as you're reading or listening to this now. Your heart is pumping without you thinking about it. You're also running plenty of stuff in the background all the time on a conscious level.

When I was in college, I noticed that I could react FAR faster if someone threw something from the side when I wasn't paying attention than if I was actually paying attention. That was my unconscious mind ALWAYS paying attention, even when my conscious mind couldn't keep up with everything.

The great news though is that you can program your unconscious mind and that's a form of automation.

Think about it — you've probably learned how to drive and can drive across town without giving it a second thought.

Have you ever made it and wondered, how in the world did I do that?

Automation.

Unconscious.

You were in the driver's seat about learning how to do that process which means you're also in the driver's seat to decide other ways of how you wish to be in the world, then have your unconscious mind execute on those behaviors accordingly.

This is why I say that mindset is really a SKILL SET. It's no different than learning how to drive a car or other skill sets you've learned in life.

Think about the payoffs.

How much have you benefited from learning how to drive? How much reward have you gotten from being able to do it in an unconscious manner so that you could hold conversations, listen to music, chew gum, eat, whatever it may be, while also driving.

That's why when I talk to people I'm so adamant and also emphatic they learn to do the things necessary to get that proper level of mindset so that they have an optimal program running in the background instead of a broken track record.

And this isn't always an easy sell.

So many of us just want to believe we're fine how we are, that how we were raised is good enough, that we don't need to learn anything more to become a better man.

Inherent in any of these admissions is that we're not fine how we are, how we were raised isn't good enough, that we do need to learn more or different things to be a better man.

Why the hell wouldn't you want to get better?

This isn't The Legendary Guide To Complacency!

This is about becoming the most powerful version of yourself possible.

So, yes, I tell people —

Sure you're fine just as you are, right here, right now — but you're also nowhere near who you could be, and while you're fine right here right now as you are, if you stay this way, you're not going to be fine in the future.

There is a serious price to pay when you refuse to voluntarily take up the mantle of responsibility and turn your potential into who you could be.

Time is going to pass either way.

Not making a decision is making a decision.

Eventually that bill comes due, motherfucker.

Also, no one is asking you to cast your parents into the fire. They did the best they could with what they had and what they knew at the time. They couldn't have done any better than that. But that doesn't mean they have the resources that you now have, so why wouldn't you want to learn, adapt and grow so that you can be better and provide better for your children one day?

All of this is about upgrading who you are so that you can be a better version of yourself, to truly unlock that man I believe exists within you.

So, part of changing your mindset is changing your beliefs.

Maybe you don't feel worthy.

Perhaps you don't feel like you deserve success.

Perhaps you have the belief that money is the root of all evil while also suffering the consequences of not having any and watching your family suffer.

Perhaps you have the belief that no amount of extra work will ever get you ahead.

Maybe you have the belief that this is just how it is for someone like you in life.

Maybe you have the belief that if you could just get one more thing, then you may finally be happy or fulfilled.

Perhaps you hold the belief that the universe is a hostile place and therefore it doesn't matter what you do.

As Albert Einstein said:

"The most important decision we make is whether we believe we live in a friendly or hostile universe."

Right there, from the man himself.

The most important DECISION.

Life all comes down to decisions.

Your ability to choose.

As the saying from Viktor Frankl goes — between stimulus and response therein lies your ability and freedom to choose.

And what are beliefs after all, anyway?

A belief is merely something you feel certain about.

You feel certain that chocolate ice cream either tastes good or bad or neither.

You feel certain that refrigerators keep food cold.

You feel certain the earth is flat.

Ah, see, beliefs don't confer truth — only that you believe it to be true.

You can believe with your entire being that the earth is flat or that gravity doesn't exist, but that only makes it true to you, not necessarily in reality.

So all beliefs are really just DECISIONS that we've made at some point.

I hold the belief that I look better in blues than reds. At some point that was a decision and as I built more reinforcement for it, the stronger of a belief it became.

In your life, at some point, you formed some beliefs that, while they may have helped you at the time, are no longer helping you.

I tell people that limiting beliefs weren't always limiting. We're highly adaptable and we usually are just doing the best we can. Most of the time, we form a belief that helps us temporarily so it's an enabling belief, that then as we progress in life, becomes a limiting belief.

As the saying goes: new levels bring new devils.

Values are the same way. Inherently, when we're young we have certain propensities to gravitate towards different things, but as we get older, we gain the ability to choose our values more or to reframe the way we see things to invariably pursue the things we wish to.

I think it's always helpful to begin with the end in mind, and to that end, the entire purpose of upgrading your mindset is so that you can become more of who you really could be.

It's so that you can achieve the mission you feel you were put on this planet for.

So that you can pursue your purpose.

So that you can find the most appropriate vehicle for you to become the man you know you could be.

Life is ultimately about growth, about progress, about meaning, fulfillment and purpose.

If you're not growing in life, it's highly unlikely that you're going to be satisfied, and to grow you need to have goals, to have a future worth looking towards. That's the benefactor of mindset.

And without mindset, you won't ever truly feel the best way you can about life.

I know this is long but stay with me here.

Some would say the quality of your life is the emotions you feel on a day-by-day basis.

Is that really true?

Let me ask you this:

If you were a soldier who went to war in 1941, isn't it possible that you were miserable for years on end and emotionally beaten down, yet still found it to be one of the most meaningful experiences of your life?

Is it really the emotions felt on a day-by-day basis or the meaning you give those emotions? The meaning you give to your experiences?

Emotion — misery from cold, hunger, et cetera.

Initial meaning: this is pointless, I hate this, my life sucks.

Other empowered meaning: I'm protecting my loved ones and other humans that deserve protection and will gladly suffer all the misery in the world to create a world that my children can flourish in.

See the difference?

How about this one? Could you be working on a big project that frustrates you to no end and you spend years in frustration working on it yet finally breakthrough to the desired result?

What if you recontextualized that project so you viewed that struggle as an opportunity for growth and rather than have it frustrate you day in and day out, instead you knew each day was just another opportunity to get better?

The quality of your life is the MEANING you CHOOSE to give it. The same is true with the quality of your day.

And isn't it true that nothing has any meaning except the meaning you give it?

As William Shakespeare said:

"There is nothing either good or bad, but thinking makes it so."

Now, isn't it possible to take both of those previous experiences and to choose a different meaning so that even if you are spending years in frustration, overwhelm or other emotions, that they at least have some meaning?

Absolutely.

Isn't it also possible that with some TRAINING for your mindset that you could actually learn to move from frustration or misery or other emotions that you don't want to feel on a constant basis to feeling the emotions you'd prefer on a more consistent basis?

Let me answer that for you — abso-fuckin-lutely.

This isn't some WOO concept. We see people do this all the time.

I'm sure you know someone who can always find something WRONG no matter the circumstances.

But I'd bet you also know someone who seems to find something RIGHT no matter the circumstances.

Here's the deal — both of these individuals are correct. Their experiences are true. Their experiences are simply a reflection of the mindset with which they approach the world.

Both of these individuals are making a CHOICE.

Conscious or unconscious, it's happening.

"Once your mindset changes, everything on the outside will change along with it."
– Steve Maraboli

Hopefully you're starting to see the sheer MAGNITUDE that mindset plays in your life.

This is a beast of a concept but also delivers a beast of rewards when you truly master it.

And let's be honest, you never really master it. There are always new levels, however, mastering it on a foundational level really sets the playing field for your life in a large way.

So, the foundation here is that we understand that mindset is predominantly the result of our beliefs and values, which ultimately comprise our paradigms and mental maps, which then dictate which actions we take and how we move through the world.

We've also said that the real goal is to live a life of meaning, of purpose, of fulfillment. And that mindset plays an integral role in actually achieving those things on the highest level.

Next, we're going to go a bit deeper and begin to get the keys to the ignition with mindset.

ACTION ITEMS

- In the last week, think of 3 circumstances where you found yourself in frustration, overwhelm, or some other negative emotion that didn't feel good. Now, how could you RECONTEXTUALIZE those circumstances so that you have positive feelings about them?
- If you simply learned to recontextualize obstacles as opportunities, how could that help you on the path to living in an empowered state and welcoming those challenges instead of resisting them and living in disempowered states?
- How has a lack of mindset mastery led you to a place in life that you find less than satisfactory?
- How could mastering the art of mindset allow you to progress at lightning like speed in life and also have a degree of satisfaction you never had before?

CHAPTER THIRTEEN

The 3 Principles of Mindset

Mindset is really just the amalgamation of all these different pieces of the puzzle that make up what is you.

It's an amalgam of your values, beliefs, habits, identity, environment, inborn traits and developed traits. It's the culmination of everything you've worked to develop up until this point in life — And most importantly, it's the primary driver that will determine what and how you develop in the future from this point.

With an EMPOWERED mindset, you'll be constantly growing, constantly getting better and constantly finding solutions to problems. You'll be creating and commanding the problems you face in life rather than allowing those problems to simply present by chance or fate.

When I talk about an EMPOWERED mindset versus a DISEMPOWERED mindset, I'm specifically referencing it in relationship to your goals and what you're optimizing for.

For instance, some people optimize for goals that are 40 years out and that's their main driver. It's not excitement, it's not happiness, it's not aliveness, it's survivingness. Those people want to adopt an empowering mindset that helps them achieve those goals, so a mindset that conflicts with that would disempower them to their main mission.

I have no "shoulds" for you here.

If that's what you want to do, by all means, go and do it.

I don't know what you've been through and what has led you here. I only know what I've found works better for me and what I'd encourage you to have an open mind to.

Growth takes place in relationship to goals.

I find that while most people may know the ins and outs of how to set goals, they struggle most with actually setting goals that matter. In short, people pick shitty goals because they haven't been taught how to optimize their goals for what they're really after.

They're thinking linearly when they need to be thinking laterally or dynamically or exponentially.

If you don't know what you're truly after, how would you even go about picking a decent goal?

Or perhaps you do know what you're after, yet have fallen prey to the cultural narrative about what goals are acceptable versus unacceptable, so while you know the goal you're after — it's not really the goal you would have picked had you the courage to delve into your soul about what you're truly seeking in life.

This is perhaps the most pervasive one I see today.

This is most easily illustrated by people who want to lose weight, so they do all the things they think they're supposed to do and go by all the "accepted" guidelines, and of course end up worse off than when they first started.

That's because RESULTS matter.

We can prescribe all sorts of bullshit for people, but that doesn't mean it's accurate.

RESULTS are the yardstick. Results are ultimately the ONLY thing that matters.

I have vegans argue with me every day about how their way of eating is superior, all while having the visible appearance of what would have been classified as an eating disorder 100 years ago.

Hair falling out, gray, thinning, loose skin, bags under eyes — swearing that bug protein is the future.

Yeah, fuck that, no thank you!

We're going to dig into goals more in a bit but just know that I really only differentiate between mindsets that either empower or disempower us in relationship to our goals.

I love Carol Dweck's concept of a fixed mindset or growth mindset, and think a growth mindset is always the empowering way.

Imagine you're talking about your mindset revolving around money.

If you want to make $1,000,000 in the next 5 years, then the only thing that really matters is if your mindset supports that or not. Choosing an empowering mindset around that goal is all that matters.

Since I foresee plenty of pushback on this concept, oftentimes it's helpful to look for examples of others who've done something similar. To see there is proof that it's obviously possible, and if you're willing to put the work in, change your beliefs, et cetera, then it's even highly plausible.

That means you may want to adopt a mindset that money:

Flows to you.

Is abundant.

Is easy to make for those who choose to allow it to be easy for them to make.

That you're capable of making $1,000,000, not only in 5 years but even in the next 12 months.

That you're worthy of making that money.

That while you're going to make $1,000,000, you're going to deliver $10,000,000 worth of value to the marketplace.

That you're going to be so good, they can't ignore you.

This is one of the biggest things that stops people.

It's so subtle yet so CRUCIAL to your success, to getting stuck from your current patterns and actually becoming who you could be.

You have to believe you're worthy.

You have to believe you can do it.

You have to recognize that which is holding you back then focus relentlessly on solutions.

Now, I said at the start that the entire goal of this book is for you to become the most powerful version of yourself as possible.

MINDSET is critical to going from someone with all that bottled up POTENTIAL and turning it into GREATNESS and most importantly finding FULFILLMENT, MEANING AND PURPOSE in that and in your life. That's the goal after all — living a meaningful, fulfilling and purposeful life where at the end, you're left looking back with no regrets and all bliss.

As Viktor Frankl said:

"What man actually needs is not a tensionless state but rather the striving and struggling for some goal worthy of him. What he needs is not the discharge of tension at any cost, but the call of a potential meaning waiting to be fulfilled by him."

So, the first part of the equation is to pursue a goal that's WORTHY of you. I refer to this as finding your vehicle by which you'll exploit your purpose, which is to become the man you could be.

It's also critical here that at some point, you believe you're worthy of this goal. And of course it should stretch you because that's where growth and courage come in, giving you hope for more.

It's to RUTHLESSLY OPTIMIZE for what you want in life.

I am with Tim Ferriss on this one — while most people tend to try to optimize for happiness, that turns out to not be a very fulfilling or even good goal for finding happiness. On the other hand, when you optimize for excitement, growth is automatically built into the system, and so is happiness since growth invariably results in that as a byproduct.

The next part of the equation is to CHOOSE how you're going to be in life, and this is the one that escapes so many.

We all get caught up in these different narratives, thinking if I could just get this next car, I could be happy, or as soon as I get this next raise, that'll do it for me.

But we all know that's bullshit.

That's what's known as **hedonic adaptation** and no matter what happens, good or bad, your baseline gets re-structured and then you're back to ground zero.

This is where the fundamentals of mindset really come in and where you have a major opportunity to reclassify your existence, to completely REDEFINE how you CHOOSE to go about your life in this world.

There's more to it than this, but for simplicity sake these are the main drivers of MINDSET and also where a real opportunity lies.

We said that mindset is primarily the offspring of your values and beliefs, and what lies behind both of those are your ABILITY to CHOOSE both.

Now, I'm not one of those personal development gurus who says mind is always greater than matter. In fact, I subscribe that the mind and body are one unit and thus should be viewed as such. A large amount of what people think causes their mindset issues is in fact particularly related to their diet or environment.

Obviously, each person has inborn traits which are unique to them, and as humans we all have a fair amount of common hardwiring manufactured into us by the manufacturer. While some would see that as a reason not to change, plenty of others have found their limitations for all practical purposes, exist mainly in their mind, not in some limiting genetic trait from birth.

So, it's primarily your ability to consciously control the DECISIONS you make in life that ultimately determines who you're going to become.

That's why Tony Robbins says:

"More than anything else, I believe it's our decisions, not the conditions of our lives that determine our destiny."

It's this process of consciously making decisions that programs your brain.

These decisions trickle into your unconscious and begin to form HABITS OF THOUGHT that ultimately will redefine your paradigm.

Mindset can be automated after all.

Just as you can automate your driving to a degree, so too can you automate your experience here in life.

So, let's dig into these key ingredients.

I've heard these referenced in lots of books that existed before Tony Robbins, but I'm going to give him credit for popularizing these three fundamentals more than anyone else. And while he talks about these, I haven't ever heard or read him talk about them in the way I'm going to in relation to mindset.

The primary ingredients that make up your mindset are what you:

Focus on or pay attention to.

The meaning you give it or how you contextualize incoming information.

And then, the decision or conclusion or actions you take based upon the former two.

To segue a bit — I was speaking with Brad Lea the other day and he said that if you can master MINDSET, SKILL SETS and HABITS, then you're just about guaranteed to be successful.

I came away from that thinking MINDSET is really just the HABITUAL application of a SKILL SET.

What do I mean by that?

Mindset is a skill set.

When you apply it habitually, you'll transform your entire world.

When you learn to focus on things that empower you, you'll become more empowered.

When you learn to give things an empowering meaning, you'll feel more meaning and also become more empowered.

When you learn to take actions or make decisions that support your goals and mission and that empower you, guess what? You become more empowered and therefore live a more empowered life.

In short — you become more powerful.

Like I've said before, this isn't rocket science.

But you can be damn sure no one teaches you this in school.

What would the world do if we had a bunch of empowered people running around?

That would just be dangerous...

But seriously, if you interpret things in life that lead to emotional places that are disempowering, you're going to live a disempowered life.

You're going to respond in disempowering ways and constantly be living in a disempowered state.

If instead you choose to interpret life in a manner that empowers you, you're going to live an empowered life and in an empowered state.

Let me ask you this:

Can you be a billionaire and have insane amounts of discipline and still be unhappy and attribute your life to having very little meaning?

Absolutely, we've all heard those stories and intuitively know it's true.

How about another one:

Can you be "successful" with a family, financial freedom, a career that is envied by others and still be miserable? Maybe you even have all the tactics and strategies such as what people would think of as good habits, discipline, leadership qualities, exceptional poise when faced with adversity or any other number of things.

Of course you can! We hear about these people all the time and we REALLY hear about them every few years because they end up killing themselves.

The reason mindset is one of the foundational pillars to master in life is because it's the one thing that transcends all the other areas of your life. When you really master it, which is an ongoing process, it actually furthers your mastery in other areas as well.

And, you can have all sorts of mastery in other areas, yet if you fail to master your mindset, still be completely miserable.

Again, mindset is a HABITUAL or characteristic mental attitude that determines what you:

Focus on.

How you choose to contextualize it.

And then the decision you make which leads to a conclusion which leads to an action based upon the former two.

I can't over-emphasize just how important this is for your life.

Can you choose your habits? Abso-fuckin-lutely.

Between stimulus and response is there a choice? Absolutely!

"Between stimulus and response there is a space. In that space is our power to choose our response. In our response lies our growth and our freedom."
– Viktor E. Frankl

This means you're actually in the driver's seat here.

You're not a passenger with no say so.

You're completely capable of adjusting your mindset and changing your entire life around that.

Now, there are plenty of men who don't want to hear this because it means they are ultimately responsible for the results they've been getting in life and they're so used to blaming and to shirking responsibility, that this is too heavy of a burden to face.

But, there are other men who are going to hear this and make a decision — to say, oh, this is super powerful and now I get it.

Take responsibility and embrace the man you could be by taking control of your mindset.

Realizing mindset is just a choice is incredibly empowering — which by the way — ding ding— is what we're after.

We're after things that are useful, that are helpful, that are empowering.

All of this is about living the most powerful life possible, living life to the highest degree, to reaching the end truly knowing in your heart that you gave it your all.

So for me, I don't distinguish between all the different mindsets out there, the fixed or growth or scarcity or abundance. I simply ask — As I take absolute responsibility for myself, does this empower or disempower me towards my potential?

I don't even care if it's right or wrong. I choose to only believe in that which empowers me.

It's about choosing to pursue greatness then adopting principles that align with that greatness.

If you don't want to do that — bad dog. Go sit in the corner.

For all the rest — let's drill down a bit more.

Principle — You believe whatever it is you repeat. Repeating is believing and believing is repeating.

If you repeatedly tell yourself you're a piece of shit, guess what? You're going to, at least on an unconscious level, believe that you're a piece of shit.

CUT THAT SHIT OUT!

As Tony Robbins says:

"REPETITION is the mother of SKILL."
(emphasis my own)

If you get up each morning and go run, before long, you'll start telling yourself that you ARE a runner.

That's an identity statement.

It's a commitment of what is and is also backed up by your actions and consistent results.

Before long, it's not even something you think about — it's automated, it's in the background, it's just something you do because it's WHO YOU ARE.

The same is true for your mindset.

Are you one of those people who always finds something wrong in any situation? The dinner could be perfect, the atmosphere just right, everything in alignment and then you focus in on the fact that perhaps the steak wasn't just as you wanted it. You don't even know why. You just had to find something wrong because it's a HABITUAL characteristic.

It's your emotional home.

It's the place comfortable to you.

If everything were perfect, that would make you uneasy.

Perhaps you only know how to operate in chaos and thrive on what's wrong and missing rather than what's right and available.

Are you starting to see just how CRITICAL this is for your life?

Repetition is the key to altering your mindset. It's not the only key for sure, but it's beyond the scope of this book to dive into all the mental hacks and processes there are for change. For our purposes, repetition is perfect.

What if instead, you decided to consciously CHOOSE what you were going to focus on, the meaning that you were going to give that, and then how you were going to respond?

What if you did that repetitively for a time until it became a HABITUAL SKILL SET?

That you only chose that which empowered you repeatedly so that before long, you didn't even have to consciously think about it?

And after a short time — it's automated.

You think you're tired from 20 minutes of running, you don't even have to think about it, your mindset is rock-solid and focuses on the fact that you have more to give, that the pain in your legs is making you stronger, that the only way is through the pain to get the reward on the other side.

You unconsciously and automatically focus on what's AVAILABLE instead of what's unavailable, and then to give that an empowering meaning, then respond in a resourceful manner.

That's the power of mindset.

It's not your circumstances that dictate how you will respond to life — it's you.

If you choose it to be, that is.

When you follow this process, your beliefs and values will change in accordance.

Your GOALS shape your identity and you are what you repeat.

A lot of people overestimate what they can do in a day or a week or even a month yet underestimate what they can do in 90 days or a year or three to five years.

You choose your goal.

That goal will determine who you ultimately become in relation to who you want to be, pursuing it along with how committed you are to being.

That's where it's important to master this on an unconscious level so that you're in the driver's seat.

And of course, once you free yourself up from wasting so much time and energy in anxiety, overwhelm or negative thought loops because you're focusing on what's unavailable or wrong, you're then freed up to do unbelievably amazing things.

For most people, this can be like getting back between 3 to 6 hours a day they spend in absolute overwhelm or just obsessing over scarcity or in this habitual disempowering emotional home that does nothing but suppress their absolute uniqueness.

Of course, when they get back those 3 hours a day, that amounts to 1,095 more hours in a year.

Assuming you have 16 waking hours in a day, that's like getting back the equivalent of 68 days!

And, not just gaining 68 days back but also getting back 68 EMPOWERED days, where you're choosing to live fully, are committed to a meaningful existence and pursuing your greatness.

When I first encountered these things and began arriving at my own conclusions, I doubted them. I thought it sounded simplistic and if it was that simple then everyone would be doing it.

But you and I both know that's not the case at all.

People know all sorts of simplistic things that could make their life better but don't do them.

It's not the education they lack, it's the APPLICATION.

In this case though, it's been my experience that people simply don't know this information or haven't encountered it presented in this manner, and that makes the difference that makes the difference.

This is the skill set that differentiates a billionaire who's contemplating suicide versus the one who's living a totally fulfilled and meaningful life.

It's also the skill set that's differentiating someone still living in an apartment, still struggling to gain some traction in the world, but who's undeniably going to get there and fast compared to his neighbors because of a mindset that gets RESULTS.

ACTION ITEMS

- What would your life be like if you chose to no longer live in anxiety, overwhelm, frustration or other disempowering feelings?
- If you focused on what's available compared to what's unavailable, how quickly could you become the type of person people simply love to be around because you see possibilities compared to problems?
- With these tools, how could you create different memories by recontextualizing anything in your past you're holding onto and transform it into an empowering memory rather than a disempowering one?

CHAPTER FOURTEEN

Mindset Multiplied

The most foundational goal we're driving towards in relation to mindset is so that you have the tools to live the most empowered life possible.

When you're living each day with meaning, fulfillment and purpose — that's when you truly begin tapping into your power, into your greatness, and your life takes a nonlinear leap forward.

Most think that you arrive at a certain destination then begin to start living with meaning, fulfillment and purpose, which is to miss the irony of it.

It's only once you start living in this manner that you then begin to break through ceiling after ceiling, surpassing destination after destination for the journey of a lifetime.

That's what you're on, by the way.

You only get this one life.

As my friend, Coach Micheal Burt, likes to say:

"This ain't no practice life."

This skill set is learning to change the way you think so that you change the way you interact with the world, and ultimately who you are and who you're capable of becoming.

There is a trickle-down effect from learning and truly implementing just these simple steps.

You stop focusing on problems and start focusing on solutions, which means you start getting solutions and actually achieving the results you actually want.

You stop being resourceless and begin being resourceful.

You go from asking low-quality questions to asking high-quality questions and in turn gaining high-quality answers that again, lead to results.

You start enjoying all aspects of life and no longer have expectations that set you up for failure and feeling disempowered.

Mindset really is the level of communication you have with yourself, right?

It's choosing what to focus on, how you communicate that meaning and what you're going to do.

This being said, mindset is more than just a mental attitude.

Think about it.

You fail a test or bomb a job interview and come out of it telling yourself how you're just an idiot. You can't believe you said what you did or couldn't figure a problem out and verbally lambast yourself.

You're probably slouching your shoulders, hanging your head, clenching your jaw, perhaps even sweating a bit.

How you've decided to FRAME things and communicate with yourself is far more than just the conversation in your head.

It starts with mindset but your mind and body are connected and now you're having congruent communication with yourself about how you're unworthy, or stupid, or whatever other disempowering meaning you choose.

This leads to you storing these things in your body and harboring all these feelings where they slowly accumulate.

You're communicating with yourself on multiple levels and your entire system is internalizing it which is why this is so important.

Your mindset is far more than just a mental attitude. It affects your entire physiology and ultimately can affect the very level of health you have in your life.

Communicate with yourself and live with an empowered mindset and you'll find yourself more empowered physically. Do the opposite and you'll find yourself disempowered physically.

Think of Pavlov's dog.

Food is introduced along with the ring of a bell. Before long, simply ringing the bell starts the involuntary processes of the dogs salivating without the introduction of food.

They built neural associations to certain stimuli and that took on a life of its own.

The same is true with your physiology.

If you've wired yourself with certain neural associations, this isn't just a brain game. Your nervous system is distributed throughout your entire body and each and every cell holds onto these things.

This is a far more complex dance than some would have you think or believe.

How you act physically is part of a cybernetic loop and if you start running a depressive pattern where you slouch your shoulders, breathe in a shallow manner and look down, guess what? You'll start having depressive thoughts along with that.

The same is true if you eat a certain diet or drink contaminated water or breathe polluted air.

All of these factors go into your physiology and affect your mindset.

Mindset is not a solo-system — you're an interconnected web of everything and you can only begin to make sense of it when you begin to recognize that there are really only subsets of the whole to be focused in on.

We're not going to delve into these nuances here but it's worth mentioning that this rabbit hole goes further. This is about unlocking the door, opening your eyes to a concept and providing some foundational principles by which you can radically transform your life.

However, as Coach Micheal Burt likes to say — a book or keynote opens you to the concept — it's the coaching and continual APPLICATION of that information that makes it transformational.

I like to think of mindset in separate ways. Mindset is oftentimes just an autopilot default that we accept as innate or unchanging or that we have no control over, and for most, that's exactly what it is because unless you confront it and yourself, that's exactly what it'll remain.

As Henry Ford is quoted as saying:

"Whether you believe you can or believe you cannot, either way, you're right."

Principle — Life reflects back to you what you believe about it.

If you want to change what is being reflected back at you, change your beliefs.

Mindset is really a collection of all the mental attitudes, emotions, beliefs, et cetera that you've built throughout your life that we could call your paradigm, philosophy, outlook, world view and on and on.

Let's not focus on semantics and instead focus on getting you some results.

Mindset is the way you view the world based upon the sum-total of what you've focused on, the meaning you've given it and then the actions you've taken based upon the former two.

If you choose to leave it to this default — you're essentially saying, I'm a victim of myself and this world and have no ability to take charge of or control my life.

However, if you choose to take the reins — then you're recognizing that you do have control over this massively important thing and then have to decide if you're willing or unwilling to do what's necessary in order to actually change it.

While it's a lifelong pursuit to constantly sculpt your mindset, it's also something that's easily done in seasons where for a time you work to sculpt yourself and build new habits. Once they're built, they're nearly automated and run in the background.

So, while mindset can be thought of as what you:

Focus on.

The meaning you give it.

The actions you take based upon the previous two.

What determines these three things to a large degree?

If you're consciously focusing on them, of course you can choose to override your default. However, if you're not consciously focusing on them, then it's your unconscious that is largely directing these.

And what rules does your unconscious follow to assess these things?

Primarily, it's your beliefs, values and physiology.

The beliefs that are the most controlling are the ones WEIGHTED with the most evidence behind them.

However, evidence doesn't always mean actual evidence but weighted evidence.

How strongly you emotionally believe something has far more to do with how strongly it's weighted compared to how much evidence you have of it.

For instance, perhaps you believe eating meat is bad.

You suffer from health problems, have no experience on a farm, have no experience in dealing with crops or land or other things, yet you've come to this conclusion and emotionally feel it solidly and with certainty in your gut. That's going to be a dominant belief that controls what you focus on, what it means and what you do. And it's important to remember that you may have arrived at this conclusion with no actual evidence other than a feeling.

That's the fun thing about beliefs — they're always true to us, but that doesn't necessarily mean they hold any accuracy in relationship to reality.

Simultaneously, if you tend to value relationships and people, you're more likely to focus on people, to draw meanings that empower that original value and similarly take actions in alignment with that. Which then creates beliefs aligned with that and so the circle goes.

Lastly, your physiology greatly affects how you show up to any situation.

Have you ever woken up and it didn't matter how positive you wanted to be, it just felt like the weight of the world was coming down on your shoulders?

Mindset is intrinsically linked with physiology. The stronger your mindset, the less your physiology will be able to influence your mindset and the more your mindset will be able to influence your physiology.

But this is also much like weight lifting or training physically. Your mindset allows you to push through intense periods of stress, then needs periods to recuperate.

If you're constantly beaten down, it's difficult to recover to bring that unbreakable mindset back.

And, it can't be overemphasized how important developing a rock-solid mindset along the way is.

Viktor Frankl is a supreme example of this as it was his heart and mindset that allowed him to survive the Nazi concentration camps. However, had he not built the fortitude of mindset and had the basic structures in place before going, he easily could have succumbed like many others did.

Here's another quote from the hardest man alive, Mr. David Goggins himself:

"Everything in life is a mind game! Whenever we get swept under by life's dramas, large or small, we are forgetting that no matter how bad the pain gets, no matter how harrowing the torture, all bad things end. That forgetting happens the second we give control over our emotions and actions to other people, which can easily happen when the pain is peaking."

These are the foundations:

Here is also a good point to stop and differentiate between thoughts and emotions. Hat tip to my good friend Michael Carrigan for articulating the distinctions between these two things.

A thought is simply that, just a thought.

It doesn't mean it's true.

It doesn't mean you have to or even should believe it.

It doesn't mean you're bad or good for having it sublimate up from your unconscious — it just is.

I have lots of thoughts and I let most of them pass right through me and hold on to a select few, then test them, ruminate over them and that's the process of actually thinking.

An emotion is just that — an emotion.

It's a feeling, a body sensation, a neurochemical representation in your body.

Here's the thing though — feelings aren't facts, just because I have one doesn't mean it's good, or bad — those are my **interpretations**.

It just is.

You could see a shoestring curled like a snake and jump in fright with a huge feeling of panic and fear.

Your response is obviously true to you based upon the meaning that you gave that representation, but that doesn't confer factual accuracy.

You may get body sensations before speaking in front of people. You can interpret those as excitement or as panic.

The feeling is just the feeling, just a body sensation. It's the representation you give that feeling that matters in how you treat it and also how your unconscious treats it.

Okay, we're going to segue here into why mindset is the most important concept you should really learn before the other fundamentals out there.

So many people spend their time studying discipline, or habits, or leadership, or any other number of topics in the personal development community, and I applaud this.

But, we've established that it's entirely possible to reach the apogee in these areas while also constantly focusing on what's not available versus what is.

For instance — have you ever woken up and just been in a bad mood for no reason at all? No matter what happens, your attitude for the day is total shit and you can't seem to get a handle on it no matter what you do?

You still have a choice.

Do you choose to focus on these feelings and all the things that are wrong, or to focus on what's right?

You can't always control what your body does but one of the last of the human freedoms is your ability to choose the meaning of something.

Remember, mindset is about heart.

When you see the world's most elite athletes performing and one of them is down so far no one thinks it's possible to come back, then they do and win, what do you think that's about?

Heart, right?

I agree.

But what do you think that athlete is telling themselves during those moments? What do you think they've told themselves repeatedly to get to that point?

They've had to have some form of CONGRUENT communication with themselves about what they BELIEVE is possible. It doesn't matter that everyone else believes it's impossible, only that they believe it's possible.

Here's something the legit GOAT Tom Brady said:

"I was a backup quarterback on an 0-8 high school freshman team.
I didn't even play.
We didn't win a game and I couldn't even get on the field.
I was kind of a late bloomer, recruited to Michigan late, started as the 7th quarterback, you know, had to work really hard to even play... thought, oh man, I'll make being in pro football, got drafted in the 6th round. You know, no one thought I'd make the team."

Interviewer: "So that drives you."

"Yeah, it still does.

I mean, I think now, now it's like, wait a minute, now you guys want me to stop playing.

No, this is when I'm having fun.

You know, now is the time when I get to do what I really enjoy.

I always had a lot of belief in myself and I always tell a lot of young quarterbacks — if you don't believe in yourself, why do you think those guys that are looking at you are gonna believe in you?

When you step in that huddle they better look at you and go — man that guy's ready to get the job done. Cause if they don't see that then they're going to start questioning — I don't think that guy can get the job done.

So you gotta believe in who you are, what you do, what you bring to the team, and then if you do that, they're going to feed off that as well."

Congruent communication and belief.

All the top performers in any industry have given themselves empowering meanings repeatedly, otherwise there is no way they'd be there.

Everyone else is saying — there's no way, that person can't come back — but what is that athlete saying? What do you think they're thinking?

Do you think they're focusing on — I'm down and this is it, it's all over and been for nothing.

Or...

These people have no idea what's coming for them. This is an opportunity for me to stage the biggest comeback in sports history and be the person I know I can.

Do you think they're focused on the pain or on winning?

Do you think they're giving themselves a meaning that it's all over or that this is their moment to shine?

What's the difference between that athlete who won versus the others?

Some would say heart — I'd say congruence between their heart and mind.

They had the desire, they had the heart, but if they also lacked the mindset to propel themselves forward, it never would've happened.

You need both.

Mind and body in harmony is what we're after — congruence makes you dangerous because you're aligned towards a single purpose while being fueled with an unquenchable desire and empowered mindset that gets results.

You can learn all the other tactics and strategies but without mindset, you're going to constantly find yourself disempowered versus more empowered and find that success without fulfillment isn't success at all.

One of the issues I've struggled with in my personal development journey is knowing where to start, what to try to focus on and master at the right time and in the right order, or even having an appropriate target to orient towards in the future.

This is one of the biggest problems I see because people go down this road a little ways focusing on self improvement yet may be focused on the right thing at the wrong time, then become disenchanted because they're not getting the results they're after and of course this is because they haven't clearly defined their target or goal.

For instance, while discipline can help you at any stage, perhaps you start studying discipline with no real compelling future or goal. Maybe you have no true reason to implement it and find yourself attempting to simply willpower your way through to impose discipline upon yourself.

Well of course that usually doesn't work out so well for most people. But, when you have a large, clear and compelling reason to implement discipline, all of a sudden it becomes far easier.

I do want to say here: I'm not convinced you need a large purpose or a why in order to activate this. Perhaps you say — I just enjoy playing football and want to be the best in the world at it.

The reason I say it's unnecessary to have a large purpose or a why is that oftentimes people's judgments enter in at this phase. They start thinking — here I am just wanting to play football, yet there are these other people out here working to solve world hunger, or eradicate cancer, or some other lofty idea — and suddenly they feel disempowered.

The goal is to feel empowered. The goal is to simply say you feel a desire in your soul for something and to follow that.

That's why I say your purpose is to pursue your potential, to pursue greatness, to pursue the man you could be and then it's really only a matter of finding the most appropriate vehicle for that.

The world needs all types.

It's also okay to not have anything that you feel really passionate about.

I have been one of those people in the past. You know that you're a person with huge drive, huge motivation, general passion in life, yet then buy up all the bullshit that you simply need to find your passion.

You need to find your why.

You need to find your purpose.

And then you spend years searching and waffling back and forth over this imaginary rendition of something you supposedly MUST have.

Erroneous!

It's important to take who you think you are and what you might enjoy into account, but ultimately, to pick something and focus on it and realize that your passion will follow.

You are built, not born, motherfucker!

You build who you want to and choose to become, you're not born into the only person you can be.

You're manufactured for adaptability.

It's your ability to adapt that allows you to create whoever you want to see reflected in the mirror.

This is a longer conversation for another time but the point I'm trying to drive home is that the sequence in which you learn things in life is important.

It's important to learn algebra before calculus.

To learn how to run before trying to organize plays on a football team.

Mindset is something that benefits you at all stages and while you can learn it at the later stages, you miss the benefit of compounded results over a lifetime if you do that.

The earlier you begin to master the fundamentals and the more focused you are on them, the longer and more robust your results will be.

Do you think it's any coincidence that most of the world's most successful people are relentlessly pursuing mastery over the fundamentals and then only move from there to higher level tactics and strategies?

Mindset is the foundation of the fundamentals.

If you think about it like a car — heart is like having a big engine and plenty of gas in the tank to go places. Mindset is how you operate that car, how you navigate to those places you want to go, how to even determine those places, how to connect all the interwoven pieces and also how to even raise your RPM threshold.

You come out of the gate with only amateur resilience, amateur ability to withstand adversity, and so you redline at 2,000 RPMs but through training and mindset, you literally increase the RPMs you can withstand. Now, you redline at 10,000 instead of 2,000. Now, you increase your horsepower from 150 to 1500. And you're pointing all that power and potential and capability in a single unified direction.

Mindset is the foundation of state mastery which is ultimately how you're going to choose to show up on a moment-by-moment basis.

When you take control of your mindset, you're a better leader, a more disciplined person, you see the possibilities in life instead of the limitations, the opportunities rather than problems.

So, with all this said about mindset — the real question I began asking myself is how could I rapidly upgrade my mindset? How could I essentially multiply my mindset?

What would that even look like?

And should this even be a priority for me currently?

Well, I first went back to Rory Vaden's book Procrastinate on Purpose because it's really about how to multiply your time which sparked my thoughts about what it would look like to multiply other areas of your life such as mindset.

From there I looked at the diagram that Stephen Covey originally came up with and then Rory Vaden built upon, adding an additional element to it based upon how SIGNIFICANT the task is over time.

	URGENT	NOT URGENT
IMPORTANT	Quadrant I *urgent and important* **DO**	Quadrant II *not urgent but important* **PLAN**
NOT IMPORTANT	Quadrant III *urgent but not important* **DELEGATE**	Quadrant IV *not urgent and not important* **ELIMINATE**

This is a critical distinction because if you do something today that has long-lasting effects where the payoff is multiplicitous of the inputs, it moves up in importance.

HOW LONG WILL IT MATTER?

For instance, if by focusing on something today, it pays additional dividends tomorrow and over the next months or years, then the ROTI (return on time invested) is a necessary calculation of extreme importance.

If you're always TOO busy to set up bill pay, or to train someone to do a job you should really be outsourcing, or too busy to re-invest in yourself, then eventually, you'll find the results you're getting in life are far sub-par compared to what they could be.

This is a simple calculation on why sports teams focus relentlessly on the fundamentals — because you can come up with all the fancy plays or strategies you like, but if you fail to dribble properly, or to fumble a handoff, everything else is for not.

This desire to go at warp speed, to multi-task our way out of everything is an affliction of productivity. It's this constant focus on being busy while lacking effectiveness and never actually catching up because proper targets haven't been set.

As Derek Sivers says:

"To me, 'busy' implies that the person is out of control of their life."

Busyness is not an excuse, yet it's one used by so many today to elevate their feelings of importance. But let me stop and ask you this — how do some of the world's top performing individuals seem to do 10X the amount of work, yet also not be constantly busy?

That's right.

It's because they've invested properly in themselves, their systems and appropriately identified how they want to structure their life, then pursued that to the point of mastery.

All of this is said to emphasize that oftentimes it's not sexy to shoot those 500 free throws after practice, or to take 200 handoffs repeatedly to ensure you don't fumble, but the end result is incredibly sexy.

It may not FEEL great to do that level of intentional practice. It doesn't feel like you're making huge progress, like you're really moving the needle. But, those are just feelings. Oftentimes it's pushing through how something FEELS that separates you from everyone else.

Everyone else quits early because they don't have that FEELING, yet sacrifice the long term payoff because they weren't willing to sit with that discomfort, knowing that to get to their target that's what it takes.

Another quote from Derek Sivers:

"If more information was the answer, then we'd all be billionaires with perfect abs."

You don't necessarily need more information, you need transformation, and in order to acquire that, you need APPLICATION of the appropriate information.

It's really that simple. That doesn't mean it's always easy though.

While most would say it doesn't FEEL urgent, anyone who's gone down this road tends to say that if you don't feel like it's urgent, or significant, or important, then it's probably the most important thing, assuming you're not actually getting the results you desire in life.

Mindset is one of the most important because it's the foundation upon which you attribute meaning and purpose in life, and the thing that allows you to persevere repeatedly because as we mentioned before — new levels always bring new devils.

Let me ask you this — if you had the option to make lifestyle changes today in order to avoid what would inevitably lead to cancer or diabetes in 20 years, would you? These are nearly a foregone conclusion unless you make those changes TODAY and don't wait another year, or two or 5 or 10. How URGENT would you say this is to you?

Unfortunately, many people make the choice not to act every single day. They choose to wait until it becomes incredibly urgent and rather than acting out of INSPIRATION, they end up acting out of DESPERATION.

Mindset is the same calculation. You can wait until life makes it so unavoidably urgent that you find yourself in a catastrophic state. Or, you can be proactive and realize that it's fundamentally urgent, especially because of its significance calculation.

The real magnitude of importance of mindset is how significant it is over time. Just like money compounding, the longer you practice, the more you master it, the more compounded results you get.

Think about it like working out. It seems like the returns are linear for someone who does this as a practice for 60 years from 20 to 80, but are they really?

That person has improved cognition, brain function, stamina, energy, vitality and zest for life, while also avoiding the addition of disease or chronic ailments that detract from many people's lives. When you start actually looking at their returns, they're not linear at all, they're exponentially superior because as others began to fall off at a non-linear rate, they were still improving.

Furthermore, they may find themselves with an additional 10-20 years of FUNCTIONAL life at the end which if you think about it is upwards of 33% more functional life, but that's not all — that life may be when they actually accomplish the MAJORITY of their massive life ambitions because they're at the peak of knowledge, maturity and wisdom, and have actually figured life out a bit more.

It's also the time they get to reap exponential rewards, perhaps spending time with grandchildren or great-grandchildren, having the time and money to explore the things they desire and develop more fully as a person.

Mindset is the same. The same significance applies to mindset where you get unbelievably compounded results over time yet is constantly discounted by so many because they fail to see the long-term benefits, or that it doesn't provide the short-term feeling of sexiness, busyness, or "factitious progress" they're seeking.

This is how you miss the target.

You miss the target by not properly identifying just how important, urgent and significant something is over a long stretch of time.

It's like eating chips. In the short-term it feels good, tastes good, provides that quick hit of dopamine. But, take it out over 10 years and the results are nearly the opposite — you have low energy, poor self esteem, are overweight and diabetic and suffer from any number of other ailments.

On the flip-side, skipping out on them isn't sexy in the short-term, but the long-term result is incredibly sexy where you're fit, energetic, full of life, have superior self-esteem and lack disease.

It's easy to miss and this is a huge part of my work because as a society, we've adjusted our targets on a grand scale and it's a massive problem.

Part of my work is to properly identify the targets I want to hit and find the most beneficial in life and to share those with others so I can triangulate my views and hopefully improve them along the way.

This struggle with orientation in life has been one of my biggest bottlenecks. There is a paradox in having too many choices and also in buying into improper targets — to not properly identifying what you want on a long-enough timeline.

Again, mindset is the foundation that's oftentimes dismissed at great cost of fumbling through life without it.

So — multiply your mindset.

How to do it.

What it looks like.

The pursuit of attempting to decipher how I could multiply my mindset in a short period of time led me to systems design and understanding the rules of multiplication.

I had to start asking better questions if I wanted better answers.

If I really wanted to multiply my mindset, what would that look like? How would I do that? How could I design my life in order to get this exponential result in a compressed time frame?

Mindset Multiplication Design

First, it's important to deconstruct what we're trying to do and appropriately identify the target.

> Multiply your mindset — on a fundamental level, this is gaining mastery over your:
>
> > Beliefs
> >
> > Values
> >
> > Physiology
>
> Because these ultimately most impact what you:
>
> > Focus on
> >
> > The meaning you assign to that focus
> >
> > The actions you take based upon the former two
>
> Everything else is downstream from this.
>
> Breaking down limiting beliefs is just a process of focusing on them, reframing the meaning, AKA recontextualizing, and making a new decision and then taking different actions that build out new neural networks to form new beliefs.

Second — Eliminate — Eliminate inputs that are disempowering — Friends, entertainment, disempowering habits.

The removal of interferences from the system is one of the fastest ways to massively upgrade yourself.

Think of it like this — if you're drinking alcohol all day every day, is it better to continually try to add coffee, medicine, or other things to help you sober up? Or to simply remove the alcohol and sober up naturally?

Exactly.

Multiply by removal first.

Third — Substitute — Your brain doesn't like a vacuum. Replace the eliminated inputs with empowering inputs — books, personalities, social media, friends, or anything else that helps to keep you on track with your desired target.

This is also a form of outsourcing and environmental design. Oftentimes we're more the product of our environment than anything else, so designing an environment intentionally that supports you in this, massively upgrades you on near auto-pilot.

Upgrading your peers is one of the fastest and easiest ways to raise your standards. On your own, it's easy to let things slip. When the expectations of your peer group sets the bar far higher, you'll rise to the occasion without trying to willpower through.

Fourth — Concentrate — In order to develop a new habit, mindset or structure for your life, you need a period of time that you concentrate heavily on a single subject in order to build this new muscle.

This is where you're laying the foundation for automation.

We could do this at a methodical, slow, lackadaisical pace but most people don't actually do so well with that.

What we want to do is heavily COMPRESS the amount of time while also having maximum concentration with the right amount of frequency in order to multiply the results.

Realistically, this is a 90 - 120 day sprint where you're obsessed with mastering this concept, anchoring it to all parts of your life and building the systems and habits of thinking so that it's essentially on auto-pilot.

> This is the shooting 500 free throws part. You think — I've got this, I don't need to focus on this any longer, to practice any longer. That's not true. This is fundamentals mastery and this short sprint will have MASSIVE effects for the coming years of your life.

Think of this like a weight loss sprint or preparing for a fitness competition. You pick a big goal and bust your tail for 90 days. You continue training after that so you don't lose the results, but at a much more sustainable frequency in order to give yourself time to bounce back then do another one.

What you'll find is that your ceiling for the first sprint is now your floor for the new sprint.

Fifth — Automate — Currently, I wake up every single morning and do 30 minutes of cardio. It's not even something I think about. It's automated.

It's doing the things today that empower me to do more tomorrow.

It's my default.

It's automated for me.

This is your automation. Having built your foundation over the last 90 - 120 days, it's taking the time each morning to reorient to the target, to identify the fundamentals to practice through the day, to know your outcome, to re-emphasize that so you repeatedly get outsized results.

This may be journaling for 5 minutes on precisely this in the morning or at the end of the day.

This may be building reminders into your calendar that go off repeatedly so you constantly re-orient.

This may be hiring a coach to ensure you stay focused and on track.

Taking the time to build this automation is how you focus on the things today in order to give yourself more tomorrow.

Taking the time to design this automation will take a short amount of time while having huge dividends for the future.

It's your new default.

And, in a short 90 - 120 day period, you've multiplied your mindset not just 2X but 10X.

Which means you're now opening up your future to 10X possibilities because you'll have the wherewithal to focus on them, to give yourself empowering meanings and take empowering actions.

Now, imagine if you take this information and actually apply it to your life.

Imagine that you apply it to your job, to your finances, to your relationships, to wherever it is you're stuck and start focusing on solutions rather than problems?

What if you start focusing on being resourceful rather than the resources you lack?

What if you started focusing on all the things that you do have, that are at your disposal instead of only concentrating on the ones you don't have?

What if you started focusing on where you DESIRE to go rather than where you DON'T want to go or how you're miserable where you are?

Perhaps you choose to focus on your partner's attributes that you enjoy instead of the ones you can't stand...

"What's wrong is always available, so is what's right."
— Tony Robbins

The goal here is to automate how you view life.

To automate always looking for what's available instead of what's unavailable.

To automate looking for what's right versus what's wrong.

To automate resourcefulness, to where it's your default, rather than slipping into resourcelessness and disempowerment.

MINDSET is a HABITUAL SKILL SET after all and once you really dial that in, just like driving a car, it's something you no longer have to concentrate on as much and simply naturally allow to run in the background.

This is your new superpower.

ACTION ITEMS

- Pull out your calendar and set periodic reminders throughout the day for yourself so that you're constantly reoriented to creating the habit of having an empowered mindset. Set these on repeat for the next 90 days or 120 if you'd prefer.
- Get leverage on yourself right now by journaling about just how significant mastering this subject is to your life and all the reasons why you must do it and what will happen if you don't.
- If ever in doubt, create a mental version of yourself in 5 years that has absolute mastery over their mindset so that when in any situation and you're confused, you can simply ask that future version of yourself what they would do with that rock-solid mindset.

CHAPTER FIFTEEN

Demystifying Your Brain

You don't have to understand how your heart works for it to beat each and every day. However, you can get vastly better results from it by understanding how it actually does work and then training to increase its stamina, reduce disease and enhance overall wellbeing.

The same is true with your brain.

It will work whether you understand how it works or not — the question is will it be working for you or against you?

You come manufactured with certain pre-dispositions such as paying attention to danger in a far higher magnitude than opportunities for pleasure.

Avoiding danger = survival, which means greater importance.

There are fundamentals to the human operating system that, when understood, can VASTLY improve the results you're getting in life and are ultimately necessary to pursuing greatness on the level you'd like to.

The sad part is, somehow no one teaches you these things in school.

Maybe we're just supposed to pick them up naturally but if you're anything like me, that didn't occur until I went out and started turning over rocks to shed some light on my missing structures.

One of the biggest problems people have throughout life is that they have this big brain between their ears, and while you would think they should know how to work it, most people have zero clue how to make it work for them.

I'm not saying the information I'm presenting here is even "technically" correct or accurate as to how you work.

I'm sure there is someone out there who is screaming, "But the 'science' says this" or "This study says that."

Let me be clear – I don't give a shit.

I only choose to believe in that which empowers me.

So what AM I saying?

This model has proved incredibly USEFUL to nearly everyone I've delivered this message to and that has applied it to their life, and that's my end goal.

I would rather have a USEFUL and HELPFUL system that produces RESULTS than an accurate system that is UNHELPFUL and produces no results.

YOUR BRAIN DEMYSTIFIED

The first thing to know about your brain is that it distorts, deletes and generalizes.

Why?

The amount of information coming in is near infinite, so in order to compile a cohesive rendering of the world, your brain has to use selective filters.

DELETES — Your brain either deletes or stores in your unconscious huge amounts of the information you take in.

Think about it. You walk into a room and can only think and focus on so many things. This is usually 7 + or - 2.

However, can't we all think of a situation where we weren't particularly paying attention, didn't consciously notice the color of the carpet, yet if we think back on it later, there it is, stored somewhere within us?

So, much of the information that reaches your conscious mind is first and foremost FILTERED.

The information that your brain deems too unnoteworthy is DELETED and never retained.

DISTORTS — Your brain distorts reality in a number of ways. One way is that it magnifies or diminishes the importance of certain things based upon the emotions we place behind them, which are usually reflections of our belief systems. In my full mindset program, I delve into all the cognitive distortions and how they can play out, such as "all or nothing thinking".

GENERALIZES — Your brain generalizes to fit the world into a structure that you can understand. You may generalize how all girls like flowers or "real men" wear jeans or that red meat leads to cancer and heart disease. But these are just generalizations and the truth is far more nuanced. While this is also a cognitive distortion, I generally only think of it as one when over-generalization occurs compared to the minimum necessary for a result.

Your brain works in a complex dance with the rest of your body and while I think it's unhelpful to try to completely isolate it from the rest of the body, a metaphor can help you understand how it works best.

Imagine your brain as a video game console with access to an infinite number of games, scenarios and all the things that come along with them.

When you search on this console for experiences in different games, you'll get all these different games with different experiences that involve different characters, storylines, et cetera back.

Your brain is like the SEARCH FUNCTION on this console.

The SEARCH TERMS or QUERIES are really just your belief systems.

And the SEARCH RESULTS are reflections of those belief systems.

So then you go act out those experiences and get the end result of what those original belief systems searched for in the first place.

The experiences you're having in life are really just like this.

Your brain is the console.

Your belief systems are the search queries.

The results are what you inevitably find yourself acting out.

Your values help determine which game you'll select from the returned query. Naturally, it's not always so straight forward.

We all have conflicting belief systems within us and depending on where we're at, different ones are dominant at different times.

Like I said — simplified metaphor that's easy to understand so you can get a macro view of the feedback loop you're playing out repeatedly in life.

All your belief systems really just want to prove themselves to be TRUE.

That's it. That's their singular purpose.

So if you have the belief that:

I'm unworthy

Not good enough

Not deserving

Not smart enough

Unattractive

Inept

A bad person

Then those belief systems want to simply seek out evidence supporting their veracity. Their truthfulness, regardless of if they are TRUE or not.

Think of these beliefs as uni-dimensional, single purpose entities within you.

These beliefs also have their own value systems.

If you believe you're unworthy, how does that belief know when it's true?

When it FEELS true. When you FEEL unworthy.

It doesn't mean that you actually are unworthy, only that the feeling is the positive reinforcement desired by that belief system.

How you FEEL is the feedback mechanism, which is why controlling the MEANING you give things is so important.

So this video game console searches out into the universe based upon your beliefs for experiences that then reinforce those underlying beliefs.

This is why Stephen Covey said:

"We see the world, not as *it is*, but as *we are*—or, as we are conditioned to see it."

And since we act out our beliefs, the inherent results we get only serve to REINFORCE the original belief much of the time. However, this doesn't play out in a logical manner. The original beliefs get reinforcement not based on logic, but instead, emotion.

Depending on your values and belief systems combined, this determines how this complex dance plays out. For instance, some people value the certainty of misery over the misery of uncertainty.

Some people search for the same experience repeatedly until one day they reach THRESHOLD, and their entire being says, that's it, I've had it, and they make a new decision and reprioritize their beliefs and values in a single fell swoop.

Have you ever met someone who couldn't get it together and seemed to fail over and over again, then one day they ran into that wall and everything changed?

Perhaps you've been there yourself at some point...

This isn't a perfect metaphor, but it's a helpful one to understand how your brain works and how it's intricately linked with your beliefs and values.

Once you understand how your brain is searching for things, and that many of the things you're attracting to you in life are really just a reflection of your underlying beliefs and values, you can begin to harness the power of your brain in order to get it working FOR you instead of against you.

This is part of settling your inner conflicts.

For instance, perhaps one part of you wants lots of money and another part says money is hard to make, or money is the root of all evil.

Or perhaps you want a relationship and one part of you says that would fulfill you and bring you joy and happiness, and another part says that would constrict you and restrain your freedom.

Or perhaps you want to be a better leader, and one part of you wants that recognition and knows that's who you can be in your soul, yet another part says the risk of leadership is too great or you're not good enough to lead others.

It's this combination of CONFLICTING belief systems that keeps so many treading water instead of THRIVING.

Your brain is incredibly complex, ridiculously so, but getting the results you want in life doesn't have to be.

Once you understand a few simple things:

> First, you act out your beliefs.
>
> The results you're getting in life are the end product of what you act out.
>
> Therefore, the results you're getting in life are largely a product of your beliefs.
>
> Also,
>
> You act out what you're committed to.
>
> Essentially, your identity is what you're committed to.
>
> So the results you're getting in life are really just a lagged reflection of your true identity — not the one you profess, but the one you produce through committed actions.

Each and every thing you do is like a vote where you're constantly voting for the type of person you're committed to being.

When you act out something different from your underlying beliefs, you begin the process of forming new beliefs and retiring the old.

The process of growth is where you're always killing a part of yourself off while also birthing new parts of yourself.

As Millard Fuller says:

"It is easier to act yourself into a new way of thinking, than it is to think yourself into a new way of acting."

Your brain is really just like that video game console, constantly searching even when you're not thinking about it, constantly searching and pulling search results into reality by the experiences you have, which are most often a reflection of your unconscious belief systems.

So, life ends up reflecting back to you what you believe about it in the first place.

The way to then change your external circumstances is to transform your internal world.

If your brain is like a video game console, all you really have to do to weaponize it is start searching for different things, which really just requires that you make a new DECISION about what to search for.

This seems overly obvious to many people, so simple in fact, that they discount it and never actually utilize this process.

DO NOT DISMISS THIS!

Your ability to harness your brain's power to pull the experiences you desire into existence cannot be overstated.

This has worked for countless greats throughout history. Their ability to first think it, to dream it, to taste it, to smell it, to tune their brain into what they KNEW was possible cannot be overstated, and then of course, they brought it into reality.

Think about Roger Banister and the 4 minute mile.

No one in recorded HISTORY had run a sub 4 minute mile, but he BELIEVED it was possible. Rehearsed it in his brain, told himself it was possible and that he was going to break that barrier, reinforced it emotionally, and gained total congruence with himself in this endeavor.

He broke the 4 minute barrier on May 6th, 1954.

The most interesting part though is that now that it had been proven possible, only 2 months later the 4 minute barrier was broken again and has since been broken by over 1600 athletes around the world.

This is an example of weaponizing your brain to accomplish whatever task you desire to tackle.

It's important to realize that emotions are the ultimate drivers of all this.

Yes, our beliefs may control the search results, but the reason we're searching in the first place is to change how we FEEL.

It's this quest to change how we feel that drives everything, our desire to feel different emotions, to achieve different, more meaningful things that powers the quest.

It's this arrival emotionally to a place that says — I want a new experience — that provides the fuel to make new decisions and then to experience new results.

Of course this can be scary, because exploring the unknown usually means expanding most people's comfort zones, which is why you need that emotional drive for curiosity to be stronger than your desire for comfort.

It's in this static state that so many get stuck. Overcoming the inertia of doing something new seems too great rather than sticking with the same, even though it's slowly killing them inside.

Their circumstances are bad but not bad enough for them to flip the switch and make a major change. First they have to build up enough emotional juice and reach that threshold point where they become INTOLERANT of not changing their circumstances.

Understanding that your brain is really just a facilitator of this process is helpful. Your brain can work for you or against you and it's largely up to you.

I do want to add the caveat though that I'm not entirely a mind over matter person. Sure, it's helpful to have this understanding of how the brain works, but that doesn't guarantee results, only your relentless pursuit of those results does.

The brain is incredibly powerful, but it also has its limitations. For instance — good luck putting any of this into practice after 10 shots of vodka.

You can't mind over matter some things, and just like that, if you're constantly clogging up your brain's capacity to work for you, then no matter how much you want to mind-over-matter your way through, it's probably not going to happen nearly as well as it could.

The better you treat your brain, the better it will help facilitate the experiences you wish to have. The worse you treat your brain, the worse it will be at helping you facilitate experiences and may even develop a mind of its own.

Your brain doesn't have to be this incredibly mystifying thing that you're intimidated by.

Sure, you can get lost thinking you need to know how many neurons the brain has or synaptic connections or other extraneous information, but does that ACTUALLY help you to get better results in life?

That's a big fat whopping — NO!

Results are what we're after to become the most powerful man you could be and in that pursuit, you need APPLICATION of the right INFORMATION to achieve TRANSFORMATION.

Information + Application = Transformation

Understanding that the RESULTS you're getting are really just a reflection of the BELIEF SYSTEMS that are driving them is so powerful and effective because you can IMMEDIATELY take action in a different direction and start getting new results almost instantly.

As Jim Rohn said:

"You cannot change your destination overnight, but you can change your direction overnight."

and...

"Life does not get better by chance, it gets better by change."

New results = new beliefs.

New beliefs = new results.

When you think you can't run 5 miles nonstop, then you actually do it, that can't be taken away from you.

You now have a new belief.

The goal is to be in the driver's seat rather than a backseat passenger on this journey.

As Napoleon Hill said:

"The only limitation is that which one sets up in one's own mind."

We both know you're here because you sense there is some part of you that desires to awaken, to pursue greatness, to be the man you know you truly could be.

You do this by having the fortitude to look into yourself, to have the courage to take the reins, to realize there is a dance with your unconscious and deeper, darker parts of yourself, and that is truly the greatest struggle you'll engage in repeatedly through life.

It's this struggle to deal with yourself and that's why mindset is so critical and also why demystifying your brain is crucial to living a meaningful and fulfilling life.

ACTION ITEMS

- For different categories in your life such as relationships, money, fitness, career, et cetera, list out 5 empowering beliefs you have surrounding those areas. Now also list out 5 beliefs that are disempowering you from the results you'd like to get.
- How is that conflict holding you back from getting the results you truly desire?

- Now, if you inspect those disempowering beliefs appropriately, identify how they're NOT actually true.

  Isn't it true that there are people who do good with money? That some people simply skip the career ladder climbing and go right to the top or simply start their own successful business? Isn't it true that someone else was dealing with the exact problems you were yet also found a way to lose that weight and become the man they knew they could be?

- Now that you've identified these beliefs as not actually true, you need to reinforce the beliefs that empower you and remove power from the beliefs that disempower you.

  Recontextualization and visualizations are your friend here.

  You don't actually have to make those old disempowering beliefs wrong. When they sublimate up, you can merely look at them and thank them for trying to help that old version of you. You can realize they were perfectly true for that older version of yourself, however, they no longer apply to the new version and then reinforce the new, empowering beliefs with more evidence.

- Visualizations can help you begin searching for new things in life at accelerated speed. Simply start clearly and emotionally visualizing that which you're after, the types of experiences you'd like to attract into your life and then the type of person you'd have to become in order to attract those experiences into your life. Become that man, and watch as these things seem to magically appear in your life.

CONCLUSION

Mindset is a beast of a subject precisely because it's so encompassing.

And it's so important precisely because it is so encompassing.

None of these different ideas or characteristics exist in a vacuum between one another.

Everything is interconnected which means we have to diligently go about understanding each, individual component and then also how to tie it all together.

Think of it like a car. You can have all the individual parts, yet their value and effectiveness is diminished unless you can bring them together under one single definite purpose.

I know these were some heavy chapters and I could've tried to make them more entertaining or lightened them, but I wanted you to have some truly powerful information to help you become the man you could be.

To close, this is really only an introduction to mindset. As a subject, it's so broad in scope it's difficult to even truly define. This isn't a skill set you master overnight, it's a lifelong practice to upgrade yourself repeatedly over time. It's never over until it's over and growth never stops until you do.

Lastly, if you're anything like me, you need each concept broken down into a step-by-step process where you can then build upon each.

You need a SYSTEMATIC approach that cuts through the fluff, through the bullshit that disempowers you, and gets to the heart of what matters most: how you can actually start living the life you know you were MEANT to be living.

To actually start BEING the man you know exists within you!

To not only answer the call that's within you, but also to get the appropriate resources necessary to maximize that call.

To get the appropriate information, in the right order, at the right time and to also focus on application so that you can achieve what you're truly after which is TRANSFORMATION.

I believe in you.

I believe you have GREATNESS within you.

And I believe you have within your capability the tools to unlock that and to start living a LEGENDARY LIFE.

PILLAR IV

Master Your Body

MEDICAL DISCLAIMER: I'm not a doctor, nor do I play one in books, on the internet, or elsewhere. While I don't believe most doctors are where you should be getting your "healthy living" advice since they mainly specialize in "sick care", I am required to give a legal disclaimer for you to speak with a medical professional before doing anything medical-related.

This book should be used to supplement rather than replace the advice of your doctor or another trained health professional. If you know or suspect you have a health problem, it is recommended that you seek your physician's advice before embarking on any medical program or treatment. All efforts have been made to assure the accuracy of the information contained in this book as of the date of publication. This publisher and the author disclaim liability for any medical outcomes that may occur as a result of applying the methods suggested in this book.

"High-performing people know that getting their food right is the number one human upgrade."
— Dave Asprey

"In the U.S., having a 6 pack is less common than being a millionaire.

3 million people have visible abs.

22 million people are millionaires.

This is why a fit, healthy body is the ultimate status symbol.

You can't buy it, it must be earned, & no one can take it away from you."

– Dr. James DiNicolantonio

If you see Dave Asprey today, he's lean, fit and healthy, however his journey was an arduous one and he wasn't always this way.

In his twenties, Dave was a tech-entrepreneur working in Silicon Valley and one of the early pioneers on the internet. He was young, gifted and on his way up, except that he had one major problem.

He was also nearly 300 pounds, suffered from severe brain fog and was under such constant stress that he couldn't enjoy any of what he was doing.

Despite the career success, his personal success was suffering, leaving him chronically sick, tired and struggling to make it through the day.

He decided that had to change so spent 18 months eating 1,500 to 1,800 calories per day and working out for 90 minutes six days a week.

While he did see some marginal improvement, the fat wouldn't go away along with his chronic sub-optimal health and energy status.

Despite trying numerous "fad" diets, Dave just couldn't seem to get his body working for himself the way he wanted.

I understand that all too well.

It's disheartening when you feel like your body has betrayed you, like it's given up on you even though you're trying not to give up on it.

It's disheartening when you feel like you've tried everything yet can't seem to make the physical breakthrough so that you are operating on all cylinders like you know you could be.

Fortunately, Dave wasn't going to accept this quality of life for the rest of his life and also knew his life would end far shorter than need be if he didn't make some radical changes.

With that in mind, he set out to hack his biology and in that has now become appropriately known as the 'father of biohacking'.

After spending years and thousands of dollars hacking his own biology, Dave released The Bulletproof Diet that went on to become a New York Times bestseller and help thousands regain their health.

Not only is transformation possible, it's likely far closer at hand than you realize.

It's likely one book away or one chapter away or one conversation away or simply just one decision away — and in that, your entire life can change.

If you're ready and committed to transforming your physique into one of power, strength and ability, this chapter will give you the basic principles to do just that.

CHAPTER SIXTEEN

Mastering Your Body

"The first wealth is health."
— Ralph Waldo Emerson

"A healthy person has a thousand wishes. A sick person has but one."
—Indian Proverb

In your quest to become the most powerful man you can be, it's damn-near impossible to actually be on that path if you're chronically unhealthy.

The obvious exception to this is if you're incredibly sick yet pushing through against all odds and staying on the path to greatness.

But that's not most people.

Most people lead a life where they're chronically unhealthy, chronically showing up at suboptimal levels, and continuously decreasing their quality of life while simultaneously attempting to convince themselves they don't care or that it doesn't matter or that they've tried everything.

You can't be great if you're unhealthy.

You can't be great if you're incapable of physically operating at the outer limits of your potential.

Being healthy doesn't have to be overly complicated, in fact, the simpler you can make it the easier and better it will be.

You have to recognize that there is a mind-body connection and so much of what goes on in your mind is the result of what you've put into your body.

I can't tell you how many I know who discount this then complain to me of anxiety, depression and a myriad of other ailments that plague their life.

I'm not saying there is a one-size fits all or that food is a panacea for all your ailments, but for most, dialing this in can make MASSIVE and IMMEDIATE changes to the upside.

Here's the thing, you're a physical being and are interacting with the physical world around you in a feedback loop system.

If you're not showing up at the level you know you could be, if you're carrying around excess body fat, if you're chronically fatigued, if you're sick and tired of being sick and tired, then it's time to change that.

I'm going to give you some simple levers to pull that can make huge shifts in your life if you'll do them.

If you're a high-performer and already have your health dialed in, skip this section, but if you're not and know you could be showing up at a higher level, continue on.

When I think of health, generally there are several different categories or ways to think of things.

You have big dials that can rapidly move the needle for you.

You also have smaller levers that may not move the needle as much or that may take longer.

There are others that may make seemingly tiny changes in the short term that end up accounting for huge changes down the line.

An example of this could be ensuring proper air quality. In the short term, you may not notice a difference, but in the long term though, improved air quality could save you from a whole host of problems.

We're going to focus primarily on a few big levers that I believe will get the majority of men huge, beneficial results in a rapid manner.

I'm going to focus on sustainability over rapid transitions, and simplicity in lieu of complexity.

To that end, I will also include a number of beneficial readings on health should you want to explore the subject further without having to personally attempt to vet books from the thousands that are available out there.

"Take care of your body. It's the only place you have to live in."
— Jim Rohn

For those who are the doubters, I've dealt with my own health problems through the years, far more than most I know, which is why I feel qualified to talk in this area.

If you've ever seen me, you might be tempted to say, "He's just genetically gifted" and yes, while I am, part of my genetics have left me prone to sensitivities, allergies, hormonal imbalances, gut issues and plenty more.

I remember one year in college, I had strep throat literally 5 times in a single calendar year.

I also had to stack my classes with strategically timed breaks which kept me on campus most of the day compared to others who could take class after class because I was unable to go that long without restroom breaks.

It sucked.

When I was 24, my girlfriend at the time had her family physician check my testosterone because I never wanted to have sex. It was 134. Pretty much that of an 80 year old male. Joy.

At one point, I had such strong IBS I was visiting the bathroom between 10 to 15 times PER DAY.

So when I say I've had my own struggles, they're real and that has also made the results I've gotten all the more real.

Today I'm fit, healthy and doing far better than at any other point in my life due to my dedication to research and finding results-oriented solutions.

In the quest for optimal, at some point, if you're wanting to push to the outer limits of your capabilities, you'll eventually want to get into the details of how to adjust the more nuanced dials. For right now, most people can GREATLY improve their life by merely making a few changes to the big dials.

90 DAYS TO MASTERING YOUR BODY

"The man who earns a million, but destroys his health in the process is not really a success."
— Zig Ziglar

This is a simple formula and one that I believe if you follow, will yield you being far better off in the next 90 days than you are currently.

It's primarily not the addition of things that will help you the most, but the removal of the things that are clogging your system.

Think of it like this — if you're drinking vodka all day, every day and then keep reaching for coffee, for pills, for food to sober you up, they may help a little, but the real major needle mover would be to simply stop drinking vodka 24/7.

That's what this way of eating will do for you.

LEVER ONE: CIRCADIAN RHYTHM

THE WHAT

I'm not going to go into the nitty-gritty on this, but suffice it to say that it's MASSIVE.

Getting adequate sleep and doing that in the same time window daily dramatically affects your overall health. This cycle controls the development and release of all your major hormones and leads to serious problems when it's disrupted.

This is more of a problem than ever because we're all looking at screens right up until the point of going to sleep which sends a signal to your suprachiasmatic nucleus that it's the middle of the day. This disrupts your body from releasing melatonin properly, which then dysregulates all your other hormones, deep sleep, REM sleep, resting heart rate and on and on.

It's a big deal.

Both the color temperature and intensity matter here which is why blue blocking glasses at night have become all the rage.

I'm a fan, but they can get tiresome.

I've installed red lights into certain lamps and even have red Christmas lights that go around my walls to provide illumination at night that doesn't disrupt my sleep cycle.

Sleep is a really big deal and routinely going to bed at the same time and getting up at the same time is crucial.

Most people have some sort of routine and developing a nightly routine that sets you up for the next day is critical.

When you put your phone down and start using red lights 90 minutes before bed, you'll see a rapid shift in sleep quality and therefore energy, willpower, decision-making quality and overall life improvement the following day.

And, while you can work to hack your sleep, or be one of those guys who tries to get away with 4 hours per night, you're far better only doing that occasionally and getting your body to a healed state before attempting to push your limits.

Most people can literally sleep themselves into better health simply by giving it the priority and emphasis it deserves.

It's when you rest and recover and it's critical to protect it ruthlessly.

THE HOW

CREATING THE IDEAL SETTING

Switch to redlights after dark. If this is impossible then 1 to 2 hours before sleep. If this is impossible, then blue blocking glasses. If all that's impossible, reduce the intensity as much as possible to create a dim atmosphere that helps set the stage for sleep.

Lower the temperature one hour before bed. You want your environment cool.

Set your intentions for the next day and ask a question of your unconscious mind that you'd like to have solved upon waking. This is soooo powerful.

Ensure total darkness.

Eliminate liquids 2 to 3 hours before bed if you struggle with urination at night.

Have your meal completed at least 3 hours before sleep and do not snack.

Note: if you're low-carb and struggling to sleep, try MCT oil, a bit of whey protein and 1 to 2 teaspoons of raw honey before bed. Less is more here.

Eliminate highly stimulative activities at least 1 hour before sleep such as television that takes you on a strong emotional journey.

Keep electronics several feet from your body at the least. Lamps that are plugged into the wall right beside your head still create an electric field that can greatly disrupt your sleep. Don't forget, we're electrical beings and while everyone would like to pretend we're not, our bodies are basically one big electrical charge and we're highly influenced by these things. Don't believe me? Brain scans measure the electrical activity in the brain. External electrical stimuli affect your internal workings.

Just go ahead and set that smart phone in the other room or at least several feet away.

Create a pleasant waking experience by having the temperature automatically increase before your waking time or set a soothing alarm clock versus having something that screeches and blares at you.

QUANTIFICATION

Quantifying how you're doing helps IMMENSELY for most people so that you can get direct, measurable feedback on where you're at.

I use an Oura Ring to quantify my sleep. If you're going to use it, only do so in airplane mode.

If you want to use something else, I still suggest turning it on airplane mode so that you're not getting blasted with close-proximity radiation all night when you're most vulnerable.

HACKS

Tape your mouth with 3M micropore paper tape. It may seem strange but this helps a ton of people. Breathing through your nose is critical for nitric oxide production, jaw and teeth formation, filtration of contaminants and a host of other processes. It's common for people's muscles to relax during sleep allowing their mouth to open and breathe this way. Nose breathing is far superior and taping is easy.

If in doubt, YouTube it.

Obviously, don't do this if you have a medical condition or consult your provider first.

SNORING

If you snore, read Breath by James Nestor or The Oxygen Advantage by Patrick McKeown. I strongly suggest learning to breathe properly and build that muscle. I'm required to tell you to consult your medical professional first but seeking help from the legacy medical does not mean to dismiss this information. However, if you have acute sleep apnea, definitely consult your physician, but still don't discard those books. It's highly likely you can rectify your issues without surgeries, machines or pills.

Get a **weighted blanket** if you feel like you need more weight on you when you sleep.

If you get hot at night, look into a **Chilisleep** or **Eight Sleep system** so that you can get individualized temperature control throughout the entire night.

BONUS POINTS

Create a nightly routine that sets you up for the next morning.

Create a killer morning routine that sets the stage for the entire day.

LEVER TWO: FOOD

In my opinion, a large portion of the — and I hate to even use the term — "mental health" crisis going on today has to do with how our bodies are interacting with the environment.

Food is not the same as it was 50 years ago. The things on and in that food are not the same.

There are a literal FUCK TON of toxic chemicals laced into nearly everything that result in opening the tight junctions throughout your gut, allowing all sorts of stuff that should never get into your body to go freely into your system.

When you manifest symptoms, we call them autoimmune disorders, or mental health disorders, or whatever other euphemism that you want.

You're being poisoned and then think the result is that you've developed anxiety out of nowhere.

I'm not saying this is everyone. I genuinely understand some have very real and serious problems and I don't want to discount that. But, I believe for a large majority of the population, many of the major ailments could be completely resolved from the removal of these toxins in their lives.

And the biggest problem with that is that they're in EVERYTHING!

They're so difficult to remove primarily because you can barely get away from them.

But, you can make some big strides that are low-hanging fruit to radically improve your health quickly.

A QUICK LOW-DOWN ON MEAT:

You can get all the nutrients you need from ruminant meats such as beef, lamb, bison, et cetera. I think veggies serve a purpose and can be helpful, but don't fool yourself into thinking that if you don't have them you'll fall over and die — you won't.

I've personally done an all meat diet for well over 6 months that consisted of only meat, salt, coffee and water and I was just fine.

However, I do think that's unnecessary in the scope of what most people are after and that veggies and carbohydrates in the proper context can be valuable additions.

A diet that consists heavily of meat and that's lower carbohydrate is generally difficult for most when they start because they're so dependent upon burning glucose for all their energy needs compared to fat. There is an adaptation period here which throws some people off, but literally 100% of the people who stick with it will make this adaptation and therefore gain greater metabolic flexibility. And of course they are 1000% better off because of it.

I'm not against chicken or pork and eat both occasionally, but I don't tend to feel as well afterwards. For this reason I am more selective when it comes to these.

Fresh ruminant meat seems to do WONDERS for so many. This could be beef, lamb, elk, venison, et cetera.

These have all been unfairly demonized by the larger agriculture industries through the years to where most think their problems must stem from the meat, but that's not the case at all.

A **VERY** strong and compelling argument could easily be made that the rise in gluten sensitivity has far less to do with gluten and far more to do with the amount of glyphosate, a weed killer introduced by Monsanto, that's also used as a desiccant and sprayed on crops. This is an insanely toxic chemical and a recent report even divulged that glyphosate has been detected in **80%** of Americans' urine.

This is a chemical that when sprayed on weeds, after just 3 days, leaves them totally dead, totally brown, just gone. And it's going into your body at astounding rates. This is a very strong reason to buy organic, but don't fool yourself into thinking you're avoiding it, you're only reducing the load.

If you're so inclined, include the veggies I have listed here, but remember that this is strongly about the things you're removing. To be absolutely clear about that up front, let me spell it out further:

🚫 TOTAL REMOVAL‼️

- Seed oils — canola oil, soybean oil, peanut oil, et cetera. (These do not come from "vegetables" and in my opinion it's rapacious and deceptive marketing.

  Literally, if you're going to cook with something, use: butter, ghee, tallow or lard. If you have to use something non-animal based, use coconut oil or olive oil.

  *As a side note, a large majority of olive oils are either diluted with seed oils i.e. soybean oil, or are rancid. These are unstable oils and have a shorter shelf life. Oftentimes people want to think they're getting avocado oil yet I read a report several years ago that tested 30 of the top brands and 27 were cut with other oils. This is a trust factor for me so I only go with reputable sources. If you're going to use it, try to verify its authenticity.

- Refined sugars, grains and processed foods. This means sodas, brownie mixes, you name it. If it comes in a box, it's not in the 90 day plan.

- Cut out any of the fake milks such as oat milk, almond milk, et cetera. They aren't even allowed to be referred to as "milk" like that in certain other countries. Don't fall for the fakery.
- Cut out the protein drinks, the smoothies, the protein bars, the snack bars, all the stuff that is highly marketed as "healthy" yet isn't moving the needle.

  * You'll be able to add these in later. Right now it's about elimination so you'll be sensitized for what's acceptable or not in the future.
- Especially cut out the stuff marketed as "keto" yet is highly refined.

Simplify, simplify, simplify!

If it wasn't around 300 years ago, chances are you're not as well adapted to it as you think you are.

This feels highly restrictive to many men, yet once you make the shift from "I don't get to have this" to "I am now free of this addiction and the ailments that come along with it and free to be healthy, energetic, and pursue becoming the man I know I could be", it's a whole different ball game.

Seriously bro, get serious about your life and your health.

After the 90 days are over and once you're at the desired maintenance weight and energy levels, you can strategically add things back in, but sourcing is key so you're not introducing lots of processed stuff into your diet again.

I've been eating this way for years at this point and love it. I am choosing to emphasize a 90 day sprint here because that's tangible, where you can get massive, rapid results, then taper into a more relaxed version of this same way of eating.

First, we're going to cover what to eat, then portions and then when to eat it.

BREAKFAST

Moderate protein, high fat, zero to low carbohydrates.

What does this look like?

Whole eggs cooked in grass fed butter along with perhaps 4 to 8 ounces of some form of beef depending on macros calculated later.

*I would suggest going the first 30 days without bacon or sausage or things of that nature to test tolerances. If you do purchase bacon or sausage, be very careful to source it. Find those which are not chock-full of additives, preservatives and other harmful agents.

CUT OUT — Oatmeal, oatmilk and all the other BS. No yogurt. No smoothies. No synthetic stuff. Just stop it and your body will thank you.

Eat as much as you want for the first two weeks to ensure you can make it to lunch with NO snacking. I'd rather you be full with plenty of calories than to be hungry and capitulate and eat some trash in between. This will be as much **psychological** as physical for most.

I find many people do best with no veggies in this meal. Animal protein and fat digest extremely well, and digestion is made even more efficient by removing the heavier things that slow it down. You'll function like a rocket ship in the morning!

* If you want some fiber, I'd suggest Acacia Fiber blended in coffee.

LUNCH

Moderate protein, moderate fat, low or zero carbohydrates through lower carb veggies.

*A quick note here — I don't think you need veggies at all, however, they can add variety to your meal and satisfaction. If you are going to have them, I'd suggest keeping it SIMPLE.

Complexity is the enemy of execution.

This may look like:

A strip steak or hamburger meat.

A good amount of lunch veggies until satiety.

Bonus points:

If you wait 30 minutes after lunch to drink water rather than drinking throughout.

Walk for as long as you can for up to 45 minutes after lunch. Even 5 or 10 minutes is far better than nothing.

Again, keep it simple and consistent. Breaking this addiction of needing to eat this wide variety of foods 365 days a year is beneficial. So many people spend untold hours debating what they're going to eat, thinking about it, fetishizing over it and then debating what they're going to eat next. Once you get that time back, you'll realize just how much it was dominating your life, and when you do pursue variety, it will taste SOOOO much better.

If you're eating out, it's not nearly as difficult as you'd think to do this either. Simply order several burger patties along with a side of veggies and make sure they only charge you for sides of patties.

Or only eat fajitas without all the extras and request a side of veggies.

A word of caution — restaurants, even the "good ones", are rife with seed oils, and basically shitty ingredients. If you order veggies, alert them that you have a seed oil allergy and that you can only have 100% real butter on the veggies. Also, most fajita meat is soaked in soy sauce which is no bueno since you're a man looking to optimize his hormones.

DINNER

Ah, at last — time to feast on some carbs.

The order with which you eat these things can matter. If you're being extra particular, save those higher carbs towards the end of the meal.

Moderate protein, moderate to higher fat, moderate to lower carbs.

This looks like:

Perhaps a large filet of fish, pork chop or slab of beef — whatever you fancy.

Nearly unlimited amounts of lower carb veggies to your heart's desire.

And perhaps an entire large sweet potato soaked in grass fed butter (180 grams) that contains 37 grams of carbs with a few moderate carb veggies to top things off.

Keep it simple. If it looks like too much, it likely is. I suggest measuring for the first two weeks so you can understand where you're at without counting as much, then dialing it in for a week or two, then it's likely you can eyeball for a while before recalibrating.

VEGGIES LIST:

Always organic to avoid as many of the chemicals as you can as I mentioned.

LOWER CARB VEGGIES: Only consumed fully cooked: collard greens, cabbage, brussel sprouts, kale, broccoli, asparagus, cauliflower, spinach, green beans.

Raw: parsley or cilantro

MODERATE CARB VEGGIES: Fresh, raw, cooked, whichever you fancy: cucumber, radishes, zucchini, cilantro, artichokes, green onions, parsley, leeks, cilantro.

HIGHER CARB VEGGIES: Squash, sweet potatoes, carrots, yams, pumpkin, white rice.

HIGHER FAT FRUITS: Avocado, olives.

FISH

A word of caution — optimize for fresh over canned and be extremely conscientious of tuna and swordfish. Tony Robbins was keeping his diet extremely simple several years ago. While only eating those two, he nearly died from mercury poisoning. It's a thing, it's real. Go for wild caught salmon, cod, halibut or others, and check mercury ratings if you're going to eat in higher amounts consistently.

PORTIONS

1 gram of protein or carbohydrate has 4 kC (kilo calories or just Calories)

1 gram of fat has 9 kC

Measure portions that you're eating for the first two weeks, then adjust in lieu of whether you're gaining weight, losing weight or staying the same.

I suggest starting with a few simple targets. Use both the Lean Body Mass calculator tool and also the macro nutrient tool to get a few rough estimates on how much you're going to be eating each day.

bodybuilding.com/fun/lbm_calculator.htm

bodybuilding.com/fun/macronutrients_calculator.htm

*Estimate your body fat percentage by searching for: men body fat percentage pictures. Plenty will pull up in the images section of your search engine. This is a rough calculation, obviously, but we want to keep things simple and it's close enough to get started.

From this, we're going to hone in specifically around targeting approximately 1 gram of protein per pound of **lean body mass** and then fluctuate carbs depending on our exercise level and to keep the body confused.

Protein — 1 gram per lb of lean body mass

Carbs — 0 to 20% of total daily calories depending upon exercise level

Fat — fluctuates to fit the gaps

For me this looks like:

Total body weight: 245

Lean body mass: 220.5 lbs (technically it's 213 lbs which I know from a recent DEXA scan, with approximately 7.8 lbs of bone mineral content.)

I selected I'd like to lose some weight and also am moderately active so arrived at a total of **2590** calories per day for a slight caloric deficit with this breakdown:

PROTEIN: 34%

220 g per day (881 calories)

CARBS: 5%

32 g per day (130 calories)

FATS: 61%

176 g per day (1580 calories)

TOTAL CALORIES: 2591

That's on a day when I'm not nearly as active or am cycling my carbs down for confusion for my body. On a day when I do a killer leg work, I may allow 20% of total calories as carbs which looks like this:

PROTEIN: 34%

220 g per day (881 calories)

CARBS: 20%

130 g per day (518 calories)

FATS: 46%

132 g per day (1191 calories)

TOTAL CALORIES: 2590

This is remarkably easy once you get the hang of it and can make tracking your portions incredibly easy. For this reason, I suggest eating the same thing consistently so you know the exact portions you are getting without having to constantly measure.

If it's too complicated, you won't do it, so make it easy on yourself.

I think targeting macros can be really helpful. It gets dangerous though when people don't differentiate between quality ingredients or not.

This is what I see so much of in the keto world where someone will hit their fat macros with loads of soybean oil and be like, "poof, healthy, great" — **WRONG**! You wouldn't pour sludge into your gas tank and expect it to run properly. You want high quality gasoline fueling your car just like you want high quality macros fueling you.

TIMING

When you eat matters – a lot.

In fact, it could be far more important than the quantity that you eat. I laid out some portion guidelines above to help most men get a grasp on the range they wish to be at, but I could also eat 4000 calories a day and not become overweight as long as I ate the right ones and also had them at the right time.

I know that's a bit contradictory, but the body isn't strictly this — a calories in, calories out (CICO) machine. It's far more nuanced and if you're over consuming but at least in high quality things, it will compensate without you having to do a thing.

Of course, if your hormones are out of whack or something like that, you can try to do all the right things and none of them may work so you have to address the right problem at the right time.

Let's first look at the timing of food over a day period, then over days and weeks.

Beef: Fattier at the start of the day and progressively leaner as the day goes on, ending with the leanest cuts at night. I find this works well because having sweet potatoes with butter or white rice with butter is far better from a taste perspective, and so I'd rather get the fats from butter there than with fattier cuts of beef.

Breakfast — eat within the first 30 minutes of waking.

3 meals a day. None of this 6 meals a day to "speed up your metabolism" stuff.

No eating within 3 hours of bed time. Bonus points if you go 4 to 5 hours or longer.

After the first 30 days we can add some confusion to the system. A mantra to live by is that nearly everything works some of the time and almost nothing works 100% of the time.

To that end, many people find it helpful to take a protein fast 1 day a month where they load up on fats and veggies or tons of buttery greens but skip the protein.

Also, to add in an intermittent fasting window such as waiting 4 to 6 hours after waking to have your first meal or shrink your day to 2 meals per day.

For some, this looks like a 16 hours fasted and an 8 hour eating window such as: eat from 11am to 7pm, then don't eat again until the next day at 11am.

Others may do 12pm to 4pm or a 4 and 20 eating pattern.

Others may add in a 24 hour fast where they have their last meal at 6pm and don't have their next meal until the following day at that time. For the more brave, this may be a 40 hour fast where they have their last meal at 6pm, skip eating the following day and wait until mid-morning the following day to break the fast.

All of these have their time and place and the more confusion you give the body, the more it will respond. To that end, I may intermittent fast on

Monday and Tuesday, have a full 3 meal day on Wednesday, not eat until 6pm on Thursday, have a full meal day on Friday, intermittent fast on Saturday and full meal again on Sunday.

This is more advanced but if you're really wanting to accelerate your results it can work well for a lot of people. If you don't, stick with the 3 meals per day and you'll be just fine.

The big ones are to never go months or years on end intermittent fasting or to constantly eat right before bed. You don't have to focus on being so smart but instead just avoid making stupid mistakes. You'll get an unbelievable advantage over time with that.

FAQs

Optimize for fresh versus packaged whenever possible. This means for fresh beef over bacon that is cured, or prepared ham or canned meats or fish.

I find frozen can oftentimes be more fresh than refrigerated meats and consider it of equal value when it comes to nutrition. So when I say fresh, I also mean frozen.

If you're worried about food costs, I used to spend $40 to $50 a day on food when I was trying to eat a ton of organic food, all different varieties and all the other bullshit I thought I needed. I didn't need any of it and it caused way more friction in my system compared to when I simplified and switched to more beef. Now, my typical food costs are around $10 - $15 per day with roughly 2lbs of ground beef, a few eggs, butter, coffee, et cetera.

If done appropriately, this should be one of the most cost effective, along with actually effective ways of eating you've ever done. But, what you get out is what you put in. If you want to spend $100 a day on tomahawk steaks, you can. Just stick with it, that is what matters.

If you're in doubt and feel like meat is going to kill you or cause adverse side effects, I suggest following Shawn Baker, Mikhaila Peterson and Dave Asprey on social media. Shawn has been a strict carnivore for over 6 years at this point and Dave extols the benefits of beef yet remains firm that plants play a positive role as well.

LIQUIDS

Let's keep this short.

The basics are:

Water

Coffee

Tea

Non-homogenized heavy cream in coffee along with butter is okay, just be sure to measure this and understand drinking calories adds up fast. A note on this — if you can't get a heavy cream brand that doesn't have any additives, skip this. Most have carrageenan or guar gum or other additives that are linked with a host of diseases. Currently, the Kalona brand which can be found at Whole Foods and other health stores is the only one I've found.

Most people are ADDICTED to the varieties of drinks they have throughout the day but if you want to master your body, you're going to have to break this addiction.

That means no sweeteners in tea. No syrups in coffee. No energy drinks. No fake milks. No bullshit. Coffee. Tea. Water.

On the water you're drinking:

Get an AquaTru Reverse Osmosis (RO) water filter or purchase water using the large 5 gallon jugs that utilize RO for filtration.

If in doubt, go to the Environment Working Group's website and look up the contaminants in your water supply here: ewg.org/tapwater

For my utility-based water here in Dallas, there are 14 contaminants that exceed the EWG's guidelines and just so you can understand, a few of them are:

Haloacetic acids

Potential Effect: cancer

Exceed the EWG guidelines by — **181X**

Arsenic

Potential Effect: cancer

Exceed the EWG guidelines by — 74X

These things are INCREDIBLY harmful to your health. Most places offer delivery on the 5 gallon bottled water if you don't have the time or stairs are another friction point. I suggest these due to their reusable nature along with getting more pure water compared to bottled water which can get heated to high temperatures, causing the plastic to leach chemicals into the water.

Keep it simple, just do something and make sure it actually works versus just makes you feel good. A cheap filter from your local store doesn't cut it in my world.

RO water can be mineral depleted so grab some Concentrace® Trace Mineral Drops.

On quantity — I think people worry about this far too much. If you're not having a bunch of other processed things in your diet, your body will let you know when it's thirsty or not. You likely don't need to drink 24 cups of water in a day or some crazy amount. Half of this has been pushed by advertising over the years in an attempt to sell more drinks. You don't need more "hydration" you need less DILUTION.

Coffee — I like bulletproof in the mornings which for me is basically with 1 or 2 tablespoons of Kerrygold unsalted butter and maybe a splash of heavy cream (it really foams up nicely and takes the cut out for me.)

Otherwise, have it black.

Definitely no milk, no fake milks, no syrups.

Tea — squeeze some lemon in if you want, otherwise, no sugars or fake sugars. That's a full hard stop.

No coffee after 2pm for most and no tea after 4pm or as is your tolerance. Most I know will do tea until 8pm then wonder why they can't sleep at night. Most tea is caffeinated, so if you want it late, opt for caffeine free.

LEVER THREE: EXERCISE

I tell people that diet, circadian rhythm and environment are 70% of the battle and exercise is the other 30%.

You can't out-exercise a poor diet in the long run. In the short run, there are plenty who can, but in the end it's going to catch up to you. If you want to get really dialed in, you're going to have to bring all these things together.

I like to keep it simple so I'm not going to break down all the different exercises here and instead am just going to give some simple guidelines of what works for many.

If you're saying, "I hate exercise. I don't want to do it," or some other weak bullshit, go look in the mirror and ask yourself what kind of man you truly wish to be – a weak, flabby one that never taps into his potential, or a man that is strong, confident, capable and competent.

You choose. You liking it is not a requirement of doing it. Just do it.

That being said, finding something you like makes it far more likely you'll stick with it, so if you need a class structure, go find one. If you need a personal trainer, go get one. If you need to enjoy it and find you want to get your cardio through playing tennis, great. Don't skip the resistance training though.

RESISTANCE TRAINING

Having healthy, strong muscles is important.

Lift weights 3-6 times per week.

Aim for 30-45 minutes. It shouldn't take longer unless you're trying to be a bodybuilder or some other goal.

CARDIO TRAINING

2-6 times per week depending on goals.

Aim for lots of zone 2 & 3 training and potentially pushing briefly into higher zones. Look up heart rate zone training for more information.

Aim for 30-45 minutes.

Mix it up. Perhaps 2 days of steady state with 1 day of sprints.

HIIT

This works really well. HIIT stands for High Intensity Interval Training. You essentially do both resistance training and cardiovascular training at the same time. You can optimize for time here versus for load, so rather than how much weight will I put on for 10 reps on bench press, how much weight do I need to bench continuously for 30 seconds, followed by some form of active recovery.

This is best done with functional movements that involve multiple muscles at one time such as dumbbell squats into shoulder presses.

20-30 minutes several times a week is a great maintenance schedule.

FUNCTIONAL TRAINING

Great for full body conditioning and complex movements that are more adapted to everyday life. If in doubt – YouTube.

CONCLUSION

I know this was a monster of a chapter, however, I also believe it is a highly necessary one.

If you're not healthy, you can't fully tap into your real potential.

There is so much in our culture that bombards us with how we're supposed to be, how we need this next supplement or how this exercise will change our lives.

I wanted to give a quick overview that hopefully cuts through all that noise to provide an easy, proven and effective system which you can apply to your life to start getting results tomorrow.

As Tim Ferriss said:

"If the answer isn't simple, it's probably not the right answer."

I know this seems like a lot, but once you fully digest it and realize how simple and easy to implement it is, it'll become far less overwhelming. You'll look back on how you operated before and wonder how you ever handled it.

The amount of time, energy and thought most people give to their food is astounding and overwhelming compared to the paltry amount of time I spend focusing on mine which frees me up to do so much more in life.

I want that for you also.

Once you start getting results, feeling better than you've felt in years, having the FREEDOM to be free of pains, lethargy and food addiction, you'll never want to go back.

It's difficult being sick.

It's difficult being addicted to foods that are keeping you from living up to who you could be.

It's difficult to cut through all the noise to even find out what foods are "healthy" compared to all the others.

Every person has their own definition and you can find books supporting either side.

The goal is not to be dogmatic, not to be a disciple of any one belief system and adhere to that until the end of time, but instead to focus on results and when something stops working, figure out why, how and where and then do something different.

The goal is to get results. I don't care if I'm right as long as I get results and when I do, then that's also how I know I'm right. Since I've gotten LOTS of results in this area, I feel confident that if you follow this system, you'll radically and rapidly see an improvement in the overall quality of your life.

Naturally, this is only the tip of the iceberg here, so-to-speak, but just this single shift can have a MASSIVE ripple effect to every other area in your life.

I'm excited for you and excited to see you tap into the man I know you could be.

ACTION ITEMS

- What's your current body weight?
- What's your ideal body weight?
- How long will it take you to get there assuming you're committed and lose at an average of 2lbs per week?
- Do the lean body mass and macro calculations and run them for carbohydrates at 5% increments such as 0%, 5%, 10%, et cetera.
- Put all these calculations into a note or print them off so that you can easily reference them each day.
- Download a tracker such as Cronometer or MyFitnessPal to keep track of your macros.
- Use a kitchen scale for measurement such as 8 oz of steak, or 150 grams of sweet potatoes.
- Don't get overwhelmed.

  You'll really only measure for a week or two and then be able to eyeball your food so it won't take forever until the end of time. Once you get this, you won't even hardly think about it.
- Throw out anything in your house that will tempt you to break this way of eating you're committing to. Remember, you're committing to yourself here and so you want to design your environment for success. Just like you wouldn't take an alcoholic to rehab and

surround him with liquor, you don't want to do the same to yourself by having junk food readily available.

- When in doubt, eat more of the approved foods versus allowing yourself to get hungry. This is ESPECIALLY true during the first 30 days. If you get hungry mid-morning, eat some meat or eggs and carry on. The worst thing you can do is allow yourself to get hungry when you're in a transition period. I'm fairly certain it's also nearly impossible to get fat or stay fat eating meat like this. I've never once encountered it.
- Get ready to see a completely different version of yourself than you've ever seen before in only 90 days.

ADDITIONAL RESOURCES FOR THE ADVENTUROUS

The Big Fat Surprise by Nina Teicholz

The Carnivore Diet by Shawn Baker

The Bulletproof Diet by Dave Asprey

What Really Makes You Ill by Dawn Lester and David Parker

* Note: I disagree with certain conclusions different authors reach, however, being exposed to the overall content is massively beneficial as I do agree with many of their conclusions.

PILLAR V

Forge Your World

INTRO

FORGE: (VERB)

to form by heating and hammering; beat into shape.

to form or make, especially by CONCENTRATED effort.

to form or bring into being, especially by an expenditure of effort.

To form or create with concerted effort.

To advance, move or act with an abrupt increase in speed or energy.

"The most fulfilled and effective people I know – world-famous creatives, billionaires, thought leaders, and more – look at their life's journey as perhaps 25 percent finding themselves and 75 percent creating themselves."
– Tim Ferriss

This is your world, your life, the only one you're going to get.

I believe you must forge your world.

Decide who you're going to be.

And then pursue that relentlessly.

When people try to tell me how reality works, I generally stop them, and say,

"In YOUR world, that may be how things work, and they work that way precisely because you believe that they do.

But, in MY WORLD, these are how things work."

Why?

Because, I'm intent on creating MY world, on setting the rules for my reality.

Tim Ferriss, author of five #1 New York Times and Wall Street Journal bestsellers including The 4-Hour Workweek said it best,

"Reality is negotiable. Outside of science and law, all rules can be bent or broken, and it doesn't require being unethical."

If you're not willing to forge your world, to set the rules of reality, then who will be?

Most of us have simply adopted the things we were taught growing up as if they were just as good as any of the other things we could have been taught, but we both know that's a lie.

Objectively, there is a reason some people get the results they want from life versus others who never get the results they profess to desire.

"Rich people don't get rich by accident and poor people don't stay poor by accident – both take effort – both are work."
– Grant Cardone

You FORGE YOUR WORLD through concentrated effort and intentionality to set the parameters you're going to operate within.

In my world, this is how this works.

I don't have to subscribe to your beliefs, your morals, your ideologies, your virtues, what you believe the world "should" be like.

This is my world, and I choose to believe that I live in a friendly universe.

I choose to believe that I can grow and get better each and every day.

I choose to believe that unlearning is oftentimes just as important as learning something new.

I choose to believe that magic happens all the time, that there is magic in these words.

I choose to believe that people are great, and that I want to support that greatness within them.

That the individual is at the heart of all greatness.

And it is the individual that must never be betrayed.

Here is a quote from John Fowles' novel The Magus:

[Maurice] "The human race is unimportant. It is the self that must not be betrayed."

[Nicholas] "I suppose one could say that Hitler didn't betray himself."

[Maurice] "You are right. He did not. But millions of Germans did betray themselves. That was the tragedy. Not that one man had the courage to be evil. But that millions had not the courage to be good."

Read that last paragraph again.

When you fail to define your world,

When you fail to forge yourself into who you truly can be,

Then you leave yourself open to become anyone and anything.

At some point, you have to stop using all the "busyness" as an excuse and actually sit down to decide how things are going to be in your world.

If you don't, then you'll keep getting the same results that you've been getting, that you're continually dissatisfied with.

At some point, you have to evaluate the things you've learned, the things you've adopted and really ask if they're serving you, and really ask if you're being the person you could be.

If the answer is no, then spend the time, sit with that discomfort and forge ahead.

Let's dig in to forging your world!

CHAPTER SEVENTEEN

Learn To Unlearn

"I was educated once - it took me years to get over it."
– Mark Twain

"Consider the average intelligence of the common man, then realize 50% are even stupider."
– Mark Twain

"To attain knowledge, add things every day. To attain wisdom, remove things every day."
– Lao Tzu

Tucker Max, legendary drinker and partier, chronicled his escapades during his twenties in the best-selling book: I Hope They Serve Beer in Hell.

Throughout the book, Tucker divulges in full, raw detail the experiences had from wild nights drinking, to butt-sex fails to defecating in hotel lobbies.

But, that's not what's truly impressive.

What's truly impressive is Tucker's ability to recognize that his behavior wasn't working for his life and to unlearn all the things he had learned were appropriate.

After the grandeur wore off from the success of his books, he realized he was unfulfilled and dissatisfied with his life.

So he decided to change it.

He underwent intense therapy for years and emerged on the other side as a changed man.

He went from partying and debauchery to husband, father and genuine human being.

Tucker took the things he learned that were helpful and applied them to starting what is now known as Scribe, a company that helps individuals write and publish their books.

It's gone on to be a massive success, having recently just worked with David Goggins to publish his book, Can't Hurt Me, which if you haven't read — it's amazing.

But, Tucker also learned to UNLEARN.

He was willing to let go of a side of himself that wasn't serving him.

He was willing to toss aside a portion of himself that was holding him back from who he really knew he could be and wanted to be.

It's this ability that we all have to transform that makes us so powerful.

Humans are the ultimate adaptation machine, if we allow ourselves to be, that is.

"It is not the strongest of the species that survives, nor the most intelligent; it is the one most adaptable to change."

This quote is often attributed to Darwin, however, since I can't find a solid source, let's just say it intuitively makes sense.

Your ability to adapt is predicated upon unlearning the things that are holding you back and learning the new things you need in order to move forward.

Oftentimes, we take this far more personally than is helpful.

We try to hold onto parts of ourselves as if they're unable to change.

We try to hold on to beliefs as if they shouldn't change.

However, I've never met someone who when asked, has the exact same beliefs today that they did 10 years ago.

We all get that we change, we intuitively know it, yet then we hold onto our beliefs from yesterday as if they're still us today.

That creates a huge amount of friction for growth and change.

Most people simply adopt the values, principles and beliefs of those around them or those they grew up with.

That doesn't mean those values and beliefs are actually the most optimal to get the life you really want though.

Tucker learned a certain set of values and beliefs, and when faced with the stark realization that he wasn't happy with who he was, had the courage to change.

Your ability to have the life you desire lies not so much in your ability to learn but to unlearn.

What you've learned has gotten you here and that's been really helpful.

But now, you have to let go of the parts that aren't helpful to move to the next things that are.

As Marshall Goldsmith says in the aptly named title of his book:

"What got you here, won't get you there"

Think about how true that is.

What got you through 10th grade won't get you through 11th grade.

What got you through your first year of marriage won't get you through your second.

What got you through your first year of work won't get you through the next.

If you want to be a successful entrepreneur, at some point, you have to unlearn the process of doing everything yourself and then actually learn how to delegate to others.

The goal is to get to the next version of yourself — in order to do that, you have to let go of the version of who you were.

If you're working 16 hour days to make $100,000 a year, it's likely that you can't increase your time working to make more.

So you have to unlearn that it takes 16 hour days and instead learn the value of automation and delegation.

If you've learned that it takes hard work to equal success, then you'll never feel successful without hard work.

If instead you learned that success equals work that is fun, then you'll find a way to make work fun while also achieving success.

You get out what you put in.

In order to get the life you want, you have to unlearn the things preventing you from achieving that life.

That next version of yourself lies in the obstacle in front of you. Avoiding the obstacle avoids that next version of you = stagnation = no growth = pain.

This is part of creating your world.

Creating the space so that you can continually unlearn in order to learn.

It's giving yourself permission to not necessarily be wrong, but to understand that this process of unlearning can help take you to the next level.

That it takes letting go of parts of yourself in order to grow into the new you.

And isn't this really natural?

Haven't you ever had a favorite movie or song or TV show that you thought would ALWAYS be your favorite, and then you outgrew it?

How about a behavior you became dissatisfied with that you wanted to change?

You had to unlearn it then learn something new.

So many of us fail to give ourselves permission to be the person we know we really could be.

We fail to give ourselves permission to unlearn our fear of failure.

Or to unlearn shame or guilt or depression.

We fail to give ourselves permission to actually just let go of the things that aren't truly serving us.

We feel as though we have to hold onto the beliefs our parents gave us as if we're guarding treasure at Fort Knox.

But how helpful is that?

This is your world.

This is your reality to do with what you will.

This is your time to decide whether you will embrace adaptability or inflexibility.

Tom Bilyeu, host of Impact Theory podcast and founder of the billion dollar company Quest Nutrition, used to love drinking energy drinks.

However, things change, and he noticed they were giving him debilitating anxiety.

He had to unlearn the process of drinking the energy drinks and learn a new way to adapt and thrive.

This isn't always easy because people around you will show up with an energy drink, or be like, "come on man, let's go get a drink."

When you inform them that you don't do that anymore, they'll push back.

I find a great way to handle this unlearning process with people is to adopt the philosophy of — that was me yesterday.

Yesterday I was someone who didn't go to the gym.

Today I'm someone who does go to the gym.

Yesterday I was a lousy partner.

Today I'm committed to be the world's best partner.

Yesterday I was inflexible.

Today, I'm flexible and embrace growth and progress.

"You're under no obligation to be the same person you were 5 minutes ago."
— Alan Watts

Much of what controls you today is the meaning you've given the world, how it operates and what you think the rules in it are.

But as it turns out, most of what you think has helped you in the past is now holding you back in the present.

Much of what you've accepted as laws of the universe are simply imaginary.

It's hilarious because once you see it, and realize that the only actual barrier there was you, you'll never be the same.

You don't have to accept life as depicted by society.

It takes courage, and while most are obedient, there is nothing saying you must be anything other than yourself.

Other people don't determine your emotions — you do.

Other people don't determine how your world works — you do.

The experience you're having in life is incumbent upon the meaning you've chosen to give it.

The rules of your world are the rules you've adopted and the only thing holding you back from unlearning those rules is you.

Do you want the outcomes that the average person is getting?

Do you want the same outcomes that haven't been working for you?

Good, then drop what you've learned and adopt a new paradigm.

If you don't unlearn these things, then you'll keep getting what you've always gotten.

As Albert Einstein said:

"We can not solve our problems with the same level of thinking that created them"

Let go of what's not serving you to gain what will serve you.

Learn to think differently.

Rather than focusing on acquisition, focus on impact.

Rather than focusing on who you were, focus on who you'd like to be.

Rather than focusing on how the world says you should be, focus on creating the world you'd like to live in.

What has made you a successful bachelor won't make you a successful partner.

What has made you a successful doctor won't necessarily make you successful at being happy or finding meaning.

UNLEARN:

- It takes 70 hr+ work weeks to be successful
- Hard work = success
- Money is hard to make
- Work isn't fun
- The world is this way thinking —

  Do you really have to dress how you dress in order to be successful?

Do you really have to be in dreary offices?

Do you really need a 5 or 6 day work week or is 3 or 4 days possible?

Does making lots of money really mean you have to sacrifice other things?

Do you really think the person working for $100,000 a year is working any less hard than the person making $10,000,000? I can find examples of both barely working and other examples of each working 16 hour days and justifying that's what it takes in order to make what they're making. Both are at the upper-limit of their capacity until they give themselves permission to simply increase their capacity.

In order to prove this to yourself, simply learn to become more resourceful, ask better questions and find counter examples.

COUNTER EXAMPLES

- Who may be some people who've actually done what you'd like to do without doing the things you think are necessary?
    - Are there plenty of ultra-fit CEOs out there? You bet.
    - How about those who limit their work day to 6 or 7 hours and that's it? Easy.
    - How about those who get paid more for less work than you're doing? 1000%
    - How about those who are making money easily rather than the hard way? Without question.

In high school, you had to ask each and every time you needed to go to the restroom.

In college, unless your professor is on a power-trip, they don't want you interrupting for this sort of thing.

In your work environment, can you imagine having to ask your boss each time you went to the restroom?

At each point, you've had to unlearn an old pattern of behavior to make room for new and improved patterns.

Yet at some point, so many of us stop this process. We feel as though we have to hold onto our patterns of behavior or lose everything we are.

And that's just not true.

You're so much more than someone who can't change.

You're nearly infinitely adaptable.

Once you embrace this, you'll be well on your way to forging your world with laws that empower you towards greatness.

ACTION ITEMS

- What are 5 things you could unlearn that could dramatically change your life?
- What are 5 things you've learned that have gotten you where you are, but will no longer serve you in getting where you want to go?
- How can you give yourself and your ego permission to let go of what's been holding you back?
- How can you use this to forge your world into one where you're constantly unlearning and learning in an iterative sort of feedback loop?

CHAPTER EIGHTEEN

Sit With the Void & Own the Bottleneck

"Wherever I go, there I am."
- Anonymous

"Success isn't that difficult; it merely involves taking twenty steps in a singular direction. Most people take one step in twenty directions."
— Benjamin Hardy

It hit me like a ton of bricks.

I was the common denominator in all my problems.

I was the single common factor in all the problems I was complaining about and blaming others for.

I had gone from having so much potential to someone who drank every single night, was up to their eyeballs in debt, was a failing partner in my relationship and who was the single most person I was supremely disappointed in.

I could barely walk past a mirror.

I could barely look myself in the eyes from my shame.

I was unworthy.

I had this deep-seated belief buried inside me and now I'd manifested it in real time into my life, only reinforcing and proving to myself and others that it was true.

If I was worthy, then how did I end up here?

I had gone from one of the world's top male dancers, a celebrated model, a published author and successful entrepreneur who worked for himself, to someone who couldn't even pay their bills.

It sucked.

But in that struggle, I gained the necessary gems to bring me to where I'm at today.

What no one tells you about personal development is that there is a trough.

There is a dip where you're transitioning from one person into another, and in that dip is where all the struggle is at.

That dip is where so many throw in the towel.

That's where you're forced to look into the void and must confront what looks back.

"Who looks outside, dreams; who looks inside, awakes."
– Carl Jung

In today's world, it's so easy to keep ourselves distracted.

To watch another movie.

To play on our phone.

To do anything but sit with that pain, to sit with that emptiness and to confront ourselves.

I realized I was the bottleneck in my life.

That everything I disliked about my life had flowed through me.

That if I wasn't happy about the friends I had cultivated, then that was me.

That if I was unhappy about my financial state, that was also me.

Literally, everything that I was trying to blame on others all came back to me.

I realized it wasn't the economy, it wasn't my zip code, it wasn't my lack of resources that was keeping me stuck.

It was just all me.

I was the one keeping me stuck.

I was the one holding me back.

I was the one disempowering myself.

I was the one telling myself I was unworthy and the world was merely reflecting that back to me.

I can't tell you how painful this was.

I ugly cried so many times I can't even count.

I was so supremely disappointed in myself because it had all been my responsibility.

All of this unworthiness, shame, guilt and horrible feelings had been brought on through me.

That wasn't okay.

I realized I was the bottleneck at every point in my life and while I couldn't change that I was the common denominator, I could change what I allowed to flow in and out of that bottleneck.

I had to sit with that pain, to sit with the void and to face myself — all parts of myself.

This began the process of me reforging my world.

Who I was committed to being.

No longer holding on to who I'd been, and instead having hope for the future for the first time in a long time.

"The most terrifying thing is to accept oneself completely."
– Carl Jung

The key in sitting with the void and owning the bottleneck is to replace that which you most need to unlearn with that which you most need to learn.

As I've said before, people don't operate well in a vacuum state.

You can only sit with that void for so long, and then you must re-emerge and if you're truly taking responsibility, you'll own the bottleneck and come out the other side as someone different.

Part of tapping into your power is to forge your world. You do that by unlearning the things that have been keeping you stuck, and then by sitting in that void until you can purposefully find the direction you're needing.

It's owning that you're the common denominator in your life, and if you want it to get better,

Then you MUST get better.

"Listen. I wish I could tell you it gets better. But, it doesn't get better. You get better."
– Joan Rivers

This is a critical point.

It's the lynchpin that so many miss.

It's the recognition that you're the common denominator behind unsatisfactory results you may be getting.

That's a painful realization.

It's also extremely empowering when you realize you're the constraining factor in your life.

It's empowering to realize that as you get better, your world also gets better.

There is serious freedom in freeing yourself.

Where are the linchpins in your life that need your attention and then how do you remove yourself as the obstacle there?

Do you need to be a better leader?

A better listener?

More present?

More disciplined?

To design your environment more strategically for your success?

Inspect your inner conflict and resolve that?

Learn to manage your emotions in a healthier manner?

The tools to change your life are right there, inside of you, as long as you'll sit with the discomfort that comes with facing yourself in the mirror.

"People will do anything, no matter how absurd, to avoid facing their own souls."
– Carl Jung

Stop the busyness.

Stop the distractions.

Stop the discursive activity that prevents you from feeling the pain of your position and instead embrace it.

Inspect it and who you are, and who you'd like to be, and how you can simply remove yourself as the obstacle of becoming that person.

I know this sounds out there, but I can't tell you how many men this has helped when I've helped facilitate them reaching this true internalization — that they're the bottleneck or obstacle in their life.

It freed them from searching and then allowed them to begin focusing on exactly who they needed to be in order to remove that and move forward in their life.

It sounds trivial, but it's not.

And truth trumps positive here.

We all hear how we need to be more positive all the time, but that's not always the case.

You need true self-awareness, true conscientiousness to have adequate self-reflection.

After all, without that, how are you supposed to get an actual representation of who you are?

Hitler had a positive self-image after all, yet committed atrocities because it wasn't an accurate one.

"The privilege of a lifetime is to become who you truly are."
– Carl Jung

The point of all this is for you to become the man you could be.

In order to do that, your world gets infinitely bigger once you appropriately identify the obstacles and start removing them.

As Ryan Holiday wrote in The Obstacle Is the Way:

"The obstacle in the path becomes the path. Never forget, within every obstacle is an opportunity to improve our condition."

You're always trying to get to that next version of yourself and coincidentally, it's nearly always you that simultaneously attempts to prevent you from this.

When you truly inspect it, I think you'll agree.

You are the one in your own way — no one else.

If you were given a car at birth that would be the only car you'd ever get in life, I'd bet heavily that you'd take care of it.

And you're the only YOU you're ever going to get!

So why not take care of you?

When your world isn't as you would desire it to be – change your world.

Change you.

It's that easy.

Everyone wants to make it harder than it is.

But the truth is, you've been changing from birth, and you're going to change a lot more in life until death.

The only real question is if you'll be intentional and thoughtful about the direction of that change.

Own the bottleneck.

Own your life.

Forge your world.

Be great!

ACTION ITEMS

- How have you been avoiding facing yourself?
- How have you been avoiding facing things in your life you know you need to?
- What uncomfortability do you need to sit with and own?
- What are the top 5 areas where you're clearly the bottleneck in your life?
- Are you committed to changing those?
- Why not give yourself permission, right here, right now, to make your life easier on yourself?
- Why not give permission right here, right now, to free yourself as the bottleneck in your life?

- Go ahead, seriously, give yourself permission to get out of your own way.
- Next time something comes up, give yourself permission to just take the easy path, to make it easy on yourself, and realize that there has always been an option between it being easy or hard, and you've always had the power to decide which it would be.
- And now realize that as you give yourself more and more permission for this, the process of that being a reality has already begun to take place and will only work to get better for you.

CHAPTER NINETEEN

Choosing Identity

"Someone's opinion of you does not have to become your reality."
– Les Brown

I've always been interested in health, fitness, nutrition and really just life in a broad sense.

When I was in college, I knew I wanted to explore those areas more, to explore things that really called to my heart's desires, yet that wasn't accepted as a practical career by my family.

People who go into those fields don't make any money — don't you know?

Everyone knows this.

That's not a real career or job.

Do something more practical.

Do something where you'll learn how to run a business, how to be successful.

Right.

Got it.

Nevermind that there were thousands of examples of people doing extremely well in all of those fields I was interested in, that didn't exist for me or my family at the time. Because that didn't exist, we didn't look for it and I doubt we would've seen it because it just wasn't a possibility in the first place.

I went on to get a degree in accounting, worked in the field for all of 3 months in a temp position and have never looked back.

Why?

Because I had focused on what I could get, not who I could be or what I could do.

I had sacrificed my dreams for something practical.

I had convinced myself of the veracity of my position then made it a self-fulfilling prophecy.

If I had focused on what life would look like if I were the best I could be in that field, undoubtedly, I could have found plenty of reasons why I'd do just fine.

But, it wasn't my **lack of resources**, yet instead, my **lack of resourcefulness.**

Sometimes you don't know what you don't know.

It's easy to become misdirected in life, to have your path warped by listening to others, by giving into fear, by having a fear-based mindset and into thinking that everyone just gives up their dreams.

That's part of becoming an adult after all, right?

Unfortunately, the social machine isn't designed for us to follow all our dreams. It's designed to propagate its own existence, its own power, its own preservation, and it does that by producing those who wish to continue its propagation.

Naturally, the antithesis of this are those who would think freely, who would live wildly, who would pursue greatness, who would follow their dreams and become the people who they could be rather than the people the machine wants them to be.

As George Bernard Shaw said:

"People are always blaming their circumstances for what they are. I don't believe in circumstances. The people who get on in this world are the people who get up and look for the circumstances they want, and if they can't find them, make them."

It's easy to be seduced by the idea that cowardice wrapped in a euphemism will lead to greatness, but just as an apple tree will never yield an orange, cowardice will never produce greatness.

We're all misdirected at times, all searching for answers, all seeking direction — a compass to follow in the darkest hour.

That compass is within you, and it's only a matter of skill set, hunger, knowledge or application that separates you from it.

Persevere always.

As Steve Jobs said —

"When you grow up you tend to get told the world is the way it is and ... to live your life inside the world. Try not to bash into the walls too much. Try to have a nice family, have fun, save a little money. That's a very limited life. Life can be much broader once you discover one simple fact: Everything around you that you call life was made up by people that were no smarter than you and you can change it, you can influence it, you can

build your own things that other people can use. Once you learn that, you'll never be the same again."

Have heart.

Give yourself permission.

Implement non-negotiable standards.

Upgrade your mindset.

Forge your world.

Become courageous.

Take responsibility and ownership.

Acknowledge your call to greatness.

Be kind to yourself and others — Tell the truth.

And most importantly — COURSE CORRECT, MOTHERFUCKER!

"What is the task of higher education? To make a man into a machine. What are the means employed? He is taught how to suffer from being bored."
– Friedrich Nietzsche

If you're not where you want to be, if you're not WHO you want to be, if you're not truly living in the greatness that's within you, then it's time to identify the misdirection in your life, and then redirect it.

Most of us are told all sorts of things we're supposed to do.

Or we have simply assumed many of the values that we grew up with.

Yet we haven't stopped to really see if they align with what we desire in a deep manner.

So many of us have picked goals or targets in life based off of what we've seen others go after, or on what we think will bring us happiness, yet at some point, we realize that we haven't stopped to identify what really leads to happiness or fulfillment or purpose or the more meaningful things in life.

This step is crucial to reorienting towards more meaningful things, to operating from your heart and gaining the leverage you need to transform your life.

That doesn't always mean making huge changes, sometimes it's just realizing that there may be more meaning to what you're currently doing than you had been associating to it and once you recognize that, your satisfaction goes through the roof.

FUNDAMENTAL REORIENTATION

Life changed for me when I **stopped** focusing on **what I could get**, whether that was material things or things from other people.

It changed when I **started** focusing on **who I could BE** and what I could DO, especially with my life when viewed from a broad lens.

I started to incorporate my DEATHBED and DEATHLINE routine into my thinking as a guide for what I said YES and NO to in life.

Essentially, I realized I didn't think I'd care so much on my deathbed if I got the new iPhone, the newest car or gadget.

I would care though if they allowed me to do something meaningful such as capture beautiful moments with others, or help connect with more people on a deeper level.

I transformed my thinking from:

HAVE —> DO —> BE

To

BE —> DO —> HAVE

I wasn't even thinking about who I could really be, only focusing on what I could get or have and then what I could do.

But that doesn't lead to happiness or meaningfulness.

Once I switched to BE—>DO—>HAVE, everything changed.

I started asking who I could be.

If I was being great, if I was being my best self, how would I show up in my relationships?

How would I show up to work?

How would I show up to fitness?

To my health?

How would I show up in life in general?

Could I be the absolute best at something?

Even if I couldn't, could I be the best that I could be?

That seemed meaningful to me.

I think at the end of our lives, we'll remember those things.

We'll remember really owning something, pushing ourselves outside our comfort zones and really fucking living.

It's who we're being in those moments that will stick with us.

We'll be proud of turning our potential into something GREAT.

That's part of this calling we as MEN have.

Of course most don't do this though.

I'm sure we can all think of someone who hasn't and looks back on their life regretfully, realizing they didn't actually have the courage to truly live.

What a fucking shame.

What a waste of a life so precious.

For so many, it's only when they're faced with an immediate, terminal end that they finally really make the decision to live and somehow seem to live more in those last few weeks, or months, or years, than in all the years leading up to that point.

As Abraham Lincoln said —

"In the end, it's not the years in your life that count. It's the LIFE in your years."

The number one regret people mention while lying on their deathbeds is, **"I wish I had the courage to live the life I really wanted."**

Let that sink in.

Like really sink in.

We don't remember days. We remember things that are meaningful, and for something to be meaningful, we have to actually be oriented towards that which is meaningful for us.

Oriented in alignment with our values.

We remember moments.

We remember experiences.

We remember that which moves our soul.

This is why it's critical to question the things that aren't working.

That your heart is just not in it at all.

To quote Steve Jobs —

"For the past 33 years, I have looked in the mirror every morning and asked myself: 'If today were the last day of my life, would I want to do what I am about to do today?' And whenever the answer has been 'No' for too many days in a row, I know I need to change something."

Society has convinced us all that we need to pursue the next car or the next house or the next gadget, but that's not where meaningfulness lies. It's certainly not where GREATNESS lies.

As Viktor Frankl said —

"Life is not primarily a quest for pleasure, as Freud believed, or a quest for power, as Alfred Adler taught, but a quest for meaning. The greatest task for any person is to find meaning in his or her life."

In the quest for a meaningful life, it's crucial to pick empowering goals or targets that align with this sense of meaningfulness.

That means focusing on who you could BE.

And what you could DO —> especially in the service of others.

And then realizing that if you do both of the former well, you'll never have to worry about what you will have because you'll be surrounded by abundance.

As Les Brown said –

"Help others achieve their dreams and you will achieve yours."

Or perhaps consider this by Zig Ziglar —

"What you get by achieving your goals is not as important as what you become by achieving your goals."

It's when you really get to the essence of who you are, of what you're really meant to pursue in life, at least for a time, that you find a huge amount of both freedom and greatness.

It's forsaking the false paths, motherfucker!

It's forsaking the social norms that have left so many dissatisfied and disillusioned about their lives.

As Mark Twain said —

"Just because you're taught that something's right and everyone believes it's right, it don't make it right."

Just look around – it's not hard to tell that we have more people disenchanted with their lives than ever before.

More men that are struggling to be good at being men.

Men who are disenchanted with the state of the world, disenchanted with their pursuits.

And they're seeking answers, seeking understanding.

Because they did all the things they thought they should do, what everyone told them to do, what society told them to do, yet here they are, dissatisfied and left with a feeling of cheapness.

We all know GREATNESS does not lie in cheapness.

It doesn't lie in shallowness.

GREATNESS lies in mastery.

Let me ask you this — Have you ever heard of a single person being on their deathbed bragging about doing nothing with their life, achieving nothing, becoming nothing, loving nothing?

FUCK THAT!

How about instead bragging about the relationships they had, the laughs they experienced, the obstacles they overcame, the things they mastered, the things they were really proud of doing and overcoming, not just sort of dabbling in, but in going deep. Really having some pride in their abilities.

I say HELL YES to this!!

If you want to do this, you have to determine your reality.

When you follow these steps, you then decide to get clear on what you're really supposed to be doing.

That doesn't mean you have to know your purpose vehicle or why. It only means that you pick a target and focus on who you could be in relationship to that target and the things you could then do.

And, you also get really clear on the importance of target acquisition, and how to pick better, more meaningful targets for yourself.

Envision who you could be in 5 years.

How would that man act?

What are the characteristics that dude would have?

Who would that guy hang around?

How would that man deal with adversity?

What would that guy be known to be excellent at?

What would people go to that man for?

How would that man have sculpted himself into someone who others look to for leadership?

How would that man have sculpted himself so that when others think of you — they literally think — damn, that person is the epitome of GREATNESS?

This is the way.

This is how you get on the road to greatness.

Be & Do —> Have

Another quote from Viktor Frankl:

"Don't aim at success—the more you aim at it and make it a target, the more you are going to miss it. For success, like happiness, cannot be

pursued; it must ensue, and it only does so as the unintended side-effect of one's dedication to a cause greater than oneself or as the by-product of one's surrender to a person other than oneself."

Here's another one to re-emphasize:

"Happiness must happen, and the same holds for success: you have to let it happen by not caring about it. I want you to listen to what your conscience commands you to do and go on to carry it out to the best of your knowledge. Then you will live to see that in the long run—in the long run, I say!—success will follow you precisely because you had forgotten to think of it."

Reorient to who you could be and what you could do.

I'm not suggesting you don't care about success. I care very much about it.

I AM suggesting you consider redefining what success looks like and that you may find all the things you want come to you as a result of all the things you become.

As George Eliot said –

"It's never too late to be what you might have been."

It's when you focus on who you could be,

The best salesman

The best father

The best waiter

The best janitor

The best insurance agent

The best student

The best version of yourself in any area

And then if you were that best version of yourself, what would you do? How would you behave? How would you act?

And then imagine, if you were the best of whatever it is, what sort of outcome would flow from that?

Personal satisfaction

Character

Confidence

Pride

Congruence

Caring

Diligence

Then, if you want more, just ask yourself what your heart really calls you to do, and if you were the best at it, what would your life look like?

CHOOSING IDENTITY

Most people think they can't choose their identity, but you absolutely can.

Have you ever known someone who didn't work out for years, they just weren't THAT KIND OF PERSON, then they decided to and now they're a fitness enthusiast?

They chose that.

Identity is whatever you're most committed to.

You choose it.

If you don't, society will for you because you're always committed to something.

At some point, you have to determine how you're going to be.

This is the time.

You want to look back on your life with pride about how you conducted yourself.

What are you going to tolerate and not tolerate from yourself?

If earlier we determined WHO you could be: world traveling, best husband, terrific father… then this is the HOW you're going to be. How will you show up each day? It's implied in the who, but we want specific.

Choosing how you're going to be is fundamental.

You're the biggest obstacle you'll have to overcome in life and repeatedly have to re-anchor to your commitment of how you are committed to being.

Ambiguity is the killer of dreams. Lack of specificity. The paradox of choice is too broad. In a world where you can do anything, you do nothing.

In order to escape reality, you have to determine how you're going to be instead.

What sort of life do you want to have?

What sort of experience on this planet do you want to have?

What's your commitment to determining that reality?

> Who could you be?
>
> Who are you WILLING to be?
>
> How do you want to feel?

What excites you?

What's the impact you'd like to have?

Here's the thing — either you determine the life you want to have or life determines it for you.

When so many people pick targets in life, they pick that they want a certain size house or a certain car or to make a certain amount, and that's great, except those aren't nearly as helpful targets.

Those are really just BYPRODUCTS of who they're being.

For most, those are the core targets, which is also why it's difficult to get beyond them.

Instead, when someone focuses on being the world's greatest inventor, or innovative founder, or caring dad, the byproducts naturally flow from that.

We see it all the time.

If Elon Musk had been focusing on being the richest man in the world, it's likely he never would've made it there.

It's only when he focused on being committed to who he could be that the financial payoffs flowed in return.

This is a fundamental reorientation for most people.

We've been led to believe that so many things we thought are the targets, aren't actually the targets and that's why hitting them is near impossible.

So many men I work with thought they had the right targets for the appropriate direction in their life, yet when I share this, everything seems to snap into a reoriented position in their minds.

They intuitively get how they've been misled and are mis-aligned and therefore can realign easily and quickly.

The goal here is to determine who you could be.

What you could do.

The impact you could have in the world.

How you could be the person you've always known you can be. These exercises will walk you through that.

ACTION ITEMS

- This is your world. Decide on who you're committed to BEING, what you're intent on DOING and then identify the potential BYPRODUCTS that would stem from the first two.
    - i.e I'm committed to being the best man I can be. I am also intent on helping other men to be the best versions of themselves. Potential byproducts may be personal satisfaction, financial affluence, a deep, meaningful network of men who all share the same mission, et cetera.
- What is your CORE CALLING? The thing that is so big it would make everything else worth it. If you could become this version of yourself that would dwarf anything else?
    - i.e To become the man I know I can be, one where on my deathbed, I look back on my life with ZERO regrets and leave a legacy of making the world a better place.
- What are 3 new targets for who you are committed to BEING?
    - i.e I am committed to becoming the best entrepreneur I'm capable of. I'm committed to developing an unstoppable

mindset so that I can never fail at anything in life. I'm committed to being a man who sets a positive example of what's possible in the world.

- What are 3 things you wish to DO in congruence with who you're committed to be?
    - i.e I am committed to starting a company that has the positive impact on the world I'd like to see rather than devaluing myself working for a company I don't believe in. I am committed to taking daily actions to forge an unstoppable mindset. I am committed to having a positive attitude, to encouraging others, to helping others see the greatness in themselves so that I'm a man who sets a positive example in the world.
- Language change strategy — Start identifying with the TYPE of person you're committed to being and also not committed to being.
    - I'm the type of person who… (insert behavior) (goes to the gym, is a devoted partner, shows up on time.)
    - I'm NOT the type of person who… (insert behavior) (skips the gym, breaks their word, lives small.)

CHAPTER TWENTY

Deload To Load

"The only time I waste is time I spend doing something that, in my gut, I know I shouldn't. If I choose to spend time playing video games or sleeping in, then it's time well spent, because I chose to do it. I did it for a reason - to relax, to decompress or to feel good, and that was what I wanted to do."
— Simon Sinek

The breakdown was inevitable.

Working 100 plus hour weeks, sleeping 5 hours a night, it couldn't go on.

Working as a New York City tech-entrepreneur, Cary Jack was burning the candle at both ends and while there was plenty of hustle going on, there wasn't the happiness he desired.

Incidentally, it wasn't until Cary finally landed a 7-figure Venture Capital funding deal with Microsoft and IBM, that he realized he wasn't living life with integrity for who he wanted to be.

It was all load and no deload.

It was all hustle yet no happiness.

We each have our breaking point where we realize things can't go on, and looking at accepting the funding with the commitment to years more of the grind he'd been doing was just too much.

So, after many tears and hard conversations with his brother who was also his business partner, they turned the funding down and made a massive pivot.

Cary moved to Bangkok, Thailand for 10 months where he forged his world and developed a new and better way to live.

From that, The Happy Hustle was born — Cary's next company where he now helps other individuals suffering from burnout and who are only hustling, find their alignment and instead get on the path to Happy Hustling.

With this change, Cary now lives in Montana where he was recently married to the love of his life, and hosts epic camping adventure masterminds with other high-performing entrepreneurs from around the world.

They hike into the Montana wilderness and embark on a 5 day digital detox and realigning deloading phase in order to get back to baseline.

It's this strategic balance of loading and deloading that makes Cary's world so successful now.

You can't always be on, likewise you can't always be off.

There's a balance, and it's often not in actual balance but in seasons.

You work hard for 90 days then take a 2-week break.

You collect a massive harvest when all the work comes in, then allow a recharge period.

Building deloading phases into your life is critical for your overall performance and success.

There is such a strong pull in society right now to constantly be loading, to constantly be on, to constantly be pushing harder and harder.

But there are consequences to that.

If you go to the gym and lift heavy every single day without rest, you'll likely plateau or burnout.

If you try to work relentlessly without ever having an off-season, you'll see your performance drop.

"People are trying to be smart - all I am trying to do is not to be idiotic, but it's harder than most people think."
— Charlie Munger

There are seasons in all our lives. Seasons where we get together with family more or we're more in tune with our relationships or where we're working diligently towards a work deadline.

Intuitively I find most people understand this, yet also attempt to break this principle.

In order to actually get more done, you have to implement planned periods of rest, recovery and time to unplug.

With the rise of social media, it appears as though everyone is on and ALWAYS on, yet when we inspect this notion deeper, it's easy to find it's untrue.

People who want to go on a month-long vacation simply record their postings for a month in advance then drip them out so it appears they're still there.

They're maintaining the illusion of omnipresence, of always being on, while actually giving themselves the freedom to unplug so they can come back stronger.

In the fitness world, I personally find it helpful to implement deloading phases in order to rest, recover and avoid the inevitable plateau.

We see this in Hollywood. Celebrities have periods where they appear to be everywhere, then seem to recede from the spotlight to rest, recover then come back stronger.

It makes sense. We are more fond of them after they've been gone for a time. When they eventually resurface, we're happy to see them again.

The same is true with most authors.

They may write a series of books quickly, then take a short holiday in order to recharge their creativity before getting back after it.

"When you say no, you are only saying no to one option. When you say yes, you are saying no to every other option. No is a choice. Yes is a responsibility."
— James Clear

This isn't a new concept at all, however, it is one I see so many attempts to ignore.

I get it.

It's tempting to think we're going to somehow be a machine, this person that never has any imperfections, that can just go go go all the time without breaking.

There may be those people out there, but they're unicorns, not the norm.

Just because they're out there doesn't mean we should all try to be them.

I can try to be over 7 feet tall all I want each and every day, but it's not going to happen.

Implementing strategic deloading phases are critical to keeping you on the path to greatness.

It's also important to identify your loading phases.

For instance, as I'm writing this book, I'm in a loading phase.

It's my single one thing to get done each and every day.

I'm working on it at breakneck speed and it's driving this project forward faster than most would think possible.

However, I know once I get done, I'm going to need a deloading phase to just do nothing.

Sit on a beach in Mexico and soak up some sun and allow my mind to recharge.

And that's okay.

"Needless commitments are more wasteful than needless possessions. Possessions can be ignored, but commitments are a recurring debt that must be paid for with your time and attention."
— James Clear

FRACTIONAL OPTIMIZATION

"If you optimize everything, you will always be unhappy."
— Donald Knuth

When I coach men around this concept, I emphasize the importance of fractional optimization.

We're all trying to do everything all at once, and invariably that leads to you doing nothing.

It just doesn't work.

Multi-tasking is a myth and a lie.

The more you multitask the worse you get at it.

Focus. Attention. These are currencies worth their weight in gold and something to be honed and mastered.

The goal is not to try to do everything all at once, it's to focus intently on the things that actually matter most.

The goal is to become a master at SINGLE-TASKING.

Optimize for what's most important and let the other things go.

This comes back to developing your ability to say NO.

To realizing that your world gets bigger when you make it smaller.

To identifying the things that move the needle and forsake all else.

If it matters most to you to be able to go to dinner each and every night with your partner, to a new restaurant, and have that experience, yet you're also trying to have the nicest new house, along with the nicest and newest car, you're not strategically optimizing. Maybe you're at a point in your life where you can do that, but most aren't.

For most, it's important to identify priorities, what matters most and what they want their experience to be like, then optimize specifically for that.

This is having the freedom to spend money freely on dinners each night without worry, while also still increasing your financial independence because you're fractionally optimizing.

"You don't get any points in life for doing things the hard way."
— Tim Fargo

For most, when they try to optimize for everything, all at once, it generally starts a race to the bottom.

You can't do it.

You only have a fractional view of the world as it is.

You have a finite amount of attention and that needs to be highly prioritized.

Rory Vaden, author of the #1 Wall Street Journal best-seller, Take The Stairs, says,

"If you have diluted focus, you will get diluted results."

To tie these two concepts together, when you're intentionally practicing fractional optimization and strategic loading and deloading, you're optimizing your life for success.

What does this look like for me in reality?

I work in 90 day sprints and optimize for only a few things during that sprint so I'm 100% dialed in.

Then, I plan in a deloading phase where I totally unplug from what I'm working on, and when I've recovered, tackle another 90 day sprint.

This works for me because I work best in these types of time frames.

Anything longer and my performance drops off. Anything shorter and it's not a big enough project to truly excite me so I'm not fully engaged in it.

During those 90 days, I may have food prepared or eat the exact same thing every single day except for dinner where I optimize for communion and social interaction.

I organize my entire life around whatever it is I'm working on so that I can load hard, then deload.

This also happens with relationships.

I know plenty of people who may have been in a relationship for 10 years and decide they need to create new passion and intensity, so they do a 90 day sprint where they're optimizing for excitement together.

That could be planning a road trip across the country or traveling around the world or simply strategically recognizing that is the single thing you're working to focus on over the next 90 days and that's what you optimize for.

"To do the impossible, you need to ignore the popular."
— Tim Ferriss

You're working to forge your world here.

In my world, this is how this works.

In my world, this is how I work and how I operate for best results.

When I'm not intentional about my loading phases, they naturally get diluted.

When I'm not intentional about my deloading phases, they don't occur, then I suffer from overloading and burnout.

When I'm trying to optimize for everything instead of fractional optimization, I am overwhelmed and end up with everything as sub-optimal.

It's critical to give your life the inspection it deserves.

It's critical to decide how you're going to live your life so that you can truly become the man you could be.

I find so many men that with only a small amount of tweaking, can get far superior results in their lives.

It only takes a small degree of inspection, intentionality and being specific in their design.

"Alternating periods of activity and rest is necessary to survive, let alone thrive."
— Tim Ferriss

Deloading is part of the loading.

I want to be clear here. I've said it before, I'm not the morality police. I'm not someone who wants to tell you how your deloading or loading should look like.

There are plenty of people who will tell you exactly what that should look like. I think it's best for you to know and decide.

The internet is rife with people trying to be positive all the time, trying to never have a single down moment. That doesn't actually work for many people.

We all have darker sides that balance our lighter sides.

We all have shadows and learning to integrate those is crucial and when you try to deny that, eventually they come bursting forth and it's generally not in a good way.

So take those into account during your deloading phases.

Give yourself time to sit with these things and deload how you need to so you can come back stronger.

ACTION ITEMS

- What would be your optimal loading phase or schedule?
- What would be your optimal deloading phase (this can be different each time)?
- How can you implement a loading phase in the next 90 days and what are you going to fractionally optimize for?
- How has not implementing a deloading phase in the past not served you well?
- How has not specifically implementing a loading phase in the past not served you or caused you to suffer from priority dilution?
- How can strategically implementing loading, deloading and fractional optimization into your life help to forge your world into the one you most desire?
- How can you become a master at SINGLE-TASKING rather than multitasking in order to get outsized, exceptional results?

CHAPTER TWENTY-ONE

Build Your Meta-Models

"If it's not a hell yes, it's a no."
— Derek Sivers

"If you're not failing, you're not pushing your limits, and if you're not pushing your limits, you're not maximizing your potential."
— Ray Dalio

In 1975, Ray Dalio founded Bridgewater Associates out of his 2 bedroom apartment in New York City.

Today, Bridgewater is the largest hedge fund in the world and Dalio is one of the wealthiest people on the planet, but it wasn't always that way.

After starting his firm, Dalio quickly gained steam and prominence until nearly losing it all in 1982, where he even testified in front of the United States congress that a huge default was coming and predicted the next Great Depression.

And that was the exact bottom of the stock market where he couldn't have been more wrong.

Everything he had been working for up until that point nearly evaporated overnight.

It went so poorly for Dalio that he had to lay off all his employees and even borrow $4,000 from his dad.

Yet, when you hear Dalio reference this today, it's a far different story, one while extremely painful, he also looks on as one of the best experiences of his life.

From this painful experience he was forced to alter his attitude towards his thinking, to shift from thinking, "I'm right" to thinking instead, "How do I know I'm right?"

This experience led Dalio from closed-mindedness to radical open-mindedness where he no longer seeks to be right, but instead seeks the right answer.

He no longer looks at pain the same either.

One of the principles he took from this experience is that PAIN + REFLECTION = PROGRESS.

This principle then became a guiding light as Dalio began attempting to figure life out.

He began to look at pain as an indicator, one that helped him stop to reflect how he could ask what he would do differently in the future.

This painful experience now becomes a puzzle to solve and when solved, you get a GEM as the end result, or a nugget of information to help you in the future.

Dalio released his book, Principles: Life & Work in 2017, where it quickly became a #1 New York Times best-seller detailing his life and also how he developed his principles.

It's these principles that Dalio credits with much of his success.

When you can distill life down to a set of foundational principles to operate from, it gets far easier and also far simpler.

You can think of principles as ways of thinking or algorithms by which you make a decision.

"Making too many decisions is often symptomatic of poor systems or process."
— Tim Ferriss

"I learned that if you work hard and creatively, you can have just about anything you want, but not everything you want. Maturity is the ability to reject good alternatives in order to pursue even better ones."
—Ray Dalio, Principles: Life and Work

All the most successful people in the world operate with high-level principles and heuristics and that's partly why they're the most successful.

They've engaged in a systematic approach towards optimizing for the life that they want and utilize highly-effective decision making metrics in order to ensure they stay on that path.

I think of principles as fundamental assumptions while heuristics are more methods of solving problems.

Discipline equals freedom is a principle.

Pain + Reflection = Progress is a principle and heuristic.

A common heuristic might be:

A person who treats waitstaff poorly will invariably also treat other people poorly.

While this is a fundamental assumption and most people leave it at that, if you choose to use it as a heuristic then you can automatically set this filter in place.

When I receive a red flag from someone who treats waitstaff poorly, I will listen to what that person is telling me about themselves and either decide to confront them about this behavior or remove them from my life.

People's actions will tell you who they are if you're wise enough to observe and listen.

Now, I've established a problem-solving heuristic into my thinking and it's always there so that it helps filter out the people I don't want in my life and filter in the ones I do.

"Life is full of signs. The trick is to know how to read them. Ghosh called this heuristics, a method for solving a problem for which no formula exists."
— Abraham Verghese

Another example could be: someone who trash talks another will eventually trash talk me.

Since I don't want to be the type of person who trash talks anyone behind their back, I will either confront this person on this behavior or remove them from my proximity.

As Mark Twain said:

"I cannot help but notice that there is no problem between us that cannot be solved by your departure."

Principles and heuristics are invaluable once you fundamentally adopt them into your life.

Another personal example would be that I've noticed how in the past I was highly susceptible to flattery so that I'd let my guard down when someone unduly flattered me, which opened me up to being manipulated and taken advantage of.

Once I realized this, I implemented a heuristic to raise my walls and be incredibly leery of someone who gives me undue flattery.

I don't completely shut them out, but I'm now cautious enough so that I'm not operating from total naivety.

You can access Ray Dalio's principles at principles.com, which I encourage everyone to do. However, developing your own as you go through life is invaluable.

When you can build meta-models, models that translate across times, fields and problems which lead you to a better version of arriving at the best solution, it gives you a superhuman advantage in life.

It's nice when you can really land on a succinct principle like another one of Dalio's:

Dreams + Reality + Determination = A Successful Life

But that's not always necessary for you to benefit massively from forming your own.

My own father is one of my favorite examples of using Dalio's principles and forming new heuristics.

Growing up, my father would always say, "I'm a good judge of character."

My father worked at my grandmother's business and did most of the hiring and firing. He hired based on the judgment of people's character.

Incidentally, he would start off saying so-and-so is a good person and has good character. How he (my dad) is a good judge of character. But invariably, six months to a year later, he's fired them. He would then say, "I can't believe this person fooled me like that. They tricked me. They were really just sleazy all along. A con artist to the core."

He'd hire someone else the next week and the cycle would repeat.

Somehow, it never seemed to register that if he was a good judge of character, he wouldn't have hired these people who lacked the character he was seeking.

He never made the mental shift from saying, "I'm a good judge of character" to "how do I know I'm a good judge of character?" or "Clearly the results I'm getting aren't what I'm desiring, so how do I create principles and heuristics so that I can actually achieve being a good judge of character quickly and easily?"

"Listening to uninformed people is worse than having no answers at all."
—Ray Dalio, Principles: Life and Work

There are very different ways of operating and arriving at principles. Heuristics are often developed through a painful experience, but it doesn't always have to be that way.

You can take the work we've done up until this point and ask: who are the people you'd like to be around in 5 years? What characteristics would they have? How can you form heuristics so that you filter in only people you truly want to be around?

For instance, if someone doesn't have the ambition or desire to be on a similar path over the next 5 years, they're probably not a good fit to have in proximity.

Another heuristic is that if I'm in a high-pressure purchasing situation and the answer isn't an absolute HELL YES, then it's no.

I don't like high-pressure situations like that so I make it easy on myself.

A heuristic I picked up from Tim Ferriss when dealing with a seemingly overwhelming new challenge is — what would this look like if it were easy?

Once you build that assumption in that there actually is an easy way to go about it, you give yourself permission to answer it, and voila — you'll have a far easier path than before.

All the greats have their own principles and heuristics for how they are going to operate.

Michael Jordan wouldn't show up to a game without a spotless car.

Heuristic — if I'm showing up to the game, this is how I'm doing it.

Grant Cardone — if I'm going to play the game of life, I want to do it at 10X.

When Grant approaches opportunities, if it's not a 10X opportunity, the answer is no.

My mentor and friend, Michael Carrigan, has a heuristic that he doesn't consider any business opportunities that won't make him at least a million dollars.

This is a simple heuristic that weeds out all the noise of anything less than he's looking for. Look at how much bigger he's made his world by giving it parameters.

Once you start defining the parameters of your life, you tune your brain like a radio, and you're only dialed into the things that fit within those parameters so you can make better, faster and more effective decisions which bring you along your path to greatness far faster.

ACTION ITEMS

- What are 3 principles you've internalized and implemented before that have immensely helped you in life already?
- What are 3 heuristics you already use to make your life better and easier?
- Taking into account who you want to be, what are 5 principles and 5 heuristics that would help you in becoming this version of yourself?
- Start a principles and heuristics journal today and begin cataloging your own so that you're consciously getting better all the time.

CONCLUSION

"Reality is merely an illusion, albeit a persistent one."
— Albert Einstein

Forging your world is all about creating the reality you want to live in.

So many people never take the time to stop, to step away from the busyness and actually hammer this out.

To get specific.

To get clear on precisely how they want their world to be, then actually pursue that.

If you've done these exercises, taken the time to give your world the degree of inspection it deserves, then you should be well on your way to forging your world.

This takes time.

It doesn't happen overnight but instead is honed over consistently returning to what you will tolerate and what you will not.

"Your complaints, your drama, your victim mentality, your whining, your blaming, and all of your excuses have NEVER gotten you even a single step closer to your goals or dreams. Let go of your nonsense. Let go of the delusion that you DESERVE better and go EARN it! Today is a new day!"
— Steve Maraboli

You choose who you want to be far more than you discover it, and in that pursuit, you will likely discover there is far more to yourself than you ever knew in the first place.

When you own the bottleneck, you appropriately identify yourself as what's stopping you and work relentlessly towards solving for that rather than other things that don't move the dial appropriately.

And, when you really adopt world-class meta-models, you'll find your personal progression goes into warp speed.

This may be the conclusion here, but it's only the beginning of a very fun and exciting journey for you if you're committed to staying on this path.

Keep hammering away, my friends.

PILLAR VI

Evolve or Devolve

INTRO

"There is nothing noble in being superior to your fellow man; true nobility is being superior to your former self."
— Ernest Hemingway

"Men are anxious to improve their circumstances, but are unwilling to improve themselves; they therefore remain bound. The man who does not shrink from self-crucifixion can never fail to accomplish the object upon which his heart is set. This is true of earthly as of heavenly things. Even the man whose object is to acquire wealth must be prepared to make great personal sacrifices before he can accomplish his object; and how much more so he who would realize a strong and well-poised life."
- James Allen

If you want to say Fuck Mediocrity, Be Powerful, Be Legendary, then it's important to realize this is a constant journey. It's not a destination to be reached but a path to follow, an orientation to sail towards and guide your way in life.

That journey will largely be determined by how many times you're willing to reinvent yourself, to transform yourself from who you were into who you could be.

Oddly, whether consciously or unconsciously, most people resist this pull of change, this process of personal evolution, yet it's the very thing that makes life worth living.

We're all striving for progress, for growth, and there is meaning in that.

And if you're not evolving, then you're devolving.

The moment you stop growing is the moment you start dying.

The moment you capitulate and say no more is the moment you get no more.

Daily marginal improvement is the goal.

Becoming better each day so that a year from now, you'll look back on your former self and nearly cringe by how naive you were, and also feel pride in the growth you've made.

"Anyone who isn't embarrassed of who they were last year probably isn't learning enough."
— Alain de Botton

Let's dig into the details of just how you can set your life up so that each and every day you're evolving rather than devolving.

CHAPTER TWENTY-TWO

Become a Transformation Ninja

"Sometimes it is the people no one imagines anything of who do the things no one can imagine."
— Alan Turing

What makes a person interesting?

What makes a person worth following?

What makes a person near contagious or infectious in their energy and vibrancy to life?

Born 6 weeks prematurely and only given a 10% chance of living, life didn't start off easily for Tim Ferriss.

But, he didn't let that stop him or even slow him down.

Despite numerous obstacles, he somehow defies all the odds and goes on to accomplish seemingly impossible feats, and just when you think it can't be done, seemingly reinvents himself again.

After somehow getting accepted to Princeton in 1996, despite scoring 40% lower on the SAT than the average, he then creates an audiobook called *How I Beat the Ivy League.*

And, proceeds to sell not one copy.

Yet, why should that stop him on his quest for transformation?

For transformation ninjas, failure is only an opportunity to learn.

After graduation, he heads to California to make his billions and instead finds himself working in a data storage company as the 2nd lowest paid employee.

Not a great start.

He decides to pivot and start a supplement company called BrainQUICKEN LLC that proceeds to take off.

Going from $40K per year to $40K per month seems great except that Tim hates his life where he is more owned by his company than owning the company, working 12 hour days, 7 days a week and heading towards total burnout.

Tim decides to remove himself as the bottleneck, sets off traveling around the world and sets the stage for what would soon become the basis for the wildly best-selling book *The 4-Hour Workweek.*

Just in case you thought it might stop there, like it does for plenty, that's not even close.

Tim is a master of reinvention, of transformation.

He then goes on to write The 4-Hour Body followed by The 4-Hour Chef.

On par with this transformation, Tim then starts what is now one of the largest podcasts in the world: The Tim Ferriss Show and follows his previous best-sellers up with two more, Tools of Titan and Tribe of Mentors.

What makes someone interesting?

What makes someone worth following?

You get a consistency with Tim, you sort of know how he operates, yet he's also always bringing something new to the table. He's always learning, always getting better, always pushing the limits, always going deeper.

And that's precisely why so many continue to follow him.

He's always intentionally evolving.

If you're just fine how you are today, then how will you get to who you need to be tomorrow?

It's a dance and it's one that those who are committed to evolving do exceptionally.

Partly, it's simply making the decision to become a transformation ninja, to constantly reinvent yourself and have constant evolution as a priority.

So many people never give themselves permission to do this, to change on a constant basis and not be appropriate and acceptable.

"Human beings are works in progress that mistakenly think they're finished."
—Benjamin P. Hardy

All transformation ninjas possess certain characteristics, certain traits that they've cultivated in their personalities and approach to life that make them exceptional. These are the primary drivers of why they go so many places and do so many things compared to your average person. We're going to break them down here.

Firstly, there is a reason to identify as a transformation ninja compared to just saying I need to constantly reinvent myself.

Your identity drives your behavior and is what you're committed to. If you're committed to that on an identity level, it will keep you on the path compared to someone who reinvents themselves once and stops.

You can say I'm the type of person who — constantly reinvents themselves.

Or

You can identify as a transformation ninja (TN) and have that as part of your core identity.

We're after change and who you become is the result of what you're actually committed to and take consistent actions towards daily.

To start, TNs possess an insatiable curiosity. They're always looking to learn, always looking to get better, always curious about the next things which is why they're always getting to it.

Nearly all of us were insanely curious as kids, yet at some point we let that die off, we lost interest in discovering more, in becoming more, and as a result, we became stagnant.

If you look at Tim's life, it's clear he's just as curious and open to learning now as he ever was and that's why he only keeps improving.

To match with curiosity is having the willingness to confront discomfort and instead find comfort in growth.

One of my teenage girlfriends once asked me what I thought my biggest strength was and I told her I just wasn't a complacent person.

That confused her.

She wanted a very typical life.

She couldn't dream of anything bigger than that which she had grown up in. Already at a young age, she was optimizing for safety and security versus excitement and growth.

It's this willingness to face discomfort that's a hallmark of all TNs. As Tim Ferriss says:

"Success can usually be measured by the number of uncomfortable conversations we are willing to have, and by the number of uncomfortable actions we are willing to take."

All growth happens as you're pushing past your own limits and inherently pushing past your own limits is uncomfortable.

However, it's this dedication to transformation that keeps TNs constantly reengaging with this discomfort because their values lie more in growth than they do in comfort.

Optimize for growth over comfort and your life will take a radical shift forward.

It's this obsession over who they're being that drives TNs forward.

They're obsessed with transformation, driven by insatiable curiosity and dedicated to learning as many skills as possible because they realize that oftentimes, where they are and where they want to go is really just a skill set gap.

Maybe that skill set gap is a very real thing such as not knowing how to peel a potato to knowing how to peel a potato.

Or maybe it's a self-mastery skill set gap such as keeping their word to themselves so that if they say "I'm going to the gym" they actually do that consistently.

Mindset and personal development are skill sets and they oftentimes have far larger ripple effects compared to what people traditionally think of as more tangible skill sets.

I think Tom Bilyeu emphasizes it well when he says,

"Skills have utility."

They do, yet somehow they are so easily dismissed as a priority, especially when people fail to realize that their current skill sets have already taken them as far as they can.

Here's the thing, everything you really want is in the unknown and that stops a lot of people.

"Remember that what you do not yet know is more important than what you already know."
— Jordan Peterson

The unknown is scary precisely because it's unknown. It lacks certainty, it lacks security, yet it also holds the keys to that which you most desire.

As a TN, it's your job to transform the unknown into the known, to forge into the darkness and push through your limits into growth.

And, your character is most revealed by the unknown, it's most revealed when you're being pushed.

That's precisely when your character will shine the brightest and you'll discover sides of yourself you didn't even know existed.

Lastly, TNs have all adopted a mutable paradigm or a growth mindset. They're only interested in being right, not in having to personally come up with the right answer themselves.

They're perfectly willing to change their entire mindset around something when they discover a better way of being.

It's this characteristic that allows them to grow so rapidly, to soar into the outer atmosphere as others are still stuck on the ground.

It's this willingness to shed that part of themselves which is no longer serving them and adopt that which moves them closer to that person they're trying to be.

As Jordan Peterson says:

"As you move through your life, you have to shed that which is no longer necessary. Otherwise it accretes around you, holds you down, and you perish sooner than you should. I think that's in large part because, if you don't dispense with your life as you move through it, then the stress of all that undone business, and of all those unmade decisions turns into a kind of chaos around you. That chaos puts you in a state of psychophysiological emergency preparedness, chronically, and that just ages you. It's necessary, in some sense, to stay light on your feet, and also, I think, to renew your commitment to your aim upward."

To recap, transformation ninjas are characterized by:

An insatiable curiosity

Possess a willingness to confront discomfort and value growth

Dedicated to transformation, to constantly reinventing themselves

Dedicated to learning as many skill sets as possible

Transform the unknown into the known

Adopt a mutable paradigm

Ten years from now you will surely arrive, so the question is — where will you be? Who will you be?

Will you be someone who faced the world, who faced themselves, who dedicated themselves to transformation, or will you be as close to the same person as you always have been?

"People prefer the certainty of misery to the misery of uncertainty."
— Virginia Satir

There is greatness within you and your willingness to confront and transform yourself will determine how much of it you manifest into life.

You can either evolve or devolve.

You can either be a transformation ninja or remain stuck trying to keep the world the same as it is.

Live the good life and commit to marginal improvement daily.

ACTION ITEMS

- Look in the mirror, in your own eyes, and actually state out loud that your goal is to constantly evolve.

- Next, tell the five closest people around you that this is part of your intention and how you want to live your life. Put it out there into the universe.
- Give yourself permission to actually adopt the identity of a Transformation Ninja, then simply recognize over the next 30 days that each day you're a little better than you were the day before.
- What is one skill you could learn over the next 30 days that would allow you to look back on who you were and see that you can transform yourself at any point, into nearly any person?
- How can you take excitement in discomfort, in breaking through into the unknown, so that you begin linking pleasure to this rather than pain?
- Mentally anchor discomfort to progression and comfort to regression so that you're always oriented towards growth.

CHAPTER TWENTY-THREE

Separation Habits are the Pathway to Evolution

"We are what we repeatedly do. Excellence, then, is not an act, but a habit."
— Will Durant

"Be the designer of your world and not merely the consumer of it."
—James Clear

"It seems, in fact, as though the second half of a man's life is made up of nothing, but the habits he has accumulated during the first half."
— Fyodor Dostoevsky

Habit:

a behavior pattern acquired by frequent repetition or physiologic exposure that shows itself in regularity or increased facility of performance.

A dominant or regular disposition or tendency; prevailing character or quality.

An acquired mode of behavior that has become nearly or completely involuntary.

The prevailing disposition or character of a person's thoughts and feelings: mental makeup.

"People do not decide their futures, they decide their habits and their habits decide their futures."
—F. M. Alexander

Oftentimes we lose sight of the goal, lose sight of the outcome we're after in life which is really to make progress, to have growth, to evolve rather than devolve.

In a quest for meaning, fulfillment and purpose, it's easy to get distracted by all the minutia comprising our day to day experiences.

Oftentimes it's the systems we have in place, our habits, that are more responsible for why we end up where we do, rather than large, one-off actions.

Tom Brady didn't get where he is by having a few brutally hard practices a few days a year. He got there by consistent daily actions and behaviors that developed him into the GOAT.

When you look at your life and the results you're getting, those results are really just a reflection of the systems or automatic playbooks you've been running and for most people those are on autopilot.

Habits are oftentimes the silent ingredient to success or failure. The difference between winning and losing, between being great or living in complacency.

As a society, we get this. We're obsessed with habits, with studying them, with wanting to know what others are doing, with writing out complicated routines that we're surely going to implement at the start of the new year and we all know how that usually turns out.

Getting the results you desire in life will largely come down to the habits you intentionally adopt or eschew.

And truthfully, most people far over-complicate this rather than just focusing on being present and intentional about the things they either allow or don't allow in their life.

There are plenty of books on habits, how to build them, how to drop the bad ones, how to link them to another anchor, but the most important ingredient in all of them is ACTUAL implementation by YOU!

You are the only one who can implement the habits you desire and cease the habits you don't desire.

The key here is that recognition.

You understand your job is to evolve in life, to go through as many iterations of transformation as you can and it's your tiny habits that will ultimately determine the outcomes you achieve or don't achieve.

I've been into fitness since I was 13. I haven't always worked out consistently, had years where I didn't at all, and then I finally decided to get serious about my life.

I finally decided to stop flirting with mediocrity, with doing things only when I felt like it, and to commit to building a series of unbreakable habits and systems.

Now, I MAKE the time to go to the gym no matter what.

My habit is to schedule my priorities, not to prioritize my schedule.

And I'm ruthless with this.

Because I decided to make that a habit.

Having that as a high-level habit has massive trickle-down effects into the rest of my life.

We're starting to tie all this together.

Because I know my habits are the key to evolving, I also know I have to implement non-negotiable habits and be intolerant of anything less.

Start analyzing your life and looking at your daily actions. Which actions are actually serving to bring you closer to where you want to be and which ones are detracting from that?

If I watch someone for a day and see the habits they have in place, I can practically predict where they'll be in 5 years unless they make major changes.

What you do repetitively is MASSIVELY important.

It's also GREATLY overlooked so many times.

We obfuscate and hide from ourselves so that we allow the excuses to come in the back door.

> "I'm tired."
>
> "I've had a long day at work."
>
> "I really want to watch this Netflix show."

We've talked about having heart and this is part of it but you have to adjust your focus.

This is a depth issue.

Those things sound great in the moment, yet will slowly erode your ability to push through adversity and attain that longer-term vision.

It's your ability to focus on who and where you want to be in five years that will pull you through these situations.

It takes heart, and that's having your heart all in on who you know you could be.

When you're clear on that, it doesn't matter about the other things, you're just going to stick to your habits — period.

Just like everything else, your habits are an emotional game.

Willpower eventually runs out which is why it's important to design your environment appropriately so that sticking with your habits is as fluid as possible.

If you know you're tired coming home from work, have your workout clothes laid out already.

If you know you'll be hungry by the time you get home and that's a weakness point for cheating, solve that the day before.

The worst time to deal with problems is in the moment you're having the problem.

"I value self-discipline, but creating systems that make it next to impossible to misbehave is more reliable than self-control."
– Tim Ferriss

Make it a habit to start predicting the future, to remove future problems before they ever occur by becoming so good at designing your reality.

This is the key to implementing habits that stick and don't wear off.

You have to be indefatigable.

By that I mean most of us are going to fall off the wagon at some point, but that doesn't mean we shouldn't just hop back on with renewed determination.

Rather than having the habit of getting discouraged when that does occur, perhaps try introducing the habit of seeing opportunity and excitement as just another chance to get back on that train.

How you frame things matters.

You can recontextualize nearly everything.

These are the high-level habits that make the difference between the ultra-successful and mediocre.

One person gets discouraged, the other gets excited at a new opportunity and also learns something about themselves.

Most of us learn things the hard way or the harder way.

Some of us need to fall off the wagon continually while others fall off once, decide they don't like that and never do again.

I have no judgments about which is best.

Some people will tell you that you can't ever drink, shouldn't ever go party and get a hangover, or to miss more than two days in the gym.

There are other people who embrace those things occasionally and they also seem to live great lives.

What's clear in this is that it's REALLY helpful to build systems that fit your personality and who you want to be.

I hear so many people say, well I "should" do this or do that, and I see absolutely zero evidence that they should or shouldn't either way.

Your life gets bigger when you make your world smaller.

It's part of this process of accepting you can't do everything so are only going to spend time on the things you most want to do. Then you don't have to say you "should" anything because you're perfectly happy to say no to the things that don't actually move the dial in your life.

Habits don't have to be a trap, they don't have to limit you, instead, I'd posit that habits are the pathway to the freedom you desire.

It's the dedication you have towards those habits that will take you from where you are to where you want to be.

Tom Brady didn't get where he is now without a plan and without DAILY HABITS that brought him incrementally closer to where he wanted to be every single day.

It's easy to see how important habits are, to logically understand that they're a huge ingredient in your life.

Yet, people still seem to dismiss their importance.

They know this universal principle, dismiss it, then bitch about how their life isn't how they'd like it.

Powerful men never do that.

Either you're committed to evolving or you will start devolving.

There are so many men out there actively and consciously evolving each and every day and if you're not, you're getting left in the dust.

It's not always sexy to have habits that separate you from everyone else.

It's not always easy to wake up earlier than everyone else, or to push through even when you don't want to, but it's also what is going to get you where you want to be.

Remember, you're out to create inequality between you and others and even between who you were.

You want to be so much better than that same version of yourself a year before and it's those daily habits that are going to take you there.

If you decide to get fit, you can't do it only doing one workout a month for the next year. You're going to spend dedicated time on that fitness daily and if you do, you'll be amazed at where you could be.

"In the end, it's about what you want to be, not what you want to have."
— Derek Sivers

Habits are a feedback loop.

You can try to force habits into place in order to be a certain type of man or decide to be a certain type of man, inviting habits to flow into place during that pursuit.

You're out to create SEPARATION HABITS.

You're out to create separation between where you are today and where you want to be tomorrow.

This seems simple and trivial but it's not.

When you start looking at life and focusing on who you could be, rather than attempting to force habits into place, you'll start asking yourself — what are the habits I need to have in order to become this man?

Next, we tie that together with non-negotiable standards. Here, you have to look in the mirror and decide if you're truly committed to that or not.

You have to be honest with yourself about this feedback, to look in the mirror, to stare into your own eyes and take responsibility on whether your behavior is in line with who you're attempting to become or not.

You know you could be playing at a higher level and we both know you won't get there unless you have every-day-actions, and that's something that can be brutal for most people.

But it doesn't have to be.

Most people want to change their habits yet don't make the vocal declaration to the universe that where they're at is not where they want to be and then make the commitment to get there.

I do this all the time with friends.

I vocalize my visions and then reinforce them with actions daily that move me towards those visions.

And I have large visions. I am out to live as much life as possible which means failing and facing times of hardship, but that's just the type of life I choose. I'm always willing to roll the dice on me because I'll bet on me each and every time.

That's what being a man is about. Facing those possibilities, facing adversity and then going forward anyway.

That's part of what greatness is and you have it inside of you also.

That's why I think it's important to declare what you're after and to identify that you're not after habits to make you the same as everyone else.

You're after separation habits.

Your goal is to create separation between who you are today and who you could be next year or five years from now and that only happens if you move the needle daily.

As James Clear, author of Atomic Habits, says:

"Habits are the compound interest of self-improvement."

Habits aren't linear, they don't just stack, there is a tipping point where all that little work seems to connect and click and then there is an exponential explosion of growth.

But you have to make it through the daily implementation first.

Remember, what you do repeatedly IS what you're committed to and what you're committed to is your identity, therefore, your habits are part of a constant feedback loop with who you are, your identity and where you're going.

Habits are one of the keys to your evolution, to your growth, and one of the most powerful ways to genuinely becoming a different version of yourself.

If you have the habit of drinking soda, you probably identify as a soda drinker. If you wish to change that identity, you could quickly change your language so that you no longer refer to yourself as a soda drinker. You then create the daily habit of drinking only coffee, tea or water, and after a brief time, you would actually have stacked up evidence to support that new identity. Then it's not simply a declaration, but a core belief.

Your brain most believes what it knows to be true on a conscious and unconscious level.

If you say you're going to exercise 3 days a week and don't, the next time you try to make a goal and commit to it, your brain automatically thinks — this guy sets goals all the time but they're worthless because he doesn't keep his word to himself.

That's why it's so crucial to be honest with yourself, to be ruthless about keeping your commitments and only committing to the things you intend on following through with.

This is the ultimate habit to have. The habit of always following through with the commitments you make with yourself so that if you say, I'm going to do X, your brain doesn't argue, it doesn't push back, it automatically says — well fuck, I guess we're doing this so I better get started on finding the best way to do it.

That's the mindset of champions, the mindset of winners, and again, you get there through habitual commitment.

"Every action you take is a vote for the type of person you wish to become. No single instance will transform your beliefs, but as the votes build up, so does the evidence of your new identity."
— James Clear

I hope you're starting to see how all of these things tie together to make you an unstoppable human being.

No one ever explained this to me or put it in this context where I could clearly see how these different concepts tied together. So that I could strategically implement them in my life and transform into the man I knew I could be, which is why I'm doing my best to illustrate that here.

To close, I could go on forever about habits, but ultimately that doesn't move the needle at all.

You are the one that moves the needle in your life.

No one else is going to implement habits for you.

No one else is going to lift the weights or do the work for you.

It's up to you and that's also the beauty of it.

The results you're getting are either working for you or not and if they're not, you have an opportunity to change that because there is greatness within you, my friend.

I truly believe that.

You get the opportunity to start analyzing your habits and make the changes you desire.

It's that simple.

But you have to do it.

No amount of reading or talking about it or analyzing it will change that very fact.

Most of my most important habits are all done in the shadows, all done out of the sight of others.

I don't receive any accolades, any congratulations, any praise over them — I just do them because I know they're bringing me closer to who I could be.

Chances are, you're not going to receive any praise or congratulations either, until you do.

It's like going to the gym at 5am every morning. First nobody notices. You grind it out for a month or two, then people notice a bit. Then after three months, everyone is asking what you're doing, how you're doing it and if you can help them do it too.

But before then — no praise, no encouragement, just good, old-fashioned work.

And that's how it should be.

You can either have reasons or results, and nobody gives a fuck about your reasons.

Hat tip to Michael Carrigan for that one.

You can have all the reasons in the world but nobody cares about those.

Or you can have results and everyone cares about those.

It's time you create your separation habits today and embrace greatness.

For me, my number one separation habit is perseverance. I have simply made it a habit to not quit, to not give up, to not give in, to just stick with whatever I have to until I get my desired result.

This is a more abstract separation habit that I reinforce with tangible ones such as going to the gym, maintaining an orderly and disciplined lifestyle and other quantifiable factors.

But, my superpower is perseverance. That simple habit separates me from so many who simply fall off the wagon, capitulate and give in when things get hard.

What will you choose to make yours?

And don't forget – BE LEGENDARY, MOTHERFUCKER!

ACTION ITEMS

- What are 5 habits you currently engage in that are not bringing you closer to who you desire to be?
- If you were to be the man you know you could be, what habits would you have that you currently don't possess?
- What changes can you make NOW to implement those habits into your life?
- How can you design your environment to better support those habits and to also minimize the ones that don't work for you?
- What sort of accountability can you put into place so that you have greater leverage over yourself to fully create this new identity you envision?
- Visualization is a powerful tool — spend 5 minutes in the morning over the next month visualizing that version of yourself in 6 months time, the habits you have, and how difficult it was at the start to push through and develop them, but how easy they are now, how much better your life is now, how proud of yourself you are that you stuck with them, that you conquered what you thought was unconquerable only a short time ago.

CHAPTER TWENTY-FOUR

Leverage The Power of Timelines

"Focus is like a muscle. If you train it, it gets stronger."
— Tom Bilyeu

"Can you imagine yourself in 10 years if, instead of avoiding the things you know you should do, you actually did them every single day? That's powerful."
— Jordan Peterson

Introducing a few, simple yet powerful principles into how you think and view your journey through the world is immensely helpful.

Principle One— What you want and where you want to go lie in the future and your ability to get there lies in your ability to negotiate with the future.

Do you want to be fit in 90 days, or do you want to have those potato chips right now? Each is a choice and each has its own consequences.

Principle Two — The Paradox of Sacrifice — Either you sacrifice for what you want or what you want becomes the sacrifice.

You have to own the paradox and understand that it's all up to you on whether you leverage the power of timelines and future vision or not.

The problem most men run into is that they are plagued by FOMO (fear of missing out) which often drives them to shorten their time horizons which ultimately then leads to dissatisfaction in the long run.

And why does this happen?

Because they're unclear on their mission and they lack the discipline and integrity to say NO.

To make choices that make their world both smaller and also bigger simultaneously.

Or perhaps you just haven't been clear up until now that this is the game you're playing, that ruling things out actually makes room for so many bigger and better things to come into your life. As Tom Bilyeu says:

"The reality is, we are all standing in a room with a thousand doors, and our job is to close 999 of them."

Your job is to close all the doors that don't lead to your vision of what you desire in the future.

It's that simple.

I like to think in terms of short, medium and long term consequences or 1st, 2nd and 3rd order consequences.

Let's establish an overall vision — you want to lose 30 lbs over the next 90 days.

The weekend creeps up and everyone is begging you to come out, have bar food and make choices that don't support your vision.

First order consequences are that you go out and have a good time, enjoy all of the food, alcohol, et cetera.

Second order consequences are you feel guilty the next day and have a hangover.

Third order consequences are you only lost 10 lbs over 90 days rather than 30 and didn't hit your targets.

Short term pleasure at the expense of long-term goals.

This is where you can leverage the power of timelines by understanding the order of consequences and then use that to say NO to anything that doesn't support your longer term vision.

You can understand that 15 minutes of pleasure of eating those chips will result in potentially years of agony because you're not living with integrity in what you're pursuing.

Short-term sacrifice no longer seems so appealing when you understand that you're going to be sacrificing either way so you may as well **sacrifice for that which you most want** and is in line with who you're trying to build yourself into.

This is the difference between the rich and poor, the successful and unsuccessful, the haves and have-nots.

One person is able to leverage and stick with a long-term vision and the other only operates from short-term pleasure seeking and doesn't understand there is ALWAYS a sacrifice.

It's critical to cut through the noise and view yourself honestly, to understand if you're over-valuing what's immediate at the expense of your longer-term vision.

And that's okay if you are. Truthfully, most people are operating in this state until they consciously decide to change and be unreasonable about developing better habits.

Give yourself some grace and also give yourself permission to change this now that you know better.

The internet is full of people who are only always showing themselves showing up at 100%. People who are telling you to never have any sort of first order consequence fun. Personally, that doesn't resonate with me.

Instead, I try to leverage long-term vision with planned deloading phases so I get to have my cake and eat it too.

I find it best to work in 90-day sprints with some sort of planned fun or reward at the end. This way I develop a vision and use that planned deloading phase as leverage to bring me to where I want to be.

However you decide to develop and plan your life, the thing to remember is that timelines matter.

There is power in leveraging timelines and in assessing 1st, 2nd and 3rd order consequences.

You can focus on what brings short-term pleasure but doesn't move the needle in your life or you can focus on what brings long-term meaning, fulfillment, reward and pleasure.

The **choice** is entirely up to you.

I will add a caveat here that it's important to take a long-term perspective while also being aware of your environment and how best to navigate that.

If you're in a country where there is tons of inflation, saving doesn't make as much sense compared to a country with a stable currency.

I see a lot of people thinking the next 20 years will somehow be similar to the previous 20 years and that's probably not the case at all. We've reached a sort of escape velocity with technology and we're also at the end of a huge financial cycle in the world so if you don't educate yourself about these things, taking a long-term perspective without adequate consideration could backfire.

Still long-term vision, you're just playing a different game.

One way I like to think about things is to ask where the world is going to be in 5, 10 and twenty years.

Those are all incredibly far off and will also be here before we know it.

The internet is not going anywhere. Things are moving digitally. They're also becoming increasingly automated, video is taking over compared to this book, the gap between the haves and have-nots is widening, there is potential for currency collapses along with civil unrest.

The man who thinks long-term and asks how they can be in the best position in 5 years down the road will fare better than the man who isn't thinking about it at all.

Some will optimize for safety and security yet fail to realize that the best way to ensure this is through adaptability and social networks compared to trying to go the "prepper" route.

The first lesson of history is that people don't learn from history and while it's not going to be the same, it will rhyme as said by Mark Twain.

Back to consequences and timelines…

There is power in recognizing the different order of consequences and also in timelines and then deciding how you want to live your life.

A crucial aspect I see all the time are people who are attempting to live with a long-term vision yet completely sacrificing their short-term circumstances.

As an example, I see people who deprive themselves of adequate meat and eat a ton of inflammatory foods that they believe are "healthy" and then feel like shit.

I ask them about this and then they proceed to **argue for their limitations**, to defend why they should feel like shit now so that they can live to 80 years old.

News flash, if you don't feel good, your body is probably trying to tell you something. Don't ignore reality to supposedly support a faux long-term vision.

Also, never argue for that which limits you. Seriously, why believe in ANYTHING that takes power from you as a man? Just stop it.

Timelines can work both ways and it's up to you to decide where that line is for yourself.

You will become far more powerful though once you start viewing the world from this perspective because you'll no longer just see a potato chip — you'll see a whole cascade of effects from there and then be empowered to make a more responsible choice.

ACTION ITEMS

- What things do you repetitively engage in that are primarily 1st order consequence based?
- How could you leverage timelines to make different **decisions** that support your vision more appropriately?
- How could you lengthen your timelines so that you make decisions that are more congruent with your overall vision for yourself, life and the man you want to be?

CHAPTER TWENTY-FIVE

Iterate Relentlessly

"You might be winning but you're not growing, and growing might be the most important form of winning."
— Jordan Peterson

"Those who achieve greatness are not those who think they are extraordinary today. It's those who invest in themselves today. Those who are learning something today. Those who are putting in the effort today. If you become complacent with what you have achieved, you will never get there. You may become good, but you will never become great."
— Tom Bilyeu

Iterate — to create something by building on previous versions or iterations, using each version as the point of departure for refinements and tweaks:

We covered that adopting the identity of a transformation ninja is one of the keys to evolving rather than devolving and developing yourself into the man you could be.

Here, we're going to get more granular on exactly how you do that and what those steps look like.

To Iterate Relentlessly, you must constantly be building on each version of yourself so that you go through as many iterations as possible in your life.

This goes back to the quote from Benjamin Franklin –

"Most men die at 25 and aren't buried until 75."

Have you met someone who was 50 or 60 and they're so impossibly naive it seems they couldn't have learned hardly a thing past the age of 20?

I know I have and they're NOT who I ever intend to end up as.

How about someone who is 50 or 60 and you're beyond amazed at the knowledge they have and the sheer breadth of life that they've lived?

I've met those people, and they got there because they follow the rule of relentlessly iterating.

They are constantly reinventing themselves, constantly building on the current version of themselves to create someone new and better tomorrow and that's exactly what you have to do if you choose to pursue greatness.

Of course, that's not always easy for most men because that also means departing from who you are today into who you could be tomorrow.

That means cutting a part of yourself off so that you can mold yourself into the man you could be.

It's like chiseling away at a piece of marble. You have to get rid of certain aspects so that you can gain others.

So principle one here is to — **CUT RUTHLESSLY.**

You have to cut the things from your life that aren't serving your overall vision and bringing you closer to who you could be.

Inherently, most people understand that you're the sum of the 5 people you spend the most time with and I'd also argue that **you're the most important of those people**.

However, most aren't then willing to cut away the people who aren't also helping to propel them forward in the way they wish.

They hang on to relationships that are advocating for their **MEDIOCRITY** rather than encouraging them to pursue greatness and be legendary.

You have to cut that shit out.

You have to cut ruthlessly on the things that aren't serving you.

Negative self talk? Cut it out.

Piss poor attitude? Just stop it.

Hanging around people who aren't empowering you to live at a different level? Gone.

Eating habits that aren't serving you? Axed.

Look, the best is yet to come.

I truly believe that for you if you'll adopt an empowered mindset and have the courage to go on your own hero's journey.

I understand that it's scary to do these things.

You've built your identity around so many things that aren't serving you and admitting that is difficult and it's painful, but it's also necessary.

You have to realize that this is simply an **opportunity** to cut those things out and then to add in the things or people which will bring you closer to the man you could be.

It sounds harsh and perhaps it is but that's what being a man is all about.

You weren't put here to live a life with no adversity.

You weren't put here to pursue weakness, comfort and mediocrity, motherfucker!

You were put here to weather that adversity with courage and honor and that means doing the things you know you should, even when it's difficult.

If you want to evolve then you have to normalize RUTHLESSLY CUTTING the things that aren't serving you out of your life so that you only allow that which serves you.

"You're going to pay a price for every bloody thing you do and everything you don't do. You don't get to choose to not pay a price. You get to choose which poison you're going to take."
— Jordan Peterson

The next principle is to **DESIGN MUTABILITY INTO YOUR LIFE**.

What do I mean by this?

Mutability — prone to change.

One of the biggest things that holds people back is that they've designed their life so that everyone expects them to stay the same rather than to evolve rapidly.

This is a **design principle.**

Generally, people want to feel like they know someone yet can still be surprised in little ways that are just enough to pique their curiosity while also not pushing their comfort boundaries too far.

That's fine but that's not how I live my life and it's also not what my friends expect from me.

I have consciously normalized rapidly changing so that people expect this from me. I have designed my life so that I am prone to change, I am prone to rapidly adapting rather than staying the same.

This seems simple but it's critical to understand and master.

I may say something today and then contradict myself tomorrow.

Initially, that can throw people off but when I get new information that abrogates the old, I don't have an ego about holding onto who I was.

I have built my ego around being someone who learns and adapts rather than being someone who argues for my limitations.

Hat tip to Tom Bilyeu for articulating this extremely well in the countless videos I've watched of his. As Tom says, what you build your ego around matters and adopting that of the "learner" is the most powerful thing because then you're not trapped, you're simply always learning, growing and adapting.

In your quest to iterate relentlessly, it's important to design that mutability into your life and also to make it conscious so others **expect** it from you.

If I'm not up to something and changing fast enough, people question if something is wrong with me or what happened to my drive or motivation. Do they do that for you? If not, consider changing that.

Seriously, when you do this and have high-level people around you, if you're not adapting fast enough, they will call you on it. They will hold you accountable because they know you have more to give and can show up at a higher level.

"Remember that what you do not yet know is more important than what you already know."
— Jordan Peterson

You're not pursuing the stuff you already know. You're pursuing a better version of yourself, you're pursuing becoming the man you know you could be and you'll only get there through rapid adaptation so adopt that and start designing mutability into your life.

Principle three — **TAKE FEEDBACK SERIOUSLY BUT NOT PERSONALLY.**

I watched an interview with Tucker Max some time ago and he talked about how he was able to transform so rapidly. In that he shared something that is easy to miss or to dismiss as trivial but it's actually a huge secret of success and that is to not take feedback and turn it into shame.

Feedback means I did something bad, NOT - I am bad.

There is a huge difference here.

If you're personalizing everything and getting your feelings hurt every time someone gives you critical feedback, how are you supposed to grow?

Exactly, you're not.

However, if you start taking feedback seriously yet not personally, you'll understand these are just opportunities to improve and that's the name of the game.

And here's the thing, so many people take feedback from just anyone and treat it as equal to their own opinion and that doesn't typically work well.

I only take feedback from someone I believe truly has superior knowledge, skills, respect or some other aspect that I value.

If Joe Schmo offers up feedback to me, I'll use my ability to think critically and determine whether it holds any water or not. I don't simply accept it as truth and certainly only adopt it if it's going to **empower** me.

Another thing is to recognize that feedback isn't specifically limited to people.

Life is going to give you feedback all the time. I know so many people who simply ignore it and don't allow themselves to receive it because they personalize rather than simply recognize it for what it is. It's not good or bad, it's just feedback and what you do with it is most important.

The next principle is to adopt the belief that you're — **SOMEONE WHO IS GETTING BETTER EVERY DAY.**

Your belief systems matter and the more you bring them into consciousness, the more you anchor them, the more they become real.

I know many people who when asked how their day is, just respond with good or okay or I'm making it.

Why would you put that out there into the universe?

When someone asks me, I say — "I'm just out here winning every day."

Why?

Because that's what I do.

Every single day is a win and even if it's the shittiest day ever, I am still winning because language and belief systems matter.

I am someone who is getting better every single day and if the day is shit, well, then it was a great growth opportunity and if it's fantastic and every single thing seems to go right, then that's fantastic also because I've designed my life well.

I can't not win.

That's the power of setting up your belief systems to empower you. Adopting the belief system that you're someone who is getting better every day starts to compound over time.

You're trying to go through as many iterations in life as you can and part of that is to recognize that the goal is to literally get better every single day.

I'd wager most people would say they're way better today than they were 10 years ago.

Why?

Because they can see the gap, and it's large enough for them to measure. But if they shorten it and focus on adapting rapidly, then they're going to be way better than they were 90 days ago.

If you implement everything I'm talking about in this book, how could you NOT be a better version of yourself in the next 90 days?

And just think of who you could be 90 days from that, even!

You can adapt and get better in real fucking time!

That's the power of belief and of adopting an empowering mindset.

It's all how you want to go through life.

"Don't ask what's the least you can do.
Ask what's the most you can bear."
— TOM BILYEU

STOP trying to defend MEDIOCRITY in your life.

Stop arguing for your limitations.

Stop giving reasons for your lack of results.

Become the man who is getting better every day and you'll be amazed at how fast your life can transform.

Lastly, I'd like to follow up with a quick synopsis of a clip I saw featuring Tim Knight on elite learners, how they think, what they expect and how that process goes.

According to Tim, elite learners:

- Use mistakes as feedback.
- Take mistakes seriously, but not personally.
- Understand that building skills takes time and effort.
- I invest the time and be tenaciously persistent.
- I understand discomfort is part of the process.
- If I avoid discomfort, I prevent learning.
- I will make mistakes and they will teach me.
- I want feedback and coaching.

That's the mindset of someone who's getting better every day.

"You've got no control over people and things. The only thing you have control over is yourself. So, take back control and work towards your potential."
— Tom Bilyeu

When I walk men through these processes, they're amazed at how simple yet effective these principles are for elevating who they are in life.

If you're anything like me, you were never taught these principles. In my life, they were never articulated, and so while I sort of vaguely knew them to be true, without consciously inspecting them, I would allow myself slippage because I didn't fully comprehend them.

If you will be the man who you know you can be, then understanding and implementing these principles is like having superpowers.

You get an insane advantage over someone who doesn't understand them or hasn't implemented them in their life.

Build these into your life and watch how fast life can change for you.

ACTION ITEMS

- What do you need to ruthlessly cut from your life? Relationships? Food? Over indulging in TV? What are 5 things that if you cut out could help you transform massively?
- How can you NORMALIZE this so that you're constantly cutting that which does not serve you?
- How can you design mutability into your life? How can you start owning the idea that you're changing and growing every single day and make that known to your relationships so they come to expect this from you?

- What feedback have you either been ignoring or taking personally that if you were to give yourself permission to hear and see, could be helpful?
- How can you adopt the identity of someone who is a learner so that your ego is no longer tied to taking everything personally and instead only taking it personally if you're not growing how you should?
- How could you build and reinforce the habit of someone who is getting better every single day?
- How can you start changing your language around this so that you are constantly reinforcing this mindset?

CONCLUSION

To close, there is massive power in here if you're open and committed to adopting it.

You know the goal is to **become the man you could be**, that there is greatness within you, that you could be beyond **powerful** if you only decide and **commit** to that outcome.

Rather than trying to be your "authentic self" perhaps try being the man you could be.

Perhaps try to become a transformation ninja, to implement separation habits, leverage the power of timelines, iterate relentlessly and watch just how quickly you can evolve and adapt.

Don't be the 20 year old stuck in a 60 year old's body one day.

No one respects that, enjoys that or wants that and I especially don't want that for you.

I believe in you and your potential for greatness.

I believe in your ability to become an UNSTOPPABLE MAN who breaks all the barriers you didn't even think were possible.

It's time you show the world that version of yourself.

It's time you show the world you're committed to being LEGENDARY.

PILLAR VII

Take Massive Strategic Action

INTRO

Superior work – that's how I'm going to smoke everyone.

I'm working as a male dancer, living a life most can only ever dream of, yet it's also not everything most think it is.

There's a dark side to it and I'm ready to leave that behind for a better life.

I've been reading the books, started speed-reading, worked to improve my efficiency and am now a rockstar multi-tasker.

I'm working on my second romance novel, modeling, doing all my own meal-prep, hitting the gym consistently and checking all the boxes of action, action, action.

Yet, I seem to be getting nowhere I wish to be.

I can't figure out why.

I'm the go-to person for anyone who has questions about tech, about how something works, about all the latest things.

I'm keeping up with it all and pride myself on my ability to smoke others who can't seem to stay as focused as I am.

I'm just going to outwork everyone. I'm convinced of it. At some point, it's going to happen.

Does this sound familiar at all?

Being on the massive action hamster wheel where you're persevering, you're putting in the work, you're juggling more things than you even understand how, yet you're not actually getting the results you want in your life?

I wish I could say this is a rare problem but for the highly driven, it's not.

In the personal development space, I hear nearly everyone espouse the phrase "just take massive action" yet then people are also surprised when they don't get the results they're after.

It's too vague, too nebulous and doesn't place the emphasis on what actually keeps people stuck and how to actually get past that.

We're all taking actions all the time, the real question is why aren't we taking the actions we need to in order to bring us closer to our desired results?

Let's deconstruct some of this so you can understand how this works and get the clarity necessary to take the actions that will bring you closer to being the man you know you could be.

CHAPTER TWENTY-SIX

The Distraction of Action

"The greatest enemy of good thinking is busyness."
— John C. Maxwell

"You can become successful with less discipline than you think, for one simple reason: success is about doing the right thing, not about doing everything right."
— Gary Keller, The One Thing

Let's agree on something quick – results are all that matter. Not how many hours you put into something, not all of the "action" you take around a thing — the results are all that ultimately matter.

I find this to be a surprising pain point for most people. They claim to be working so hard, to be taking all this massive action, yet still aren't getting the result they proclaim to desire.

When asked why not, they then say they don't have time to slow down and analyze their process because they just need to work harder.

Don't be that person.

Action has a tendency to make you feel important or validated, like you've actually accomplished something and perhaps you did, but if it's not the appropriate something, does it really matter that much?

No.

Busyness is simply an excuse to not be honest with yourself and to have a critical conversation about how you're really using action as a distraction to avoid the satisfaction you're professing to want.

"Being busy is most often used as a guise for avoiding the few critically important but uncomfortable actions."
— Tim Ferriss

It's important to not confuse busyness with effectiveness.

This happens all the time as well. We're convinced we need to listen to one more podcast, or just read another book, or try to power through whatever we're working on rather than ensuring we're taking the most strategic actions possible.

This often manifests itself as "learning as an escape from doing".

We're convinced we're making progress because we simply need to learn more yet we haven't actually embraced the learning-doing feedback loop which is far more effective.

No amount of learning can replace action and no amount of action can also replace learning. It's an iterative feedback loop.

Everyone agrees that the action takers are the money makers yet I see a plethora of people who are taking tons of action yet aren't making any money — that's because they're not strategic in their actions.

"Success and greatness is not related to the volume of tasks that you complete, but simply the significance of them. And ultra performers are able to get themselves to do the things they know they should be doing, even when they don't feel [like it]."

— Rory Vaden

The truth is that the art of taking strategic action is all in saying NO to all the other things vying for your attention.

This is where most people fail.

They think they need to clean the house first or get the proper workout clothes or find the right supplements before they can go to the gym and entirely miss getting the results they're after because they're failing to do the ONE thing that moves the dial in their life.

CUT THAT SHIT OUT!

What you say yes to and say no to matters.

When you do all the other things that don't actually progress you forward and say NO to the ONE important thing that needs to get done, then you're just distracting yourself.

You're fumbling.

You're not being honest with yourself about what you're committed to.

You have to close the possibilities in your life so that you can open new possibilities.

Seriously, you have to be OBSESSED with results, not simply take action, action, action, and then congratulate yourself on all that action even though it doesn't mean anything.

It's distracting at best and self-sabotage at worst.

You know this is true. This isn't rocket science. It is just that you haven't taken the time to get the clarity you MUST have in order to progress forward.

"Creative avoidance is different, and this is something that people do as an art form. Creative avoidance is subconsciously creating things for yourself to do so that you can do those things as a means of feeling productive, but really it's a giant scheme for avoiding doing the things you know you should be doing even when you don't feel like doing it."
— Rory Vaden

You're taking action all the time so the real question is what are you truly committed to?

You're disciplined, just disciplined to the things that aren't actually taking you where you want to go and this is why being brutally honest with yourself is so important.

What you build your ego around matters and it has to be built around being a learner, around getting better and valuing that above all else, rather than simply being a "hard worker" who's miserable because you're busting your ass yet not getting the results you desire.

Look, we're goddamn goal achieving machines. We can't NOT take action. The only problem is we mostly take action towards things that don't lead to actual satisfaction.

Recognizing this is the first critical step towards moving in a different direction.

"Make sure every day you do what matters most. When you know what matters most, everything makes sense. When you don't know what matters most, anything makes sense."
—Gary Keller, The One Thing

Your identity is defined by that which you're most committed to.

And what you're committed to is always defined by that which you're most willing to sacrifice for it.

The RESULTS you're getting are a reflection of what you're committed to in life.

Action isn't the problem.

It's that you're not truly committed. If you were, you'd be willing to sacrifice nearly anything to follow through with that commitment.

But if you want to be, if you make that decision with every fiber of your being...

Then all action must stem from the pursuit of future goals and your commitment to those which means saying NO to anything that's not in congruence with those goals.

When you do that, you change your actions and simultaneously change your beliefs and develop your identity along with those actions.

You are what you repeat.

"The third type of procrastination is called priority dilution, and this is fascinating, ... [because] priority dilution is the chronic overachiever's form of procrastination. What's different about it is, unlike the first two, ... priority dilution is not about being lazy or disengaged or distracted, but it is the same net result of the first two, which is ... you leave the office or you end your day with your most significant priorities incomplete, not because you're lazy, but because you allowed your attention to shift to less significant but perhaps more urgent tasks."

— Rory Vaden

I'm hammering this home because it's something so simple yet we fall into this trap over and over and over again in life.

It's paradoxical, but sometimes perceived "inaction" really is the most important action.

It's having that commitment towards absolute clarity that is what will drive you forward.

There is no such thing as inaction. You're constantly in action.

But, here's the thing — your obsessions become your possessions.

You just have to be obsessed with the results that are going to get you where you want to go.

Action is thinking about what you want, visualizing it relentlessly to the point that you're so clear on it it's practically already there.

It's feeling what you want.

Tasting it.

It's writing.

It's reading.

It's pursuing a goal.

It's all the unsexy work that leads to the sexy end result.

Action is long hours contemplating a single move, rehearsing a single thing.

Action is deciding who you want to be then becoming obsessed with that.

I know that seems paradoxical, but it really is this process of every single day reorienting yourself to what's most important then actively saying NO to anything that doesn't move you towards it and truly saying YES to a single, large task that moves you forward.

Clarity is a rarity.

Seriously.

"If you have more than 3 priorities, you have none."
—Jim Collins

This may sound harsh, but fuck your "shoulds".

I hear people say this all the time, I should do this or should do that.

No.

You need to cultivate the art of not shoulding all over yourself and feeling pride in your ability to happily say no to any and everything that doesn't move you towards the man you could be.

It's that simple.

"Don't be on your deathbed someday, having squandered your one chance at life, full of regret because you pursued little distractions instead of big dreams."
— Derek Sivers

In 10 years, you're not going to remember all those little actions you're taking day in and day out but you will be living with the RESULTS of whatever you're truly committed to.

You will almost certainly thank your former self for having the fortitude to fight through the fuzziness around who you could be and it's also an opportunity to give your future self a gift.

You won't remember procrastinating on doing whatever menial task 10 years from now, but knocking down that one thing that matters most each day will certainly reveal itself in where you'll be in 10 years.

Don't fall into the trap of using action as a distraction.

Get next-level clarity and commit to less in order to get the results of more.

That's how it works.

"If everyone has the same number of hours in the day, why do some people seem to get so much more done than others? How do they do more, achieve more, earn more, have more? If time is the currency of achievement, then why are some able to cash in their allotment for more chips than others?

The answer is they make getting to the heart of things the heart of their approach. They go small. Going small is ignoring all the things you could do and doing what you should do. It's recognizing that not all things matter equally and finding the things that matter most. It's a tighter way to connect what you do with what you want. It's realizing that extraordinary results are directly determined by how narrow you can make your focus."

— Gary Keller, The One Thing

Don't have clarity, be a rarity in your life.

This is both harder and easier than you think.

It's simple yet we're in an attention economy where so many have had their ability to hone in with singular focus on a single thing wrecked.

We're reaching for the phone, reaching for social media, reaching for distraction after distraction.

But this is a muscle just like anything else.

So while it feels difficult at first, once you've retrained yourself to only accept dedicated focus, that's what you'll get and that's what will change your life.

Your ability to focus on a single thing, repeatedly, is what will separate you from others.

Your ability to stick with something when it gets difficult.

While others will be distracting themselves with discursive actions, you'll be focused singularly on what you have made the decision to pursue.

You'll be making daily, incremental progress towards that goal.

It's not always sexy, but the results are always sexy.

Take the time to step back, to strategically analyze and then to move forward with a more narrowed and lasered focus.

Do this and watch just how fast your life will transform.

ACTION ITEMS

- What actions are you taking that are acting as distractions that don't move you towards your goals?
- How are you allowing priority dilution or creative avoidance to stop you from doing the things you know you need to do today in order to change the results you're getting in life?
- Take an hour — yes an entire hour — don't allow any interruptions, no cell phone, no stimulus and focus on your life, what you want, who you want to be, how you want to be, the things you want from life, and all the daily actions you're taking that aren't moving you towards that place and write them down.

- You need to create the space to give your life the attention it deserves. You've got to get off the distraction machine.
- How have you been allowing trivial actions that are casual in nature, that don't move the needle in your life, to act as little distractions to avoid doing the big things you know you should?
- How does that make you feel?
- Now use those feelings as fuel.

CHAPTER TWENTY-SEVEN

Better Questions Get Better Results

"The quality of your life is a direct reflection of the quality of the questions you are asking yourself."
– Tony Robbins, Awaken the Giant Within

"The way that you become world-class is by asking good questions."
– Tim Ferriss

When I first heard how important it is to ask better questions, I completely dismissed it. In my mind, I was already asking the best questions I could and it sounded like mumbo-jumbo garbage.

However, after going deep in the personal development space, I realize now that there is another level to asking questions and it's something so many people dismiss because of its seeming simplicity.

As Tony Robbins says, **"It's not the lack of resources, it's your lack of resourcefulness that stops you."**

In order to take massive strategic action, it's imperative to ask a better quality of question so you get a better quality of answer, otherwise, you may be doing what we just talked about and using action as a distraction which never leads to satisfaction.

When you start studying how incredibly successful people move through the world, you'll quickly see that they ask different levels of questions.

As the saying goes by Orson Scott Card, **"We question all our beliefs, except for the ones that we really believe in, and those we never think to question."**

Successful people know that one of their primary directives is to cut through what's real and what's not and asking what appear to be absurd questions on a surface level, ends up providing the keys to altering reality.

What do I mean by this?

If you think it's going to take you an entire year to lose 30 lbs and never stop to question it, it'll take the entire year to do that.

On the other hand, if you ask how you can do it in 90 days, you'll get a different answer.

You'll have to seek out greater resources because that's the constraint you've placed on it and since you know others have done it, you know it's entirely possible.

If you believe the only way to have financial stability is by working a job you hate for 40 years, then that's exactly what you'll get. On the flipside, if you ask how you can fire yourself from that job in the next 6 months and have a successful business of your own, that also becomes possible.

What you ask from the universe matters.

What you believe is possible matters.

This is why I tell people to entertain the idea that magic exists.

Once you start asking higher level questions, it's literally magical how fast your life can transform if you'll give yourself the permission to go there and then of course take massive strategic action towards that goal, shunning all else.

This is one of the most underrated superpowers out there and if you become a master at question-smithing, you'll be on your way to tapping into a greater source of power within yourself.

One of my favorite questions I heard years ago is from Peter Thiel —

"Take your 10-year plan and ask yourself, 'Why can I not achieve this in 6 months?'"

On the surface, that sounds absurd, right?

But, what if you actually spend the time to cut away all the stuff that doesn't matter then work relentlessly on this?

I can guarantee that you'll be further along than if you were working lackadaisically on a 10 year timeline.

"If you want confusion and heartache, ask vague questions. If you want uncommon clarity and results, ask uncommonly clear questions."
— Tim Ferriss

All these people get it.

My question is what will it take for you to get this?

This isn't a skill that's developed overnight, but it is a skill you can decide to master in this single moment.

You're on a journey to become the best possible version of yourself and it's time you started asking ridiculous questions so you can start living a ridiculous life.

As Grant Cardone said, **"The single biggest financial mistake I've made was not thinking big enough. I encourage you to go for more than a million. There is no shortage of money on this planet, only a shortage of people thinking big enough."**

Not asking big enough questions is one of the main reasons why you never get bigger results. When you start asking bigger and better questions, the results start becoming possible too.

Tim Ferriss has a blog post where he explores just this. It's titled — **Testing The "Impossible": 17 Questions That Changed My Life (#206).**

It's that relentless focus on asking different questions that opens up different possibilities.

In fact, that's why this very book exists and you're getting to read it right now.

I knew I wanted to do something else in my life yet didn't know how.

I looked around and saw life coaches not making the kind of money I wanted to, I saw how challenging it was to make it financially as an author and how long it took so many people to actually get where I wanted to go.

So naturally, I asked a different quality of question.

I sat down and started writing out questions and answers such as how could I help men in the way that I needed help when I was younger, and how could I do that in 6 months rather than 6 years?

Who else is out there doing the things I want to do in a successful manner and how can I model that while staying true to my purpose in this world?

And guess what?

Boom — answers like you wouldn't believe.

I had already committed. I knew I was destined to go down this path even though I didn't know HOW but that's the point — ask and you shall receive.

But, I didn't want this to take me 10 years.

I knew there was someone out there TODAY who needed to hear this message so I needed to ask better questions so I could work with the urgency and focus I needed to.

As Grant Cardone says, **"You be patient... I'm in a hurry."**

I'm in a hurry also and if you're in a hurry, one of the best things you can do to speed yourself along is to create the space to ask those high-level questions.

And it gets even better if you do it in a group setting. You'll be amazed at what people come up with if they're given permission to ask the most outlandish questions and then the results that they can achieve from that.

"Ask and you shall receive, but I'm sure it meant Ask intelligently. I'm sure that's what God meant. I'm sure he didn't mean Bitch and you will receive, Whine and you will receive. I don't think that was the instruction. To ask intelligently you'd have to ask specifically. Clarity is power. The more clear you are about exactly what it is you want, the more your brain knows how to get there."
— Tony Robbins

Rather than asking questions such as, "How can I quit my job in the future?" start getting granular with your questions such as:

How can I quit my job in the next 6 months and work for myself where I'm able to set my own hours, have financial freedom which looks like $20,000 per month in revenue, only work with people who make me a better person and enjoy the entire process?

It's this process of placing **constraints** on what you're asking that leads to clarity.

Define your dream job, such as location independence (meaning you can work from your laptop), only working with those you want to versus being forced to work with people who repeatedly choose misery, being able to work in a set time frame during the day rather than being on call 24/7, outsourcing all the parts of the job you either don't enjoy or aren't what you're most uniquely qualified to do.

Once you have these parameters in place, you've effectively narrowed your focus to a certain criteria of jobs. And if you say you want to be able to scale to $10 million per year in the next 5 years, that places a further constraint.

If you don't believe that's possible, well that's on you because there are plenty of examples out there of people who've done exactly that.

In your journey of taking massive strategic action, you must know what you're moving towards with absolute precision.

It's not enough to know what you're moving away from.

You can say you want to move away from wherever you're living, but if you don't have a destination, how do you book a plane ticket?

You can't.

You need to know the precise destination and the precise time you want to arrive.

Which means you're saying no to all the other times of arrival, to all the other things you could do so that you can do that exact ONE thing.

There is clarity in saying no.

I get it, you don't always have a clear map or destination.

Perhaps you feel like you're surrounded by fog but you visualize this big mountain in the distance and you're going to have to sort of stumble around until you get there.

But just like fog, you have to move towards it a little bit and then you'll be able to see another 20 feet in front of you.

You may not know the entire journey but you know enough to get to the next step and that's what's important.

Questions are your guides along the way to ensure you're operating from a place of clarity rather than murkiness.

If you feel like you're underwater or not showing up how you could be, it's time to start asking a better quality of question so that you can start getting the results you know you could in life.

Clarity is power and high quality questions lead to clarity.

Powerful men ask powerful questions.

ACTION ITEMS

- What questions could you ask from life that you haven't been asking?
- What questions could you ask to ensure you have absolute clarity so that when you take action, you know it's specific and focused?

- What parameters have you been leaving out of these questions that could help you further narrow them down?
- If you look at your questions, and ask how you could 10X those instead, what might that look like?
    - There is less competition when you set 10X goals because everyone else is setting "realistic" goals which makes them far more crowded. Go where others are not with big, audacious goals and they're generally easier than trying to compete on the lower-level goals with everyone else.
    - These also often require a similar amount of energy to complete yet are far more energizing because they are far more exciting and audacious.
    - It also rules out 98% of other possible options leaving you with only the best, high-level results remaining.
    - Lastly, most people set small goals and achieve them simply because they don't currently know how to go about achieving the larger goal. Don't be that person.

    As Robert Brault says:

    "We are kept from our goal not by obstacles but by a clear path to a lesser goal."

CHAPTER TWENTY-EIGHT

Design Your Results

"I have been called a lot of things due to my commitment to action – a workaholic, obsessive, greedy, never satisfied, driven, and even maniac... I have never had someone who is more successful than I am considering my excessive action to be a bad thing – because successful people know firsthand what it takes to achieve this kind of success."
– Grant Cardone

"The truth is, if you are not putting in the time, effort and energy every single day, someone else is."
– Ed Mylett

Results are all that matter.

All the things we've covered up until this point are finally coalescing into focused, relentless strategic action.

All of these tenets come into play here in your quest to become that next version of yourself and your ability to bring them all together is imperative for your success.

We covered in the last two chapters the importance of not getting stuck in the distraction of action, getting absolute clarity on what those results look like and how to ask better questions to hone in on that vision.

In order to avoid the take-massive-action hamster wheel that keeps you stuck, I'm going to dissect the importance of designing the results you want and how to tie it all together so that you get 10X results in your life.

The first step in this process is to get as clear as possible on where you're trying to go and who you're going to be.

That's not always easy because you don't know what you don't know and sometimes you haven't even fully fleshed out exactly what that is.

But, this first and foremost means placing **constraints** on what you're willing to tolerate and not tolerate in your life.

When I first started down the path that I'm on now, I knew I wanted to help other men who were struggling how I once had. I wanted to provide them with a sort of roadmap or cheat codes for life that I'd never had, but I had no idea how I was going to do that.

At first, I thought I'd do a digital course on mindset. What I learned as I progressed in my knowledge was that my vision and what I was trying to do was far greater than that. I learned that who I am destined to become is also much greater. So naturally, I adapted and expanded my vision.

I got as clear as I could based on the limited information I had at the time and as I got more information, I continued seeking clarity.

This is what I call engaging the **action-iteration feedback loop**.

You have to take action, then step back, assess the feedback you've received from that and what you've learned, integrate that, and then take more action.

If you don't actively assess the feedback life is giving you, you're not going to progress nearly as fast.

Think of this like you're a football player. You're going to go play a game then watch hours of footage over and over again on that game, dissecting all the mistakes you made, then practicing to clean those up, then play another game.

That's how the pros do it, while the amateurs just keep on practicing and playing without cleaning up the sloppy mistakes.

You're trying to be a PROFESSIONAL on all levels so start acting like it and heavily engaging the action-iteration feedback loop.

Action is great but again, the most important thing is results which requires action + learning simultaneously and being truthful about that feedback so you're constantly moving towards the results you're after.

Along with that is to decide how you're going to **measure your progress**. If your goal is to lose 30 lbs and you spend all day cleaning the garage and doing miscellaneous shit that prevents you from going to the gym, you may get to the end of the day and feel like you were really productive yet you also failed in your larger goal.

We talked about this before – having non-negotiable standards and setting metrics by which you're going to live your life.

You have to get clear on how you're going to assess feedback and what that looks like.

The next step in taking massive strategic action is to **chunk down** the exact steps you know right now that you need to take in order to get where you're going or become who you're trying to become.

If your goal is to start your own company, that can be an overwhelming process until you break it down into daily steps that you must take in order to get it off the ground in the timeframe you've allotted.

You have to design the results you want, then create a step-by-step roadmap for yourself as clearly as possible, then put in the fucking work.

One thing I see people fall into here is getting too caught up in the planning and not actually doing the work.

You have to be fast.

You can't spend a month working on this.

I know I'm talking about these steps and getting absolute clarity, but you also have to avoid getting stuck there.

The faster you can move, the faster the action-iteration feedback loop works and the faster your life will transform.

And here's something that stops people for some reason — they believe they should automatically be good at whatever new endeavor they're after.

That's ridiculous.

You're always going to suck at something when you first do it compared to yourself having done it for 3 years.

Why would you ever have any other sort of expectations?

Part of the beauty is that you get to grow, to expand from where you are to a state of mastery.

This is why adopting the mindset of the learner is so important, because you're not taking it personally.

Of course you're going to suck whenever you first do something but you also know you're going to get better so the faster you do it, the faster you're going to get better.

The next step here is to **optimize for design**, not necessarily discipline.

While I believe discipline is fundamentally important, the ability to get yourself to do the things you've committed to doing even when you don't feel like it, I also believe it's important to realize you only have so much willpower in the day.

The most successful people understand this and optimize for it.

Oftentimes, **design trumps discipline**.

What do I mean by this?

If the top five people you hang around all go to the gym, and are asking you to go to the gym with them, you're far less likely to need that willpower to push through and go compared to if your top five people are all asking you to go get drinks instead.

If you wake up every morning to the smell of freshly baked donuts that are sitting on the kitchen counter, you're far more likely to give in compared to if they're not there and you'd have to go out of your way to acquire them.

Too many people understand this principle yet dismiss it, but it's a critical lynchpin here.

These are the same people who believe if they just work harder then they'll eventually get where they want to go.

WRONG!

If you keep doing the same things over and over again, you're likely going to keep getting the same result.

"We can not solve our problems with the same level of thinking that created them."
— Albert Einstein

There are plenty of people working extremely hard making $60K a year and plenty of other people working at that same level making $6 million per year.

Hard work doesn't guarantee success.

You must be strategic in life, have a plan and work that plan.

And when you have that plan and truly understand how imperative it is to optimize for design, that's exactly what you'll do.

Don't try to discipline your way through a poor design.

If your environment is constantly causing you to deplete your willpower over trivial bullshit, well you already know what you need to do.

CUT RUTHLESSLY all that which is not serving your goals.

Seriously.

If it's not providing 10X returns, then why is it in your life? You could have something else that **IS** providing 10X returns if you'll just have the courage to cut away that which is not.

For most people, they can cut 50% or more of things from their life that aren't adding extreme value.

"Don't hold on to someone who's leaving, otherwise you won't meet the one who's coming."
— Carl Jung

"I've enjoyed a lot of the women that have come into my life through the years. I've also enjoyed it when most of them left at some point also."
– Michael Carrigan

If you're focused on designing the results you want in life, ask your future self who they'd be hanging around in 5 years, how that person would need to think to be where they're at and exactly the type of person they'd need along with characteristics, values, et cetera to embody that vision.

Would that person go from making $100K per year to $10 MILLION per year by hanging around the same dumb-ass people?

Probably not.

So why are you trying to hold on to your limitations?

Why are you trying to hold on and argue for that which holds you back?

Either those people have a similar desire and are encouraging and helping you get there or they're not.

Either way is fine, but it's important to stop lying to yourself and to be truthful about this.

This is part of being a modern, masculine man.

It takes strength to have this level of mental fortitude.

It takes strength to overcome your weaknesses and that's also where all the growth occurs.

None of the stuff in this book matters if you don't take action on it.

Simultaneously, if you take a bunch of action yet don't apply the stuff in this book, what are you going to get?

These are principles of life for a reason.

These are timeless and universal.

"If the ladder is not leaning against the right wall, every step we take just gets us to the wrong place faster."
— Stephen Covey

Strategy matters just as much as the action. The two are **yolked** and your ability to implement the action-iteration feedback loop makes all the difference in how quickly you progress.

"I'm not a 'self-made millionaire'. I'm a team-made millionaire. Other people helped me get there. Nobody does anything great alone."
— Ed Mylett

Lastly, if you're struggling with these principles, with implementing this into your life, get some **accountability**.

Get a friend who will help hold you accountable.

If you want to level it up, get a coach.

All the top people in the world have coaches.

Entertainers, athletes, celebrities, financial traders, real estate agents, mortgage brokers — you name it. The top people all have coaches and not just in their field but in many different fields.

They may have health coaches, financial coaches, career coaches, accountability coaches, strategic design coaches.

There's a reason for this and a reason they're all willing to pay hundreds of thousands or millions of dollars per year for these coaches.

Paul Tudor Jones, a financial trader who made a half a BILLION dollars in one day famously paid and still may pay Tony Robbins a MILLION dollars per year to be his coach.

I've spent thousands upon thousands of dollars for coaches, courses and to simply be in the room with other like-minded people who had similar values.

That's one of the fastest ways to hack leveling up and meet the people you need in your life compared to trying to source your friends from who you meet at a job or at the local gym.

"Massive thoughts must be followed by massive actions. There is nothing ordinary about the 10X Rule. It is simply what it says it is: 10 times the thoughts and 10 times the actions of other people...You never do what others do. You must be willing to do what they won't do – and even take actions that you might deem "unreasonable".
— Grant Cardone

If you want to truly design the results you want in life, get around other people who have either done that or who are also attempting to do that very thing.

If everyone around you accepts MEDIOCRITY, you're more likely to accept it.

If you're surrounded by nothing but EXCEPTIONALISM, you're more likely to end up exceptional as well.

A last word on **CONSTRAINTS**.

"Would you tell me, please, which way I ought to go from here?"
"That depends a good deal on where you want to get to," said the Cat.
"I don't much care where ..." said Alice.

"Then it doesn't matter which way you go," said the Cat.
—LEWIS CARROLL, Alice in Wonderland

I coach a lot of men who struggle to find what they're truly after in life. Starting with constraints of what you wish your life to look like is incredibly helpful.

For me, I believe that 10X is easier than 2X.

As Tim Ferriss says in The 4-Hour Workweek:

"Doing the Unrealistic Is Easier Than Doing the Realistic."
"Ninety-nine percent of people in the world are convinced they are incapable of achieving great things, so they aim for the mediocre. The level of competition is thus fiercest for "realistic" goals, paradoxically making them the most time- and energy-consuming. It is easier to raise $1,000,000 than it is $100,000. It is easier to pick up the one perfect 10 in the bar than the five 8s.
"If you are insecure, guess what? The rest of the world is, too. Do not overestimate the competition and underestimate yourself. You are better than you think."

Lifestyle design is about saying NO to all the extraneous things that don't serve you, placing constraints on your options so that you ONLY focus on 10X possibilities and that narrows your potential vehicles substantially.

So what does this look like in action?

- I'm not going to entertain any vertical (specific niche market) that doesn't have the possibility of making at least $1,000,000 within the first 24 month period and won't generate at least that per year indefinitely. It also needs to have the capacity to reach 8 figures of revenue per year minimum.

- I require any new avenue I pursue to be locationless or able to be done from my laptop so I have near total freedom in where I live.
    - A caveat is selected speaking gigs, in-person podcasting, et cetera but on an approval only basis that doesn't comprise the majority of my cashflow.
- I don't currently want to manage a large team, so it must be capable of scaling with automation and outsourcing to other companies so I'm not needing to micromanage my business.
- I must own the business, not have it own me.
- I must be able to take care of business duties within 10 hours per week so I spend the majority of my time doing what I'm best at such as coaching, consulting, developing content, learning new things, et cetera so that I can better serve my community.
- I only work with those who are coachable, have a desire to grow and have a good attitude.
- I only accept opportunities where I'm celebrated and do not engage ventures disguised as "opportunities" where I'm truthfully only tolerated.
- I only pursue opportunities where I feel like I can deliver 10X more value than the price I charge for services.
- I only work with those who also want to be a force for good in the world, to live into their potential, to be the men they always knew they could be.
- In all these pursuits, I must focus on becoming the man I know I could be and these are simply vehicles to help me actualize that

purpose – to be a beacon for possibility, for encouragement, for empowerment, for betterment, for the transformation that's possible in life.

See how that works?

By creating CONSTRAINTS, I narrow the potential avenues.

So many men have too many options. It's the paradox of choice. You don't need more options, you need less that are more congruent with the man you wish to be and the life you wish to build.

You don't have to even know the exact vehicle, you need to simply identify constraints, even ones that seem ridiculous or impossible in nature.

Once you do this and commit to finding a way to make it happen, you'll be amazed as answers start pouring into your life on exactly how to make that a reality.

To close, massive strategic action isn't necessarily like: I need to make 100 sales calls today.

Instead, it may look like — how do I build a funnel and webinar so I can sell to 100 people at a time?

There are levels to the game of life and once you decide to work your way up them and start leveling up, you'll realize there is a whole world out there you never even realized.

I believe you have greatness within you, and a key to unlocking it is taking massive, strategic action. Every. Single. Day.

ACTION ITEMS

- Begin with the end in mind — what are the results you're after?

    - If you don't know, start with constraints and tighten. Remember, your job is to say NO to all that doesn't have 10X returns.

- What does a step-by-step process look like for taking you there?
- How could you improve the design of your environment so that it supported you in this result?
- What steps can you take now, today, to start down that path?
- What do you need to cut from your life in order to support this result and not drain your willpower?
- Who do you need to find in order to help support you in this goal? A group of guys? A coach? A mentor?

CONCLUSION

"Every single successful person has had to face moments when there was no reason or logic that indicated they should continue, zero motivation and inspiration. Still, they showed up and put one foot in front of the other anyway."

– Ed Mylett

At some point, all the biggest names in the world took an **unreasonable** amount of action.

They decided to change their lives and then paid the price in order to do that.

They decided to change the legacy of their entire bloodline by showing up in what appeared to others as unreasonable and even maniacal action takers.

This is what you must do.

I believe in you and the man you can become.

That dude is in there, just waiting to emerge, for you to step up and do what you know you must in order to become that version of yourself.

Here's a transcription from a clip I heard by Ed Mylett on doing just that.

For the original clip, here is the link.

https://www.youtube.com/watch?v=0Ko2YXrIpIE&ab_channel=kingoftalk

*Emphasis my own.

"You meet somebody wealthy,

Their family at one point was not wealthy,

And then the ONE shows up.

One person changes the family tree forever.

In my family I'm the ONE.

And it wasn't because I wanted it or hoped for it,

I fought for it.

I want to fight for my family.

I want my mom and dad proud of me.

I want to be proud of me.

I want to look in the mirror and be happy with the man I look back at.

That he gave it everything, that he went for it.

That's what I want for you.

I want you to be happy with you. Not cool.

I've seen all kinds of cool guys my whole career.

Cool guys go BROKE.

They have a good two or three years.

Players who implement strategies that get focused and intense,

They win decades.

You have to win year after year after year.

I'm almost 50 years old man,

I've got a loaded calendar.

I'm after it.

I'm not casual.

I want to win.

WAKE UP!

You want to win?

You want to be a millionaire?

You got to quit being so casual.

You walk slow.

You implement things slowly.

You talk a good game like you're going to be somebody.

Business is a sport, it's competitive.

You got to get FOCUSED and get in a HURRY.

Wake up Brother.

If you make some of these adjustments man, you could change your life.

You could change your family forever.

It's not casual.

You could change the chapters in the book of your life if you want to.

You're the author.

It might be year two, three, four before you get your big win.

But you could DECIDE now, I'm going to walk, talk, and be a different person.

You're the lead character in the story of your life.

But too many of you let what I call the "extras" of life dictate where you're going.

Y'all hear me?

Here's the truth — most people's dreams can be bought.

With enough failure, they will sell their children's dreams.

They can't still fight with a little success or a whole bunch of failure,

Most people will sell their WILL to win

Some of you have sold it because you're making a little bit of money,

You don't work like you did when you were making nothing.

Some of you will sell your win for some failure,

You're probably buyable.

But if you decide my will cannot be bought.

I will keep fighting for my family,

I'm the ONE,

I'm going to change my family tree forever.

Decide now.

You're gonna keep negotiating the price or can you NOT be bought?"

I believe in you. DECIDE right now. Make the decision to believe in yourself and become the ONE.

PILLAR VIII

Be The Best Man You Could Be

INTRO

"It is my firm belief that the best way to fix the world—
a handyman's dream, if ever there was one—is to fix yourself.
Anything else is presumptuous."
— Jordan Peterson

"Man is made or unmade by himself. By the right choice he ascends.
As a being of power, intelligence, and love, and the commander of
his own thoughts, he holds the key to every situation."
- James Allen

This is the final section and it's time to tie this all together.

Ultimately, this book is about unlocking the greatness that resides within you and actually becoming the man you could be.

You know you have more potential, you know you're leaving pieces on the table, you know you can get your life in better order and be a better version of yourself.

Hopefully by this point, you have a set of tools that will help you actually implement the things you need to in order to become that version of yourself.

There are plenty of people out there who talk about being a "good" man or what makes a "real" man.

I don't give a shit about any of that.

I do care about helping you become the best version of yourself, whatever that may look like.

I do care about helping you to become good at being a man, however you choose to define that.

I believe this last step is critical to acknowledge, to declare to yourself and the world what you're after.

It's not easy to be the man you could be.

It's not a walk in the park.

It's a dedication.

It's a lifelong pursuit towards excellence and mastery.

It's a commitment towards yourself and others and this world.

It's you standing up and acknowledging that you have a role to play and you're going to accept that duty and responsibility voluntarily.

"A man who is more concerned with being a good man than being good at being a man makes a very well-behaved slave."
— GARRETT J WHITE, BE THE MAN

Once you can acknowledge and integrate these things into you, you'll stop having unrealistic expectations that at some point life will be easy.

That you shouldn't have any problems.

That you should just accept mediocrity and comfort in lieu of the man you could actually sculpt yourself into.

That you should simply sacrifice that which you could be for a bit of empty, soul-sucking temporary distraction.

This is about greatness and you have greatness within you if you'll commit to it.

Commit to that and you commit to being LEGENDARY!

CHAPTER TWENTY-NINE

Become More Than Yourself

There is a paradox of being a man. While I believe we're all motivated by selfish desires, in order for us to reach our highest potential, those desires intrinsically turn out to be for others more than ourselves.

When you live life passionately there comes a point where you find you can only muster so much passion for yourself alone.

It's tempting at times to believe that a man is a castle unto himself and that he alone can conquer the world with no other means or motivations.

However, that's never true.

You're not only playing the game for yourself but for others as well and when you embrace that, you become far more powerful, far more motivated, far more devoted.

Oftentimes in my conversations with other males who are attempting to discern what it means to actually be a man, they will describe how they're attempting to reach self-actualization — some bullshit state where they'll reach "enlightenment".

Firstly, I'm not certain how to define "enlightenment" and if that's something you're after or think you've achieved it then God bless, more power to you. I just can't comment on that.

I relegate my expertise to trying to be the best version of myself possible and helping other men do the same.

I'm all for "self-actualization" in a sense, however, the problem I see so many run into is actually an EXCESSIVE focus on self, an excessive focus on me, me, me and this leads them to misery and coincidentally being less actualized.

They continue down the solipsistic path thinking that if they can just give themselves enough "self-care" or introspection or focus that their problems will somehow disappear and that they'll somehow reach this theoretical state.

It's bullshit.

You have to master yourself, to understand the principles, but excessively focusing on yourself does not lead to an "enlightened" place.

The truth of self-actualization is that this state most occurs when you're in the SERVICE OF OTHERS.

There is a sense of self-transcendence when your mission is larger than yourself, when you are no longer the most important thing and instead you're more than yourself.

According to Viktor Frankl:

"By declaring that man is responsible and must actualize the potential meaning of his life, I wish to stress that the true meaning of life is to be discovered in the world rather than within man or his own psyche, as though it were a closed system. I have termed this constitutive characteristic "the self-transcendence of human existence." It denotes the fact that being human always points, and is directed, to something or someone, other than oneself--be it a meaning to fulfill or another human

being to encounter. The more one forgets himself--by giving himself to a cause to serve or another person to love--the more human he is and the more he actualizes himself. What is called self-actualization is not an attainable aim at all, for the simple reason that the more one would strive for it, the more he would miss it. In other words, self-actualization is possible only as a side-effect of self-transcendence."

And of course this is paradoxical as we're all motivated by selfish desires, yet in another sense, as we selfishly desire to become the most we can, at some point we understand that the only way to do this is through a sense of service to others.

One of the core things I see young males struggling with today is their constant focus on themselves, constantly focusing on how they could be happier, or could get this new thing or that thing without considering others in the least.

This myopic and self-centered approach keeps them perpetually stuck and wondering why they feel empty and unable to become the man they know they could be.

One of the quickest ways to solve this is to simply recontextualize and move your focus outside of yourself.

You're broke and can't find the motivation to get off the couch for yourself?

Do it for your family.

Don't have a family yet?

Do it for your future family.

Ask yourself how you would act if you did care for yourself and love yourself — then do that!

Here's another thing, selfishness has to be taken in the **context of time.**

Things can be all about you today but how does that affect future you?

What about you in 20 years?

While I believe we're all selfishly motivated to a degree, when you can expand that time horizon, you become infinitely more powerful.

This is why someone who can be committed to their 10 year vision will outlast someone who can only conceptualize a one year vision.

That person who is selfish about not compromising on that 10 year vision has a ridiculous advantage over the other person who either can't be selfish enough to have the assertiveness necessary to stay committed to that or when that person is simply caught up in selfish desires that are immediate in nature such as eating that cake now at the expense of their future self in 6 months.

Again, you see how important timelines are and your ability to harness them is critical to success.

This is part of becoming the man you could be. If life is all about you, it turns out not to be nearly as fulfilling compared to if it's all about us.

It's not necessary to be able to articulate all the nuances about relationships, why they're important, why it's important for you to live in a manner congruent with fulfilling your soul — it's only important that you actually do it.

You ultimately service your heart by serving others at a high level.

That can be simultaneously selfish and fulfilling.

Look at all the people out there today sacrificing immensely in order to serve others, to help make the world a better place how they see fit.

Part of that is their idealism and the other part is the fact that they wouldn't be able to look at themselves in the mirror if they didn't do it.

These things aren't mutually exclusive.

While we all understand many of the things that are associated with traditional masculinity such as being a provider, a protector, a leader and a sense of strength for those around him, I believe there is more to it than I can adequately articulate here.

There is a calling in your soul, something deep inside you, a whisper from the universe about how you need to live, about who you could be, about actualizing the greatness that resides within you.

Only you can decide your purpose.

Only you can decide THE MAN you want to be.

Only you can decide what it means to be more than yourself,

To rise above who you are and voluntarily adopt the mantle of who you could be.

To be legendary.

Each of us has stages in life.

Many males stay in the entirely selfish stage where they have no greater purpose and life is entirely about them.

Many other males adopt traditional roles where they abdicate their selfishness to take on a faux role of serving others by sacrificing self. This is where they're emasculated, unappreciated and find that they've signed on to serve a false ideology that doesn't actually turn out to be on-purpose for them and the life they desire or who they could be.

A select few understand that they can simultaneously be selfish while also serving a cause much larger than themselves.

They understand that if they don't take care of themselves, then they can't adequately serve their larger mission.

They understand that they're far more powerful if they love themselves fully and therefore take care of themselves adequately so that they can fully commit to their purpose and mission in life.

They understand that the mission is a higher calling and in order to fully pursue it, they must fully align with that.

They understand that life is about more than themselves and in order to navigate it appropriately, they have to be the best version of themselves possible.

These are the MEN who live for a greater purpose, who are inspirational to their children and I don't mean in the way that children always idolize their parents. I mean in a way where they see their father not giving up on his dreams, living on purpose, having integrity and doing the things he needs to be doing.

There is something magical about that.

This concept is a dance yet I believe an important one.

Too many think life has to be one way or the other.

It doesn't.

You can be selfish while also being more than yourself simultaneously.

Think of the fireman who runs inside a burning building knowing there's only a 1% chance he's going to live.

He has no choice.

Selfishly, he wouldn't be able to live with himself if he did any other thing.

He also knows it's not all about him, there are people who need saving and he has a duty to himself.

He must maintain the honor he has within his soul.

Selfish and selfless simultaneously.

However, let's say there's a 100% chance of death and also a 100% of certainty that he's not going to be able to save anyone.

Selfishly, he has to weigh this and understand that if he goes in that building, then he condemns the potential victims in future fires by making a useless sacrifice.

It's a dance, nuanced and one only you can decide is right for you.

Look, I've said it before and I'll say it again – I'm not the morality police here.

I'm only attempting to articulate the conversation you need to have with yourself in order to get in alignment so that you're living in congruence with who you want to be.

That's part of greatness.

We all know that when we have something larger than ourselves driving us, we become infinitely more powerful.

Infinitely more dangerous and focused.

Yes it's selfish, but it's also selfless.

And since your purpose is to become the best man you possibly can be, you need both in order to fully become that man.

This conversation is important because so many want to water men down, tell you that you are evil for being selfish, that you're somehow toxic for wanting to become the best version of yourself that you can.

FUCK THAT!

I vehemently disagree.

The best thing you can do in life is to become strong, to have courage, to have honor, to become the best possible version of yourself and to direct all that you are towards something greater than yourself.

Be selfish.

Be strong.

Be unwavering.

Be unfazed by all life throws at you.

Be who you know you could be.

Tap into that greatness that you know is within you.

Become the man you know you can be and be unrelenting in that pursuit.

BE LEGENDARY, MOTHERFUCKER!

ACTION ITEMS

- How have you been neglecting yourself by trying to avoid being "selfish"?
- How could being "selfish" about your mission help propel you rather than trying to be a good little boy and be "selfless"?
- If you were to become the strongest, most capable, most competent version of yourself possible, how would that benefit all those around you?

- For those who would criticize you becoming this version of yourself, who would criticize your selfish desires to become this version of yourself, you know what you need to do with them.
- How could becoming the strongest, most capable, most competent version of yourself serve something greater in life, in a far more profound way, rather than if you were weak, incapable and incompetent?

CHAPTER THIRTY

Mind Your Intentions

In the pursuit to be the man you could be, it's critical to not only look at your intentions but also the results those are going to get.

So many men want to focus on being a "good" man rather than being good at being the man they're trying to be.

You can have the best of intentions and those intentions lead to incredibly dark places.

My grandparents on my father's side had good intentions for their children. They coddled them, didn't allow them to experience the world how it truly is and never truly let them fail. As a result, they're all hampered in who they could be rather than actually going out and being a force for good in the world. Neither of my aunts have worked an actual job, whether for someone else or themselves, in over 25 years.

That's astounding.

They were both highly capable and intelligent women who completely abdicated all responsibility in life, gave up on themselves and never had the courage to become who they could've been.

They're debilitated adults as a result of **good intentions.**

My father was forced to shoulder far more responsibility as both a man and someone who chose to have seven children, yet even still, because of this coddling he never truly went out and chased his goals or became the man I believe he has the potential to be.

There was always a safety net. Always the whisper of comfort, of inheriting the wealth my grandparents had amassed and my father helped to build. So instead, he chose to sit and wait on that rather than simply going and making his own mark on the world and building his own fortune.

You can have good intentions telling your kids they can be anything that they want to be, but if you're sitting there having totally given up on yourself, then what do you think they're going to model?

Intentions aren't enough.

To be the man you could be, you have to be cognizant and can't capitulate to other's definitions of what a "good" man is.

You have to decide and then become that person.

I heard Andrew Tate say, **"You build your value as a man."**

No one else is going to build that value for you.

Only you can do the work.

Only you can decide what's worth building or not building.

And struggles are to be sought after.

You don't build your value by taking the easy or comfortable path.

Oftentimes, we're told to be softer, to be more compassionate, to be more comfortable yet that doesn't lead to where you want to go most times.

Just watch the PragerU video on YouTube — Why The Road to Hell is Paved with Good Intentions. Here's the link:

https://www.youtube.com/watch?v=Fu11dLnlNOE&ab_channel=PragerU

There is value in struggle.

There is value in overcoming obstacles and building yourself into who you could be.

Intentions aren't enough though.

I know plenty of people who've had the intention of doing exactly that for a decade now yet still haven't built themselves into a person they love and respect.

If you're not getting those results or if the results lead to a darker place, then you have to get critical with yourself and stop hiding from the fact that what you're doing isn't working to build you into the man you desire to be.

It's important to look at where we're at in the world today and to ask what's real and not real.

We're being told that eating animals is harming the planet.

That drinking soy "milk" (which we all know is bullshit and as I said before, isn't even allowed to be referred to as "milk" in certain countries) is somehow healthier than something we've eaten for thousands upon thousands of years.

That slaving for someone else for 40 years is a dream to be sought after.

That sickness and disease is normal.

That "dad" bods are actually more desirable than being physically capable and fit and something to be proud of.

That being able to chug beer and name off stats of your favorite sports team is actually more important than being capable and competent in whatever endeavor you're pursuing.

You and I both know that you were put on this planet for more than that.

You and I both know you have a greater capacity than to sell yourself short for a little comfort.

"Those who would give up essential Liberty, to purchase a little temporary Safety, deserve neither Liberty nor Safety."
— Benjamin Franklin

Supposedly "good" intentions sound nice on the surface yet as history shows, they can lead to horrible atrocities over the long-term.

I believe it takes strong, competent and capable men to stand up against these seemingly "good" intentions in a world where these virtues are ridiculed.

In order to do that, it's imperative to recognize just what type of man is capable of doing that. To quote a segment between Jordan Peterson and Joe Rogan:

Peterson: "You should be a monster. You know, cause everyone says

'well you should be harmless, virtuous, you shouldn't do anyone any harm, you should sheath your competitive instinct, you shouldn't try to win, you know, you don't want to be too aggressive, you don't want to be too assertive, you want to take a back seat in all of that.'

It's like – NO

Wrong

You should be a monster, an absolute monster,

And then you should learn how to control it.

Rogan: "Do you know the expression: it's better to be a warrior in a garden, than a gardener in a war."

Peterson: "Right, right. Exactly. That's exactly it.

And that's exactly right.

So when I tell young men that, they think... well lots of them are competitive, they're low in agreeableness, you know, cause that's part of being competitive temperamentally.

So is there something wrong with being competitive?

There's nothing wrong with it.

There's something wrong with cheating.

There's something wrong with being a tyrant.

There's something wrong with winning unfairly.

All of those things are bad.

But you don't want people to win?

What's the difference between trying to win and striving?

You want to eradicate striving?"

https://www.youtube.com/watch?v=04zsJa5wd0Y&ab_channel=Kalevra

It's this tension, this competitiveness, this threat of potential malevolence that keeps individuals and society civil.

This is why I say to mind your intentions.

It's not enough to have the intentions to be a "good" man.

The RESULTS your intentions get in life MUST reflect accurately, otherwise you run the risk of trodding a very dark path.

Marxism sounded like it had good intentions yet resulted in hundreds of millions of deaths.

If you spoke to many Germans in 1936, they would have extolled the "good intentions" of the Nazi party, yet we also saw where that led.

There are supposedly "good intentions" to allowing eighteen year olds to take out thousands or hundreds of thousands of dollars worth of debt to get a degree they can't wipe their ass with afterwards yet I speak to many men who're still paying that off in their 40's and 50's and would've been better off with a trade.

You can't be naive.

You can't be incapable of assertiveness.

You must be capable of striving, of standing up when you see something in the world that doesn't make sense, and you must have the well-developed wisdom to be able to actually discern when that is so, compared to the man who lacks these traits.

Let me ask you, does a naive fool who has good intentions that result in catastrophe truly have good intentions?

If we're taking full responsibility, then wouldn't intentions need to be yoked to results?

And if results were a catastrophe, then wouldn't that reflect the original underlying intention to be incompetent, incapable, naive and a fool?

Otherwise, this person would have done whatever necessary to actually alter these traits, to change their behavior, to develop themselves into a competent, capable, sophisticated man of wisdom.

Many find this harsh yet if you're going to navigate the world appropriately, working to become the absolute best version of yourself is critical to actually getting the results you desire.

We understand that the world can be a difficult place and that's part of the nature of the world.

We understand that while it seems "nice" to help others, it's also imperative we let them have their struggles, otherwise they'll fail to become the person they could be.

In Jordan Peterson's 42 rules for life, the 24th and 25th rules read as follows:

> 24. Do not try to rescue someone who does not want to be rescued
>
> 25. And be very careful about rescuing someone who does

This is a prime example of minding intentions.

While it can be incredibly tempting as a man and protector to wish to rescue someone, to wish to alleviate whatever is going on in their life, it's also important to separate your intentions from results.

I've been here many times in my own life and found that rather than rescuing, I simply ended up prolonging, enabling, and encouraging unacceptable behavior.

I had "good" intentions, but they led to shitty results and why is this important?

Because I wasn't the best man I could be in those circumstances.

If I had been a stronger, more capable, more competent, more wise man, I would've been able to see and understand this and then do what is sometimes painful, which is to allow people to learn the lessons they need to without me intervening.

I know this seems like a tangential topic, but I truly believe this is one of the easiest areas for us to get sucked into and then go off-purpose.

It gives us a cheap sense of importance, of fulfillment, of doing "good" in the world without the actual results matching our "intentions".

In order to be the best man you could be, you'll need all that we've covered up until this point.

Being a force for good in the world means having the perspicacity to recognize the end result of whatever it is you're after.

It means having a base understanding of humans, of human nature to therefore be able to extrapolate and do what's necessary.

"What one does is what counts. Not what one had the intention of doing."
— Pablo Picasso

Mind your intentions.

The goal here is to live a highly intentional life where your results also align with those intentions.

It's imperative to be highly intentional while also having the capacity to understand what is truly necessary to get the end result of those intentions.

As we've covered, results are all that matter.

The best of intentions can lead to only imagined hells unless those are tempered through a degree of wisdom and an appropriate emphasis is placed on the desired outcome.

ACTION ITEMS

- What are 5 examples of times when you've had "good" intentions that have led to undesired and less than satisfactory outcomes?
- If you had been a better man, more capable, more full of understanding, how easy would it have been to make different decisions to get more satisfactory outcomes?
- How can you align your intentions with results today so that you learn to not only have good intentions but to measure those intentions by the results they produce?
- If you were to become a monster, then learn to control it, what would that look like?
    - Would you need to train? To work on emotional regulation? To work on assertiveness? To work on discernment and wisdom? To work on being capable of malevolence even though you NEVER wish to actually wield it?
- How can you develop yourself into a monster that you also have control over?

CHAPTER THIRTY-ONE

Become The Most Capable, Confident, Competent and Strongest Man You Could Be

"There is only one way to avoid criticism: do nothing, say nothing, and be nothing."
— Aristotle

"For every reason it's not possible, there are hundreds of people who have faced the same circumstances and succeeded."
— Jack Canfield

The destination after all we've covered is for you to ultimately be the most capable, confident, competent and strongest man you can be.

That's power.

That's what will make you a powerful man and a force to be reckoned with in the world.

The entire basis for all we've covered is to emphasize and focus on the fundamentals in life.

If you do these things well, then whatever else you want will be yours assuming you're willing to do the work and make the necessary sacrifices for it.

The first step to becoming powerful is to gain power over yourself, to gain mastery over yourself and your life, in your ability to hit the goals you desire and actually develop goals worth desiring, to do the things you say you're going to do, to keep your commitments and not negotiate with yourself on these things.

As the last principle here, "become the best man you could be" is an edict for you to step up in your life, for yourself, for others, for all that's within you.

Like the rest of what we've covered, it may seem trivial, however it's anything but that.

Most men never take the time to acknowledge this, to articulate it, to declare it to the universe that they want to be the most capable, confident, competent and strongest version of themselves possible.

It's powerful when you acknowledge this though.

It's powerful when you set this as your target for WHO you are choosing to become.

As a man, I view it as my duty to become the best version of myself, whatever that may look like.

There are plenty of people out there who will try to tell you what a man is, what makes a "good" man, what makes a "real" man, and if you want to hear that, then go seek those people out.

I'm here to encourage YOU to define those things, to encourage you to inspect your life appropriately so that you decide who the best man you can be is and more importantly to encourage you to simply focus on being good at being a man, whatever that is to you.

There are plenty of social media gurus who will tell you to give up all vices such as alcohol or smoking or whatever, to wake up at 4AM, to take cold showers, to meditate for 20 minutes, to journal for 20 minutes, to hit an infrared sauna for 20 minutes and there is some merit to that depending on who you are and your circumstances, however, I'm not convinced this is the appropriate solution for everyone and it's important to allow nuance.

Plus, I've done this and spent inordinate amounts of time doing all these things that made me feel productive yet didn't move me any closer to my goals or desired results.

I recall hearing somewhere that Tim Ferriss wrote a majority of the 4-Hour Work Week between 1 A.M and 4 A.M.

There might even have been some malbec wine involved.

What if Mark Twain had never drank?

What if Aldous Huxley had never experimented with psychedelics?

What if people had never embraced coffee because it is a stimulant and could be considered a "vice"?

There are all these considerations and I believe they're nuanced and the problem so many people run into is that they don't take the time to inspect these nuances.

"You get what you think about, whether you want it or not. Commit to thinking about what you want, rather than how impossible or difficult that dream may seem."
— Dr. Wayne W. Dyer

Only you can decide what will make you the most capable, confident, competent and the strongest man you could be.

I'm not here to tell you what that is.

All of these things are relative.

There is always a trade-off on what you decide to be capable and competent in compared to something else such as maybe you know how to cook really well but don't have a clue as to what to do in the gym.

The world needs all types and whatever type you decide to be, it just needs you to be the best at it.

Fundamentally, what we've covered here are the most important facets of life that will allow you to do any of these things well.

If you're the type of man who lives passionately, has non-negotiable standards, is always upgrading his mindset, who masters his body, who is the author of his world, is committed to evolving, and takes massive strategic action in whatever he does — how could you not be the man you could be?

How could you not be immensely successful in whatever you apply yourself to?

"The best way to predict the future is to create it."
— Abraham Lincoln

There are plenty of people who scoff at this sort of thing, but seriously — why the fuck would you desire to be anything less than the man you could be?

This book isn't about how to have a life of mediocrity.

FUCK MEDIOCRITY!

It's about how to become POWERFUL as a MAN and unlock the GREATNESS that's within you!

And it all starts with you and your commitment to pursuing that.

Your commitment to never wavering on that path.

Your commitment to BEING LEGENDARY!

"What lies behind you and what lies in front of you pales in comparison to what lies inside of you."
— Ralph Waldo Emerson

There is a reason this chapter is less of a how-to and more of a call-to-action.

As you now know, you don't need to know "the how", you only need to make the decision and follow that up with unreasonable commitment and "the how" will reveal itself in due time.

This is simply a principle and declaration for those who would be the BEST version of themselves.

It's the last step in this book because that in and of itself is the root of all your power — YOU.

Whether you want to climb to the apogee of the corporate ladder, become a 9 figure entrepreneur, or simply be the best father or husband you can be — it all lies in becoming the best version of yourself.

The power you gain along the way in those other pursuits is simply a reflection of the power you've gained over yourself and who you've become along that journey.

Plenty of people will tell you to lay off the gas along the way, to just settle and accept mediocrity, to stop being such a high-performer.

What those people are really saying is that you're "making" them feel bad and uncomfortable for not having similar standards for themselves.

Of course in those very statements reveals their nature because you know to take responsibility and in that, no one can "make" you feel bad unless you allow it. Your emotions are your responsibility.

What they're really saying is that they lack the COMMITMENT to play on the level you are.

What they're really saying is that they haven't committed to themselves and their lives, that they aren't prepared to go to battle each and every day the way you are, to tap into their potential how you are.

This isn't a signal to lay-off the gas, it's a sign that you're on the right path, that you're making progress, that you're actually changing and adapting in REAL-TIME and becoming that next BEST version of yourself.

It's also a sign that you're becoming a BEACON of excellence to others.

It's a sign that you're starting to be seen as the man you know you could be and also that you may have a few naysayers, but more importantly, you're going to be a source of inspiration for those around you.

You're now on the path to being someone others look up to for guidance, who commands respect.

That's powerful and so are you.

You have no idea just how capable you could become.

How competent you could be if you committed to that.

How confident you would be from actually embracing that version of yourself.

And the strength you would find within along the way.

If you let it, this will be the single most exciting, illuminating and discovery-filled journey of your life.

It'll be like being a kid all over again.

You'll blast through a barrier you didn't even know was there and then, take a moment to be present and soak it in, and enjoy the wonderment that comes from going places and becoming a person you didn't even know was possible.

I believe in you.

I believe you have greatness within you.

I believe you have potential beyond belief.

And I look forward to seeing you become the best man you know you could be.

I look forward to you becoming LEGENDARY.

ACTION ITEMS

- What does being the most capable, confident, competent and strongest man you could be look like to you?
- What sort of qualities does that man have?
- How would he act in all areas of life?
- How would his mastery over the fundamentals of life allow him to become the most powerful and best version of himself?

Additional Resources

I love hearing feedback from readers.

Email me specifically with your feedback to this book at: BeLegendaryMan@gmail.com

For free trainings, routines, and other kick-ass content go to CaelinKompass.com and enter your email to get periodic emails from me.

Also, all of my programs such as fitness, coaching, group coaching, bootcamps, masterminds and more are all there as well.

As the saying goes: The book is the what, the coaching is the how. Or the book introduces you to the concepts, the coaching ensures you integrate them over a period of time with accountability and instruction.

I'm active on the socials, and each and every follow is a vote for my content, the value I provide and encourages me to continue on this journey.

Instagram: @CaelinKompass

Twitter: @CaelinKompass

YouTube: www.caelin.tv or @caelinkompass

Rumble: @caelinKompass

Linkedin: @CaelinKompass

I will be switching my main focus to Instagram and YouTube over the coming months and that will be where I interact with my followers the most. Going live on YouTube or Insta is a great way to get real time interaction if you'd like to connect.

Acknowledgments

I owe a huge debt of gratitude to so many who have supported me along this process, not only with this book, but throughout life in general.

First, to my mother and father, whom without their endearing and never-ending support I would never have made it this far in life. To both of you I am eternally grateful and cannot express the gratitude I have in my heart for you both.

To my brothers and sisters. You've supported me, you've encouraged me, you've loved me even when I didn't love myself.

To my best friend Zach Fitzgerald. You've believed in me always and helped me push through all the times of adversity when I was sure I couldn't go on any longer. Many thanks, brother.

To Stela, for the endless conversations of listening to me sort through my thoughts and always believing in me.

To Carlene, my dear friend and editor of this book. I cannot thank you enough for the encouragement, the help and your dedication to making the world a more beautiful place.

To Michael Carrigan. For making me RIGHT.

To Cris Cawley of Game Changer Publishing. You've made this process easy, fun and most of all accessible to those who would establish their expertise into a book. Many thanks!

To Jason Harper, for coming through last minute for the most serendipitous photoshoot and for being a wizard behind the camera.

To Rory and AJ Vaden along with the entire Brand Builders Group team. You helped me codify my thinking more clearly and provided the necessary structures for me to move forward at warp speed.

To my strategist, Schell Gower, who helped push me and put up with me breaking "all the rules" because I don't subscribe to other's realities.

To Coach Michael Burt. Thank you for helping to show me how to monetize my knowledge and passion and create a category of one.

To Brad Lea, for mentoring me on social media strategies and mindset.

To my many other friends that supported and encouraged me along this journey. I couldn't have done it without you.

To the haters and naysayers – thank you for fueling my fire and helping to turbocharge my drive, my passion and my mission in the world. The world needs powerful men and you're helping to empower them out of apathy into ambition and to legendaryness.

To all of my extended online social media family. The internet is a beautiful and scary place and you make it all worth it. I want to personally thank each and every one of you for liking, sharing, and engaging in the content I produce. Without you, none of this would be possible.

About The Author

Caelin Kompass is a speaker, coach, author, entrepreneur, and all around obsessed individual. He founded FREEDOM 2.0 to help men get unstuck, achieve their true potential and become better versions of themselves.

Caelin believes in the power of the individual. Also, the more men who pursue masculine excellence as well as aim to achieve mastery in all aspects of their life will make the world a more safe and vibrant place. In "BE LEGENDARY", Caelin lays out the foundations, principles and structures to help men become just that - LEGENDARY.

Caelin has spent years delving into physical and psychological fitness to fully understand himself and the near unlimited possibilities of human potential. As someone who lives it, Caelin believes that the mindset you adopt throughout life matters far more than any personal circumstance. To that end, he believes what's wrong is always available... but so is what's right!

Caelin is a highly sought after peak-performance and mindset coach and an authority on personal transformation. He is devoted to making the world a better place by helping to create strong, capable, competent and empowered men. It's not about being a "real man" but instead simply about being the best man you're capable of being.

In his free time, Caelin can be found in the gym, at the lake, buried in a book, cycling, hiking, attempting to conquer the internet or any other number of activities. Life is meant to be lived and Caelin believes in doing just that.

Disclaimer

This book contains advice and information relating to health care. It should be used to supplement rather than replace the advice of your doctor or another trained health professional. If you know or suspect you have a health problem, it is recommended that you seek your physician's advice before embarking on any medical program or treatment. All efforts have been made to assure the accuracy of the information contained in this book as of the date of publication. This publisher and the author disclaim liability for any medical outcomes that may occur as a result of applying the methods suggested in this book.

THANK YOU FOR READING MY BOOK!

DOWNLOAD YOUR FREE GIFTS

Just to say thanks for buying and reading my book, I would like to give you a few free bonus gifts, no strings attached!

To Download Now, Visit:

www.CaelinKompass.com/Freegifts

I appreciate your interest in my book, and value your feedback as it helps me improve future versions of his book. I would appreciate it if you could leave your invaluable review on Amazon.com with your feedback. Thank you!